ASPECTS OF INDIA

ASPECTS OF INDIA

Essays in Honor of Edward Cameron Dimock, Jr.

Edited by
MARGARET CASE AND N. GERALD BARRIER

MANOHAR

AMERICAN INSTITUTE OF INDIAN STUDIES
New Delhi
1986

ISBN 81 - 85054 - 07-X   ISBN 81 - 85054 - 07 - X

First Published 1986

Published by Ramesh Jain, Manohar Publications, 1 Ansari Road, Daryaganj, New Delhi - 110002 for American Institute of Indian Studies, D-176 Defence Colony, New Delhi - 110024. Phototypeset by The Word, 807/95 Nehru Place, New Delhi - 110019 and printed at P.L. Printers, C3/19 Rana Pratap Bagh, Delhi - 110007.

CONTENTS

Preface

This collection of essays, written in honor of Edward Cameron Dimock, Jr., and presented to him by a few friends on behalf of scores of others, should perhaps be called a symposium as well as a festschrift. For whereas a festschrift is a colleciton of writings for a feast, a symposium is a convivial gathering of companions to drink and converse on intellectual subjects. There are many friends, indeed, of Cam Dimock who wish they had been invited to the feast, for he has drawn to himself over the years a large and devoted band of companions. But many, if not all of us have engaged in symposia — in this real sense — with Cam in India and Chicago and elsewhere. The writings of many have seen the light of day thanks to his encouragement and support, and so have joined the wider symposium of scholarly studies on South Asian subjects. The present volume to honor our teacher, friend, patron, and colleague is but a sampling from ten of the many students of Indian culture who wish to record their thanks to him.

Margaret Case
N. Gerald Barrier

Aspects of India

The Prince Who Married His Own Left Half

A.K. RAMANUJAN

In 1962, Edward Dimock invited me to collaborate on a paper with him on a favorite subject of his, the Goddess of Snakes in Bengal. I was innocent of Bengali, but I'd been dabbling for a while in folktales, motifs, and such. The enduring part of that paper is still Edward Dimock's textual analysis and synthesis of variants in the Manasa myth. Working with him on that paper raised questions that I'm still trying to answer. For instance, in folk narratives, what is the relation of one variant to another? When we "synthesize" a composite text out of several "variants," what is its status and use? When, as happens all too frequently in Indian tales, several "types" get mixed together to form new texts, is the admixture random and promiscuous, or does it add up to a functioning unity, serving an artistic, meaningful whole?

In this essay, written to honor and celebrate a dear friend's many-sided work, I'd like to address his love of tales, and tell one that Kannada villagers tell. And I'd like to attempt answers to some of the above questions—not theoretically, but through the analysis of a tale, its "archtype," the "mixture of types," the "variants," and how they mean what they mean.

Here is the tale, collected in Ghodageri, Belgaum District, Karnataka, in 1968.

The Prince Who Married His Left Half

The king had a son. When the prince came of age, the king wished him to get married. But the young man didn't want to get married; he listened to no one's advice, not even to the elders'. His father became rather desperate and threatened to hang himself if the prince didn't get married. The son then yielded and said,

"All right. Split my body in two, bury my left half in flowers. A woman will be born out of it. I'll marry her. I won't marry anyone else.

The king was terrified that his son would die in the operation, when they were cutting him in half. He asked the prince,

"Is there no other way, a simpler way?"

The Prince said,

"There's no other way. Other women are uncontrollable. It's hard to keep them in line."

The king finally agreed. An expert cleaved the prince's body into two halves, and buried the left half in flowers. In a few days, a lovely woman came out of the flowers. The right half grew whole and it was as if the prince had never been cut in half. The king got her married to his son according to the proper rites.

The prince had a wonderful palace built in a deserted place outside town for his wife, and visited her there. The king also was very fond of his daughter-in-law. He too would visit her now and then, and see that everything was right for her.

One day a wizard came to that place. On his way to some far-off country, he saw this wonderful palace in a deserted area and he started walking around it. The king's daughter-in-law, who was standing at her window, saw him and smiled at him.

The wizard took shelter in an old woman's house in the nearby village. The old woman used to make garlands for the king's daughter-in-law every day. The wizard made a fantastic garland one day, gave it to the old woman, and said,

"Take this to the king's daughter-in-law and tell me what she says."

The old woman took the garland to the king's daughter-in-law, who opened it and got the message. Though she felt happy inside, she pretended to be angry; she pressed her hand in vermilion and slapped the old woman's cheek. The old woman came home weeping and showed the man her cheek. He consoled her by saying,

"Don't worry about it. It's nothing. She just wants to let me know that she is having her period."

A few days later, he made another garland for the palace, and gave it to the old woman. This time, when she received the garland, the king's daughter-in-law dipped her hand in white lime and slapped the old woman's breasts. The old woman came home weeping. When the man saw the white marks, he said,

"Don't worry. She wants to tell me that it's full-moon time."

In a few days, he sent the palace a third garland. This time the king's daughter-in-law dipped her hand in black ink and hit the old woman on the backside. She came home crying and told him what happened. The man said,

"You must read these things right, old woman. She wants me to go to the back of the palace on a dark new-moon night."

When he went there on the dark new-moon night, a rope was hanging from the back window of the palace. He gripped it and hauled himself up, and went in through the window. The king's daughter-in-law was waiting for him; she was happy and they made love. She said to him tenderly:

"If you come in your natural shape, the guards at the gate will not let you in. So disguise yourself, and you can come here often."

The young man said, "That's easy," and used to visit her in the guise of a snake. He would enter the palace through the drain-pipes; as soon as he came into her room he would change into a man, and they would make love. Many days passed this way.

One day when the king came to see his daughter-in-law he saw a snake slithering in the drain-pipe. He at once called his servants and got it killed. He asked them to throw the dead snake outside the palace, and went to his daughter-in-law's chambers. When he said, "You know, I saw a snake coming into the house. Your luck was good. I saw it, got it killed and thrown outside," the daughter-in-law cried out, "Ayyo! What a terrible thing!" and fainted.

When she came to, after much first aid, she was grief-stricken that her lover was caught and killed; but outwardly she pretended to be terrified of the snake, and her narrow escape. Before he left, the king tried to comfort her by saying,

"Why are you scared? The snake is really dead and gone."

From that day on, she was in mourning; she gave up food and sleep. One day a dāsayya, a holy mendicant, came to her door asking for alms. She called him in and asked him a favor:

"Look here, Dāsayya, I'll give you a rupee. It seems there's a dead snake lying outside. Will you go check if it's there?"

He went out, checked and found it there. She said to him,

"Go take the dead snake to a cemetery, cremate it and bring me the ashes. I'll give you two rupees for your trouble."

The dāsayya agreed, took it to a cemetery, cremated it according to proper funeral rites, and brought her back the ashes. She gave him two rupees first, then added three more.

"Go now to a goldsmith and get a talisman," she ordered.

The dāsayya went out again, and came back with a talisman.

She placed her dead lover's ash in the talisman and tied it around her shoulder. Mourning her dead lover's death all day, she grew thinner. The prince heard about her emaciated state and thought, "My wife has some secret sorrow, I must go and console her. She's growing thinner each day."

He came to the palace and asked her why she looked so thin and sick.

He talked to her in any number of ways. He asked her to tell him whatever was happening. But she didn't part her lips once; she didn't tell him a thing. He made her sit on his lap and used all the arts he knew, and persuaded her. Finally she said,

"What else can I do? You've kept me here in a jail. I get to see your face here once on full-moon day, and once on new-moon day. How can my heart be happy and content?"

The king's son felt very contrite when he heard of her sorrow.

"Then I'll stay here all the time, every day," he said to console her.

She then said,

"I'm going to tell you a riddle. If you answer it, I'll throw myself in the fire and die. If you can't answer it, you must throw yourself in the fire and die. If anyone asks afterwards why this happened, neither of us should tell them why. If you agree to these conditions, I'll tell you the riddle. Otherwise, let's quit."

The crazy prince agreed. He placed his hand in hers and gave her his word. Then she said,

"One for seeing,
Two for burning,
Three for wearing on the shoulder —
A husband for the thigh,
A lover for the shoulder!
Tell me what it means."

The prince struggled and groaned to get the answer to the riddle. He could not, for the life of him, find any answer; so, according to his word, he fell into a fire and killed himself. She took another lover and lived happily.

Anyone who hears it can see that such a tale works on several levels at once. The disciplines of literary criticism, anthropology, and psychology, especially the different schools of psychoanalysis, will see different aspects of the tale as important. In the rest of the paper, I shall reconstruct a tale-type from its many tellings (a word I prefer to "variants," which implies an underlying "invariant"), and discuss its structure; compare it with another telling from an anthropological point of view; and comment briefly on a possible Indian view of "narcissism," as embodied in tales like this one.

In addition to the telling I've translated above, ten others have been recorded. Nine of these are in Kannada. The tenth, in Suzanne Hanchett's recording (Hanchett, in press), and four of the Kannada recordings have all three sections of the story:

I. the self-division of the prince and the marriage to a woman born of his own body;

II. the arrival of a magician/snake who becomes the wife's paramour;
III. the death of the snake, the riddle, and the consequences.

Five of the Kannada versions have only the second two parts. We may reconstruct an archetype, a composite of all the motifs in the ten versions, as follows:

I. a) A prince distrusts women, refuses to marry. b) He agrees to marry only the woman who is born of his own left half, when it is cut and buried in flowers. c) When he is cut in half, and placed in a box, one part becomes a male body, another a female. Or, c1) The woman is born of a bowl of his blood, and d) a drop of blood falls on the ground and becomes a snake, which appears later as the woman's paramour. e) The princess is housed in a palace outside town.

II. a) A magician comes to the palace and b) woos the princess through a go-between, an old woman who makes garlands. c) He reads her three signs, meets her on a dark night, and becomes her lover. d) He enters and leaves the palace as a snake.

III. a) The father or a1) the prince happens upon the snake-lover and kills him. b) The princess pays c) a holy man or c1) some boys one coin to find the snake's remains, two coins to cremate it, three to make a talisman for her shoulder or neck, in which she wears her lover's ashes.

IV. a) She sets the prince a death-riddle, which summarizes her love affair and her present situation, usually by the phrase, "Lover on the shoulder, husband on the thigh." If he cannot answer the riddle, he should throw himself into the fire; if he does, she would die. b) He is unable to answer it and kills himself. She takes another lover and lives happily. Or, b1) His sister learns about her brother's desperate wager, often through a dream, and comes to see him. On the way, she hears birds talk about her sister-in-law's riddle and his answer. With her help, he answers his wife's death-riddle, and the wife kills herself. And c) He marries his sister's daughter.

A search through the motif indexes (Thompson and Balys 1958, Thompson 1955) revealed that none of the striking motifs that open the story had been recorded. Though some important motifs appear in later parts: H 607.3, man sees princess who makes signs to him; H 611.2, he (or his friend) interprets them; H 805, riddle of the murdered lover; H 575, accidental discovery of answer to the riddle. I offer some additional numbers and descriptions as follows: A 1275.1, man creates his own wife from his own left half; A 1275.2, man creates his wife from a bowl of his own blood.

It may be worth dwelling a little on this motif sequence before we go on with our tale. A 1275.1 is 'deity creates princess from prince's body and gives her to him.' Obviously Adam and Eve belong here. It is tempting to think of the parallel between the Adam-Eve-Serpent triad and the one here. Also relevant is the *Bṛhadāraṇyaka* (1.4.1–6) creation myth of the Primordial Person dividing himself into male and female to beget all living beings by successive couplings. In any larger study, such comparative material should be considered, chiefly to point up the remarkable differences among the three uses of the motif of sexual fission. For instance, the *Bṛhadāraṇyaka* myth begins with loneliness and its conquest by creating another out of oneself. It is a creation myth, not a cautionary tale like our folktale. It is about creativity, progeny, transformation ("life, liberty, and the happiness of pursuit"). I don't know if the tellers of the folktale knew of the classical precedent. The folktale certainly reverses the outcomes: not creation, but destruction, not the overcoming of loneliness but a perpetuation of it; not procreation, but illicit affairs, betrayal, and barrenness. The First Man could split himself in two without being a "schizo," because he had no choice but fission and incest: pre-sexual reproduction appears as a precursor of the sexual. As we know, "sex" means "division," division of function, division of labor. After the division into sexes, there is no return to the original unity without regression and even self-destruction.

In the type indexes (Thompson 1964, Thompson and Roberts 1960), one finds that the closest type to which we may assign the present tale is *851 Turandot: Princess sets riddle to her suitors to be answered on pain of death.* So I suggest here a number and description (with the above reconstruction, which may be further refined, as more variants are found) to future folktale scholars and type-indexers: *851 Indic, The Prince Who Married His Own Left Half.*[1]

At any rate, this search for motifs and the construction of an archetype from the various tellings we have so far reveal some interesting features:

1. half the tellings do not have I at all;
2. none, except the one above, has II, the princess' sign language;
3. all the stories have III, the riddle;
4. where tales have both I and III, we have two subtypes: a) where the prince cannot solve the riddle and kills himself, b) where the prince solves it with the help of a sister, whereupon the wife dies, and the prince marries the sister's daughter.

I'd now like to consider the structure of variation in these tellings and what they tell us about the meanings of the tale.

Stith Thompson expresses a commonly held view regarding Indian tales: "The structure of the complicated tale is very loose, so that the plot is often very difficult to fit into the patterns determined by European analogues. Sometimes the story-teller seems to have a repertory consisting of merely single motifs which he strings together almost at will" (Thompson 1946, 16). If we take such a view, we need only list the above differences. We may attribute these to the whims and powers and deficiencies of individual tellers, and the vagaries of oral transmission. But if we take the view that differences in Indian and other tales are structured and motivated, unless otherwise proven, we must ask why only some things are "changed," "forgotten," and not others. When, in the fuller versions, certain motifs appear that are not in the others, one may ask, "Why these?" One of the uses of making a synthetic archetype is, I think, not so much to trace the history or geography of a tale's migrations (though that was why archtypes were first constructed), but to distinguish fuller, more richly articulated tellings from the others, and to ask questions of form and meaning. Even garbled and less articulate tellings contribute to our understanding of the fuller versions.

Now to return to our version, which is rather a detailed one, we may ask "What function does II have, with a full elaboration of the princess' secret language of signs?" If we look up the indexes, we find that our section II occurs in another independent tale and was striking enough for the type-makers to give it as the name for the whole tale-type: *516A, The Sign Language of the Princess.* It is an ancient story that has been re-reported in twenty versions all over India (and from nowhere else). The *Kathāsaritsāgara*, the classic collection of tales in Sanskrit, has the earliest version (see Tawney 1968, IV, 251–261). Here is a summary (Thompson 1964: 185):

516A The Sign Language of the Princess

I. The Friends. A prince and a youth of lower rank (vizier's son, etc.) are close friends. (a) The Old Woman as Trouble-Maker [M301.2.1, T12]; (this element appears sometimes as a separate tale). (b) For other false reasons the prince commands that his friend be executed. Compassionate executioner. Later, the friend appears to interpret signs. (c) The two friends are banished. (They break the villager's water pots, etc.) (d) The prince dreams of a princess [T11.3] and he and his friend search for her.

II. The Princess and her Sign Language. The prince sees a lovely princess who makes signs to him [H607.3]. The friend interprets them [H611.2]. (Example: the princess strikes her teeth with a rose [Z175.1, Z175.2], signifying that her father's name is Raja Tooth).

III. Winning the Princess [*K1300*]. *They travel to the city where dwells the princess. (a) Through the help of an old woman (flower-seller, etc.) they gain access to the princess. (b) The prince, disguised as a girl, gains access to the princess* [*K1321.2*]. *(c) The princess tries to poison the friend, but fails. (d) The friend drugs the princess and brands her back. In the guise of a fakir he then tells the king he has driven a witch away from a human corpse which the witch was eating and has branded the back of the witch. The king, believing the princess to be a witch, drives her out and his friend carries her off. (e) The prince, disguised as a woman, is left in the care of the king by the friend. The prince then escapes. The friend returns and demands the "woman." The king is forced to give the princess instead. (f) Other means of winning the princess.*

Note how the prince is unable to interpret signs, and needs a friend to help and protect him, though he is quite faithless toward his friend. Note also how the prince obtains his wife by first becoming a "woman" himself. In the fuller versions there are two older women, too: a troublemaker who separates the friend and almost gets him killed, and later in the tale a helpful old woman who helps the prince get access to the princess. Note also how the princess tries to kill the friend, and later the friend accuses her of being a witch eating human corpses. The accusation is a ruse and patently false, but tells the truth about this female figure in a deeper symbolic sense.

Thus, *Tale 516A, The Sign Language of the Princess,* is full of signs that are read or not read at some risk to one's life. One doesn't have to be a Jungian to see that the whole tale is about the prince coming to terms with his wiser alter ego (friend), who alone can read the signs, befriend the Old Woman, identify the princess (or the feminine side) as a cannibal before she can be won; and he has to help the prince himself to "become a woman" before he can relate to one. I would suggest further that the whole group of tales listed in the index under 516, 516A, and 516B have to do with related themes, but this is not the occasion to elaborate on their significance.

I think I've said enough to show that the presence of 516A in our tale is not random. The claim is strengthened by the fact that the prince begins by distrusting women, and can marry only his left half, which too he keeps at a distance—and that he cannot understand her or himself. The tale is making the important psychological point that our Prince Narcissus cannot read. Like many riddles, the princess' riddle tells the literal truth. All that the prince needed to do was to relate her words directly to herself and himself.

By contrast, the magician, a stranger, does just that and reads the signs of the princess by relating her signs to her body, her condition, the time of the month, the phases of the moon. The old woman is used as a foil, for she too cannot read: the slaps she receives on breast and buttock stun her understanding. So it is the magician who understands and wins the princess, gives her pleasure, makes her happy, earns her love and her mourning, as the prince never does. He also has an animal self, a snake who enters the house through the drain hole (how Freudian can you get?). But the prince, out of touch with women (significantly, there is no mother in the tale), out of touch with his own left half and his own woman, cannot read the riddle she sets him—a riddle which is both an act of cruelty and a cry for communication, in which she blatantly gives everything away, summarizes his and her situation, flaunts her unfaithfulness, almost crying to be found out, to be understood. It offers him a second chance to know himself; both a death sentence and a possible new spell of life.

So part II (The Sign Language) of the story is intimately related both to I (the prince's distrust of women) and to III (his inability to read his wife's riddle). Part II introduces other symmetries: for example, the magician befriends an old woman who makes garlands. After all, the princess herself was born of flowers, and responds to them.[2]

Once we see these themes, others become clear, too. These are brought into relief by the other subtype, which we mentioned above, where a sister solves the riddle and saves the prince's life. (I'm indebted to Suzanne Hanchett for allowing me to see and use her translation and analysis.) Here is a slightly adapted version of the tale she collected in 1977 in Gorur, Karnataka from an Adi Karnataka woman:

There were five brothers, four of whom were married. The fifth brother would not accept any girl who was offered to him as a bride. So the parents and the other brothers told him to go find himself a bride, that they could not do any more for him.

He then made a knife and set off on a horse. He went along for a while until he got to a banyan tree. There he put a new clay vessel under the tree. And stabbing himself in the chest, he let some of his blood flow into the vessel. Covering the vessel with a pure, white cloth, he removed the knife from his body and put it down. A drop of blood dropped from it on to the earth. The drop of blood at once turned into a snake and crept away before he could see it. He took the vessel and left that place

He then went into a forest and tried to hide the vessel somewhere. But as he set it down, it turned into a beautiful girl. After twelve years she came of age, and he married her right there in the forest. After the marriage, he built a house and left her there, saying, "It has been twelve or thirteen years since I saw my people and my country. And I also want to go hunting." He forbad her to go out of the house until he returned, as there was no one in the forest. He told her that, even if a holy man or beggar should come to the door, she should not come out and give him alms. Then he left her.

Meanwhile the snake had made its way to the house in the forest. Wherever the man went, the snake would watch him but move in the opposite direction. As the man went away from the house, the snake approached it, and took the form of a young man. And as it left the house, it would become a snake again. So the young man and young woman began to see each other, and soon began to like each other, the way boys and girls like each other.

This had been happening for a while, when the husband returned. Now he would often see a snake leaving the house as he entered it. He became suspicious, wondering what was happening. This could be an enemy that might harm him. So one day, he took his knife and cut the snake into three pieces. He put the three pieces in a pile, one on top of the other, and went out.

After a while, a holy man came to the house begging for alms. The girl told him, "I'll give you anything you want. Just tell me if you saw anything on the way." The holy man said, "I only saw that somebody has killed a snake and cut it into three pieces." She said to him, "I'll give you money. Please get those pieces for me." The holy man went and got them for her.

She then took the three pieces and made them into three charms by putting them in tube-shaped amulets, which she hung from a single thread around her neck.

When her husband returned, she was lying on her cot. He asked her what was wrong with her and she said, "I've a headache. I'm going to tell you a riddle. If you solve it, then my headache will go."

The riddle went as follows: "With one coin, I got it. With two coins, I got it made; with three coins, I've put it round my neck."

Then she said, "If you solve the riddle, you win and I will jump into the fire. But if you do not solve it, you lose and you'll have to jump into the fire."

He thought very hard but he could not solve it. The wife made a platform of firewood, and invited people from the seven surrounding villages to attend the cremation.

Now the man had an elder sister who had been given in marriage to one of the seven villages. On her way to the cremation, she happened to sit under the same old banyan tree. On the tree were two birds talking to each other. One said, "It seems there was a fellow who felt that if they brought a girl from another family she might turn out to be a cheat or a woman of bad character. So he cut himself . . . . ."

And the bird related the whole story to its mate, concluding with, "Now he has to jump into the fire."

The elder sister had now heard the riddle and could read what it meant. She hurried to the place and arrived just as the man was about to jump into the fire. She had written out the whole story on a sheet of paper and she handed it over to the village leader. They all read it, and the people decided that the man had been cheated. They made the wife jump into the fire instead of him. He married his sister's daughter and lived happily thereafter.

Notice how here, too, the young man accepts no one as his bride; he creates one out of his heart's blood. A crucial detail is added when the snake/lover is also born of his blood, though he knows nothing about it. He is cheated by his own unrelated and unacknowledged selves, his wife and her lover. When he kills the snake, she sets him the death-riddle which he cannot solve. As the woman who told the story said, "The very blood from which he hoped to make a trustworthy girl of his own, that blood became his enemy" (Hanchett).

But his sister, who is a benign female figure, who can read signs and the language of birds, solves the riddle for him. The birds who reveal the secret are perched on the very same banyan tree where he had stabbed himself, and the birds also represent a couple who talk to each other. Furthermore, as Hanchett points out, "the elder sister's daughter is one of the preferred choices in this kinship system." By marrying his sister's daughter, the man is back in family and society; through the sister, the people of the village are involved in his story. She, being married into another family, represents an outward branching, even a severance from the natal family. Such a sister is a specially appropriate dispeller of narcissistic spells. She is both family and not family, both blood-kin and in-law, knits the realms of kin and nonkin safely for bride and bridegroom. Thus, the story does dramatize "the dilemma of exogamy and incest, the paradoxical need to use outsiders (wives) to produce insiders (children)." One might add further, given the man's fear of outside women, and his near-fatal solution of marrying someone born of his own blood, this telling gives him a *via media*: by marrying his sister's daughter, he marries one who at one remove shares his blood and yet is a socially acceptable outsider—an unthreatening Other. Traditional Indian patterns of marriage take this dilemma into account. With their taboo on certain forms of endogamy (the extreme form of which is marrying oneself or one's daughter, etc.), combined with the taboo on caste exogamy as well, they balance the insider/outsider relations. A man cannot marry a sibling or certain close cousins, but can (in the Dravidian pattern) marry a sister's or paternal aunt's daughter. He/she cannot marry within a *gotra* or clan, but still has to marry within the caste or subcaste. The prince's story is an extreme enactment of the problem and the solution.

Another aspect of variation, the context of the telling, needs to be considered. The first telling is a domestic one; the tale is told within the house to children by an elder. The second, reported by Hanchett as a vratakathā, is a tale told as part of a woman's ritual during a Nāga-pañcami or Cobra Festival. The first feels free to explore the negative side of the problem and end it even with a death. The second offers a socially acceptable solution to the riddle, a marriage, a reunion of brother and sister, the presence of a whole community, and the creation of a new family. It does not dwell on the love affair and the sign language of the princess, as the domestic tale does—the latter genre seems freer to explore the unconscious, without the fears and favors of social pressure. The ritual tale itself is a public event, told during the Cobra Festival to propitiate snakes, to ensure safety and fertility within marriage. So it socializes the self-involved hero.[3]

Thus, while different tellings or variants throw light on each other, each has an integrity of its own, and functions uniquely according to its genre and context. They are what one meets when one hears a tale. In collapsing them into Proppian functions or the Aarne-Thompson archtypes, we lose a great deal of information and significance. Motifs, functions, and archtypes are useful heuristic abstractions only when they help us return to the concrete tellings in which the culture carries its meanings. The so-called variant, what I've called a "telling," is the true unit of folktale analysis.

I have, in passing, alluded to narcissism.[4] I shall content myself here with remarks on this theme. In all the tellings, and in other tales as well, the concern is with family continuity. Hindu conceptions of person and relationships of life and afterlife are a part of this cluster. Narcissism, interpreted in the Hindu sense, is not only the inability to love a contemporary other; it is also the turning away from ancestors and offspring, from one's place in the orderly sequence of generations; it is to refuse to be generative. Our first variant shows the dangers of suicidal self-involvement, the second the communal, familial solution. Of the four stages of life (celibate student, householder, forest dweller, and world renouncer/sanyasī), Manu and other thinkers valued most the stage of the householder. Though holy men and renouncer/sanyāsīs are respected, even revered, one detects in the literature a suspicion of them, an ambivalence toward them. They are suspected, and frequently convicted, of the charge of sterile self-love, of missing out on the natural cycle of life which often comes back at them with a vengeance. As in the following example, a sanyāsī who had embraced celibacy prematurely has not cared enough for the fathers and forefathers who cannot reach heaven unless the family continues. An old etymology for putra or "son" suggests that a son is one who saves the father from going to a hell specially reserved for those who do not have sons, a hell called put. The Hindu death anniversary ritual (śrāddha) performed by sons and descendants stresses the importance of offspring in keeping forefathers happy and out of hell. In the Hindu conception, the dependence of parents and children is mutual—self-love, the incapacity to love another, cuts deep into this mutuality.

The following classical story from the *Mahābhārata* (condensed from the translation by J.A.B. van Buitenen 1973, 103–10–7) is particularly apt in expressing the suspicion of self-absorption and guilt of holy men:

Jaratkāru the ascetic traversed the entire earth, abstaining from food, living off the wind, drying out his body day by day.

He saw his own forebears hanging in a cave with their faces down, hanging on to a single remaining strand of grass; and he saw a rat that lived in the cave gnawing slowly through this string. They were bereft of food and emaciated and wretched in their cave; they suffered and yearned for deliverance. He spoke to them: "Who are you? Seeing you upside down, fallen into this dire distress, I am seized with grief. How can I help? Ward off your downfall with a quarter, a half, even all my austerities? I am willing to do so."

The ancestors said: "Old man, you are magnanimous. Listen. We are the seers of strict vows, who have now fallen from heaven, because we are wanting in offspring. Our sacred austerities are lost, for we have no more thread. Yet there is one single thread left to us still, but it might well be lost: the one unfortunate son who remains to us unfortunates in our line is solely given to austerities. He is known as Jaratkāru, scholar of the Vedas, controlled, great-spirited, of massive mortifications. He is the one who out of greed for more austerities has brought us to this pass. He has no wife, or son, or any kin . . . . This string of grass from which you see us hanging, tat is the string of our family from which our lineage grows. And the plant fibers that you see here, they are our threads, eaten away now by Time, good brahmin. And this half-eaten fiber you see, we are hanging by it—and he, the last of our line, is practicing austerities! The rat you see is mighty Time itself, brahmin. And bite by bite he is killing off that foolish ascetic Jaratkāru. . . . See how we flounder in Hell like sinners! And when we have sunk here with all our ancient ancestors, he too will be cut down by Time and shall travel to Hell. Whether mortification, or sacrifice, or any other great purification, nothing equals offspring. When you see him, friend, tell the wretched Jaratkāru what you have witnessed, and tell him, "Thy wretched forebears are hanging face down in a cave. Take a wife as is proper, masterful man, and get children!"

Hearing all this Jaratkāru became utterly miserable with grief, and told them who he was in a voice blurred by tears. "It has always been the purpose of my life, O ancestors, to contain my seed and carry my body whole to the world hereafter. But now that I see you hanging like bats, my mind recoils from a life of celibacy, grandfathers." Then he promised them that he would marry a wife but one who bears his own name and who will be given to him as alms by her own free will, and one he should not have to support.

He roams the world till The King of Snakes brings his sister to the hermit; the virgin's name is also Jaratkāru, and her brother undertakes to support her. Jaratkāru then marries Jaratkāru.

Finally, one may add that in India the study of psychology has been, by and large, philosophical, or part of the techniques of ecstasy and salvation, as in yoga. There is no major tradition of introspective personal psychology, as in later Europe, out of which, especially after the sixteenth century, the *Confessions* of Rousseau (or earlier, those of St Augustine), the self-portraits of Rembrandt, the novels of Richardson, and all their heirs, as well as the modern psychoanalytic schools have arisen. But we may suggest that in tales like the above, probably even more than in myths, one finds a psychoanalysis-like exploration. Psyches are fearlessly probed and artistically presented to be experienced concretely rather than abstractly. Told as they are to children, much before the myths are told, such tales form, along with other child-rearing practices, the early bases for the Hindu Indian's aesthetics, ethos, and worldview.

NOTES

1. I've heard that such a tale has been reported from Newari in Nepal also (Robert Levy, personal communication), but I have not been able to trace it. If it is also told in Newari, thousands of miles away from Karnataka, the tale has a wider Indian distribution than our present collections lead us to suspect.
2. It is important to remember that, as an independent tale, 516A has all these motifs (the princess, old woman, flowers, sign language), but their meanings are changed. Different aspects are picked out and highlighted by the presence in our tale of a princess born of flowers and a prince who distrusts women, who cannot read signs. Motifs and incidents do not have fixed, "archtypal" meanings; they are interpreted by the presence of other motifs in context. When one tale incorporates another, we have to read the whole tale anew, see the parts in relation to the new design they make.
3. In formulating this thought, I'm indebted to a conversation with V. Narayana Rao.
4. At this time, I've shied away from the relevant psychoanalytic literature on narcissism, beginning with Freud's famous essay (1914). Hamilton (1982) has a useful bibliography and a detailed critical discussion, especially regarding early childhood development. I've also refrained from going into the contrasts between the self-love of our hero and that of the Greek Narcissus.

REFERENCES

Freud, Sigmund (1914). "On Narcissim: an introduction," in *The Standard Edition of the Complete Psychological Works of Sigmund Freud*, XIV (1914–1916), London, 1957, Translated by James Strachey et al.

Hamilton, Virginia (1982). *Narcissus and Oedipus: The Children of Psychoanalysis*, London.

Hanchett, Suzanne. *Colored Rice*, In press.

Jung, Carl G. (1953). "The Relations Between the Ego and the Unconscious," in *Collected Works, VII, Two Essays on Analytical Psychology*, New York, Translated by R.F.C. Hull.

Tawney, C.H., tr. (1968). *The Ocean of Story, Somadeva's Kathāsaritsāgara*, 10 vols. [reprint of 1924–1928 ed.].

Thompson, Stith (1946). *The Folktale*, New York.

——— (1955). *Motif-Index of Folk Literature*, 6 Vols, Bloomington, Indiana.

——— (1964). *The Types of Folktale*, 2nd revision, Helsinki.

———, and Jonas Balys (1958). *Oral Tales of India*, Bloomington, Indiana.

———, and Warren Roberts (1960). *Types of Indic Oral Tales*, Helsinki.

van Buitenen, J.A.B. (1973). *The Mahābhārata, 1. The Book of the Beginning*, Chicago.

Horses and Snakes in the Adi Parvan of the Mahabharata

WENDY O'FLAHERTY

Throughout the *Mahābhārata*, but particularly in the *Ādi Parvan* (Book One), snakes are the shadows of horses.[1] The horse is the right animal to sacrifice, the animal on which one rides triumphantly up to heaven; a horse sacrifice represents the culmination of the career of an Epic hero, a sacred act that leads to the fulfilment of *dharma* in the Kṛta Yuga. The snake is the wrong animal to sacrifice, the animal that drags one down into the underworld; a snake sacrifice is a satire upon the paradigmatic heroic act, a sacrilege that leads to the final inversion of *dharma* in the Kali Age. Vedic literature does tell us of a snake sacrifice, but it was a sacrifice *by* snakes, not *of* snakes; it was a sacrifice by which the snakes obtained immortality, by sloughing their skins. And two of the priests that officiated at that sacrifice were Takṣaka (the serpent who is the object of Janamejaya's sacrifice) and Janamejaya himself![2] Though Janamejaya's priests tell him that the gods themselves devised a ritual called "the snake sacrifice," they add that no one but he can do it [1.47.6–7].[3] As J.A.B. van Buitenen remarks of Janamejaya's sacrifice of snakes, "to the ancient Indians, among whom the non-Aryans must be counted, such a sacrifice must have been an abomination."[4] The snake sacrifice is a dark mirror for the Epic as a whole, brilliant, sinister, and surreal.

The massacre of the snakes is an intentional genocide; the massacre of the Bhāratas is an accidental genocide. Yet the very first story told, even before the listing of the contents of the Epic that is about to be narrated, is the story of an intentional genocide: the slaughter of all the Kṣatriyas (kings) by Paraśurāma. Though it is told briefly, in just three verses [1.2.3–6], it is most vivid: in order to avenge the death of his father, Paraśurāma filled five lakes with blood and offered his oblations into them. The ostensible excuse for telling this story at this moment is rather thin: several hundred verses earlier, the bard has mentioned the name of the place where the great Bhārata battle was fought, and the listeners ask him to tell them about it in greater detail; it turns out to have been the place where Paraśurāma filled his lakes with blood. The real reason, however, is to set the scene for two other oblations of blood: first the official ritual slaughter in the surreal snake sacrifice of Janamejaya, and then the unofficial ritual slaughter (of Kṣatriyas again) at the real Bhārata battle that culminates in the horse sacrifice of Yudhiṣṭhira.

Horses and snakes are associated explicitly throughout Book One (and elsewhere in the Epic), but they are also implicitly connected through the mediation of a third animal: birds. The opposition between birds and snakes, well known throughout ancient Indian texts, plays an important role in the *Ādi Parvan*; the identification of birds with horses, though less obvious in the Epic, is also important in ancient India (particularly in the *Ṛg Veda*),[5] and plays a significant role in the mythology of the snake/horse sacrifice. Thus birds and horses may have been originally identified because they share certain characteristics (such as swift flight), but they came to be further identified because (like grandparents and grandchildren) they share a common enemy: snakes. Moreover, both birds and horses are connected with fire: both represent the sun, and fly in the brightness of the sky; the Garuḍa bird is said to blaze like a fire; Agni, the god of fire, becomes incarnate in a horse; and so forth. But fire is the enemy of the snake, a cold-blooded animal whose element is water, particularly dark, subterranean water.

Madeleine Biardeau has demonstrated that the Armageddon depicted in the *Mahābhārata* is a representation of the cosmic doomsday or *pralaya*, and Alf Hiltebeitel has gone on to show how that final battle functions as a ritual sacrifice.[6] This sacrifice that is performed on the doomsday battlefield is reflected in the Epic not only in the official, "white" ritual of the consecration (in Book Two, the *Sabhā Parvan*) and the horse sacrifice (in Book Fourteen, the *Āśvamedhika Parvan*) but also in the unofficial, "black" ritual of witchcraft—the snake sacrifice in Book One. Many scholars have been puzzled by the prominence of snakes in the opening book of the *Mahābhārata*. Van Buitenen notes that "much of the *Beginning* must be regarded as extraneous to the story,"[7] and that "the structure is loose and associative . . . a presence of Snakes, largely forgotten in the rest of the epic."[8] But the snake sacrifice in the first book sets the stage for the tragedy that is to be the subject of the entire Epic to follow, the story of a sacrifice that goes horribly wrong. For not only is the snake sacrifice the wrong sort of sacrifice to undertake; in addition, Janamejaya's sacrifice is never even completed. This latter danger, which is a constant threat in all Vedic sacrifices, also infects the consecration of

Yudhiṣṭhira in Book Two, a ritual that is disrupted by the evil Duryodhana; only after a long exile and a disastrous battle is Yudhiṣṭhira finally able to perform his horse sacrifice, in Book Fourteen. It is that final sacrifice that is so bitterly undercut by the snake sacrifice in Book One.

After the introductory invocation, the very first words that the bard says are, "I was at the snake sacrifice of Janamejaya the son of Parikṣit" [1.1.8]. The ostensible significance of that sacrifice is, at first, merely to set the stage for the central Epic: that is, the reason that Janamejaya is mentioned at all is because it was at his sacrifice that the *Mahābhārata* was narrated, and that is all that the listeners ask about: Do tell us the *Mahābhārata*, they beg. Indeed, throughout the introduction to the *Mahābhārata*, the concern to know the events that led to the telling of the Epic seems to outweigh the concern to know the events that led to the experiencing of the Epic battle; and Janamejaya is the pivot of both of these concerns: his perverse sacrifice is the end of the experience and the beginning of the telling.

There then follows a 400-verse summary of the Epic [1.1.20–210, 1.2.1–243]—a summary that condenses into only two verses the two connecting sets of snake myths: "In the book about Āstika are told the birth of Garuḍa and all the snakes, the churning of the milky ocean, and the origin of Uccaiḥśravas, the stallion of Indra; then comes the beginning of the story of the *Mahābhārata* as it was told to Janamejaya the son of Parikṣit at his snake sacrifice" [1.2.73–74].

Only after this summary does the bard return to his original subject, Janamejaya, and begin to tell his story. The story is not told chronologically; it starts in the middle and goes back to the earlier causes of the snake sacrifice, meandering sideways into apparently irrelevant episodes (such as the adventures of Uttanka) and then flashing back to still earlier causes of the snake sacrifice (such as the churning of the ocean). And this whole labyrinth of snake lore hardly touches upon the importance of Janamejaya's role in the so-called central theme of the epic: the fact that Janamejaya's father, Parikṣit, was the only survivor of the holocaust of the Kurus and Pāṇḍavas. For, though the historical role of Janamejaya may indeed have been central to the skeletal narrative of the *Mahābhārata* (the battle of the Pāṇḍavas and the Kurus), the mythical role of the snakes is far more central to the symbolism of the Epic, and it is this symbolism that is tangled up in the coils of the *Ādi Parvan*.

Several other important threads run through this first book, around which the scattered stories are not so much strung as coalesced, like crystals in a supersaturated solution: the history of the family of the Bhṛgus,[9] the conflict between Brahmins and kings (or Kṣatriyas), and the unnatural begetting of heroes. The book within a book that tells the main portion of the snake sacrifice is called the Book of Āstika; now, Āstika was so named because, at his birth, he said, "It *is*" [1.44.19–20], but his name is an obvious contrast with the better-known designation, Nāstika, "One who says it is *not*," the usual Hindu word for a heretic.[10] Āstika's story is therefore the story of the affirmation of good religion (in which one does not sacrifice snakes) against bad religion (in which one does sacrifice snakes). All of these themes play a part in the tales of snakes and horses, but they are so complex and so omnipresent in the Epic that I have thought it best to leave them in the background in order that the more specific zoological patterns may emerge more clearly in the foreground.

To unravel the thread of snakes and horses (and birds and dogs) in the first book of the Epic by following the order in which the events are presented would be possible, but rather confusing. I would prefer to rearrange the basic episodes according to their historical (or should I say mythical) chronology, supplementing them with secondary episodes (from the first book and occasionally from the fourteenth) in order to demonstrate the underlying structure of the equine and serpentine cosmogony of the *Mahābhārata*.

CATEGORIES OF SNAKES AND HORSES

Snakes are liminal creatures, on the borderline between animals and the anthropomorphic categories of beings (men, gods, and demons). In fact, the word that I have translated as snakes (following general usage) does not really mean snakes at all; it is *nāga*, that designates half-anthropomorphic half-serpentine creatures who live in the underworld (Pātāla) and in deep waters on earth. The translation as "snakes" is somewhat justified by the fact that to the *nāgas* are often assimilated more ordinary snakes or reptiles (*ahi, sarpa*, etc.), but the *nāgas* remain creatures betwixt and between. The Epic gives several recitations of the lineages of the snakes, treating them as families of individuals like the families of sages, worthy of respect [1.31.4–18; 1.52.3–22].

The moral ambiguity of the snakes is an essential point on which the plot of the Janamejaya sacrifice turns; when the gods ask Brahmā why he did not stop Kadrū from cursing her own sons, the snakes, he replies, "There are too many poisonous snakes. The mean, evil, virulent snakes who love to bite are the ones doomed to die, but not law-abiding ones" [1.34.9–10]. This process of culling the over-numerous herd, leaving only the virtuous behind, is a basic justification of the Epic genocide,[11] but it is particularly appropriate to the liminal snakes. As soon as the snakes are cursed, one of them, Śeṣa, rejects his wicked brothers and performs awesome acts of asceticism. (In this he imitates the paradigmatic figure of the good demon who abandons the demons to help the gods.)[12] Eventually he becomes Ananta, the serpent of infinity, who supports the earth, and he is even given Garuḍa as his helper! [1.32.1–25]. Once Ananta is permitted to violate the category of evil snakes, he is able to violate the category of snakes who are enemies of birds; all boundaries are erased. And when the gods and demons become incarnate as the heroes and villains of the *Mahābhārata* conflict, Śeṣa is the only snake who joins them, and as a hero: he becomes incarnate as Baladeva, the brother of Kṛṣṇa [1.61.90].

Later, at the time of Janamejaya's snake sacrifice, there is a sharp contrast between a bad snake (Takṣaka) and a good snake (Vāsuki). Takṣaka is already branded a villain by his various nefarious deeds, and here he cares only to save his own skin; Vāsuki is already established as a good guy through his service to the gods and demons at the time of the churning of the ocean, and here he is the one who takes measures to save all the other snakes [1.48.9–26]. When the genealogies of snakes are listed, Vāsuki is the author of one line and Takṣaka of another [1.52.4–9], but *both* sets are sacrificed, which seems to violate Brahmā's pious intention — as does the slaughter of *both* families of Bhāratas.

A blurring of boundaries sometimes occurs in the categories of snakes and horses. Generally, snakes are the enemies of horses, but there is also a confounding of snakes and horses. Takṣaka's son, who plays an important role in the episode of the burning of the snakes in the Khāṇḍava forest [1.218–219], is called Aśvasena ("Possessing an army of horses") [1.3.145]. In other parts of the Epic, too, snakes and horses are subtlely linked. When Nahuṣa becomes king of heaven, usurping the place of Indra, his downfall occurs when he uses the wrong sorts of horses: he yokes sages instead of horses to his chariot, and when he goes so far as to whip Agastya, Agastya curses him to become incarnate as a snake [13.102]. When Nala rescues a tiny snake from a forest fire (a strong parallel to the rescuing of the snakes from Janamejaya's sacrificial fire and from the Khāṇḍava forest), the snake turns into the great serpent Karkoṭaka, whose bite transforms Nala into a charioteer, peerless in his knowledge of horses [3.63].

One list of all the evil creatures in the universe uses the formulaic phrase, "Dānavas, Rākṣasas, Gandharvas, and Snakes" while in the very next verse the formula is repeated, but the Gandharvas are left out [1.59.5–6]. Later the groups are listed as "Gods, Gandharvas, and Rākṣasas," [1.61.102] and immediately afterwards as "Gods, Dānavas, and Rākṣasas, as well as Gandharvas and Apsarases" [1.62.1]; here, the snakes are left out. Sometimes the list includes "Gandharvas, Yakṣas, Rākṣasas, and Snakes" [1.218.23]; sometimes "Gods, Rākṣasas, Piśācas, Daityas, and Snakes" [1.216.23]. When Arjuna is born, and all creatures in the universe rejoice, "the brood of Kadrū and Vinatā, the Gandharvas and Apsarases, and all the creatures" pay honor to him [1.114.40]. Elsewhere, the lineages of birds, snakes, and Gandharvas are listed together in one group, set off from other lists [1.59.39–43].

From these formulae it would appear that the snakes are often connected with Gandharvas; sometimes they replace Gandharvas and sometimes they are grouped with them. The Gandharvas themselves are morally liminal,[13] listed sometimes with the gods and sometimes with the demons, and so from the standpoint of moral categories it is fitting that they should inhabit the twilight zone with the snakes. But, more important for my argument, the Gandharvas are closely associated with horses.[14] When Arjuna defeats the Gandharva Citraratha, Citraratha gives a hundred magic horses to each of the five Pāṇḍavas [1.158.45–51].

The Epic says, "Gandharvī gave birth to the horses, Surasā, the daughter of Kadrū, gave birth to the snakes, and Kadrū gave birth to the serpents; Vinatā had two famous sons, Garuḍa and Aruṇa" [1.60.65–68]. From this cluster of begats it is clear that horses, snakes, and birds form a subgroup in the plan of creation, with horses mediating between birds and snakes (generally, though not always, in association with birds and opposition to snakes), just as Gandharvas mediate between gods and demons (generally, though not always, in association with gods and opposition to demons).

Passages such as these suggest that horses, snakes, and birds are intimately related in the *Mahābhārata*. How they are related and why they are related are questions that are addressed in the complex cycle of myths about the snake sacrifice of Janamejaya, to which we will now turn. Since the stories are well known, I will not retell them here, but will merely give a summary of each episode in the Appendix.

THE CHURNING OF THE OCEAN
(1.15–17; see story 1 in the Appendix)

The myth of the churning of the ocean, an important cosmogonic story, is told in the *Ādi Parvan* explicitly in order to explain the origin of Uccaiḥśravas, the stallion of Indra. In this version of the story, a snake, Vāsuki, is used as a literal tug-of-war rope, a liminal figure as always, in the eternal battle between the gods and the demons. The churning finally produces, simultaneously, the white solar horse and the lunar Soma (together with the sun and the moon themselves, which are swallowed and revived periodically). The head of the demon Rāhu becomes immortal, but his "tail" (that is, the rest of his body) is mortal. But the contrast between the head of the snake Vāsuki, which spews fire upon the demons, and his tail, which is held comfortably by the gods, is a reversal of what one might naturally expect: a contrast between the "good" head and the "bad" tail. Reversals of this sort characterize the world of snakes in general, and the benign Vāsuki is no exception. We might outline some of these contrasts as follows:

gods/demons ≡ head/tail ≡ [tail/head] ≡ sun/moon ≡ horse/snake

THE FIGHT BETWEEN KADRŪ AND VINATĀ (1.14–30; see story 2 in the Appendix)

The story of the emergence of the divine stallion from the churning of the ocean is told in the *Ādi Parvan* only in order to explain the origin of the quarrel between birds and snakes; indeed, the churning is inserted as a kind of digression in the story of that quarrel. The Book of Āstika—that is, the section that the *Mahābhārata* regards as the beginning of the story of Janamejaya's sacrifice—begins with the contest between Kadrū and Vinatā (an important story that is also retold later, to Āstika [1.49]).

Both Kadrū and Vinatā are evil mothers, though in different ways. Vinatā inadvertently deforms her son, the dawn, producing a creature that is, like a *nāga*, "stunted" from the waist down,[15] a creature that, like Rāhu, has a good head and a bad body. Kadrū asks her sons to commit a dishonest act and then curses them when they refuse to do it. (Apparently they *do* do it later, as Kadrū wins her bet, but she never modifies her curse.) Though Vinatā is depicted as a loving mother, she does send her son on a dangerous journey. But it is the enmity of these two women toward one another, rather than toward their sons, that begins the trouble; and that trouble is about a horse. This myth may well be the earliest attested example of betting on a horse; significantly, the horse is "fixed," and not for the last time in human history (nor is this the last crooked wager in the *Mahābhārata*: a loaded dice game robs the Pāṇḍavas of their kingdom). Thus Kadrū wins her bet by a trick, and by another trick (Garuḍa's double-dealing with Indra about "putting down" the Soma) she loses what she had won.

Transporting the snakes to the Ramaṇīyaka island is a device intended not only to give them a pleasant vacation (flight included), but a way of dealing with an evil that, though it cannot be destroyed, can at least be moved out of the way. Kṛṣṇa similarly transports another group of snakes to the island of Ramaṇaka [*sic*] in order to keep them from killing the little boys in the pool in his village; that pool was the only pool that Garuḍa was forbidden to enter (this being his curse for eating off-limits fish there), and so Kṛṣṇa promises the snakes safety from Garuda on Ramaṇaka.[16]

The themes that we will see repeated throughout this corpus are the enmity between birds and snakes and the connection between snakes and horses (particularly horses' tails). That the tail of the horse—white for birds, black for snakes—is the pivotal point may well be a reflection of the episode in the churning of the ocean when the *head* of the snake spews fire on the demons, while the *tail* of the snake rains upon the gods. But it is also a reversal of the Vedic emphasis on the horse's head; where gods (and kings) use the head of the horse, snakes (and demons) use the tail. The bird/horse/sun fire that threatens the snakes is another recurrent theme. We might therefore set up a series of oppositions:

gods/demons ≡ birds/snakes ≡ fire/water ≡ white/black ≡
horse's head/horse's tail

The gift of immortality almost won but then lost is a theme that we have already seen in the tale of the churning of the ocean; there it was the demons who lost the Soma, and here it is the snakes. The careful distinction between proper and improper eating is here applied to one of the many theriomorphic multiforms of the warring Pāṇḍavas and Kurus: an elephant and a tortoise. Normally, these are positive symbols of power and support, the great tortoise (Kaśyapa or Kūrma) and serpent (Ananta) or elephant (both called *nāgas*) on which the earth rests. But here that function is reversed; the giant elephant and tortoise are set down precariously and destructively on *top* of mountains, and their sibling rivalry makes them fodder for Garuḍa. This culinary touchstone is then itself tested with the liminal case: the pure, inedible Brahmin and his impure, edible wife:

cosmic tortoise + elephant/warring tortoise + elephant ≡
Brahmin/Niṣāda ≡ man/woman ≡
forbidden food/permitted food ≡ immortality/death

We will see other cases of inversions of the simple rules of food tabus in other myths in this cycle.

THE DEATH OF PARIKṢIT
(1.36–40; see story 3 in the Appendix)

The snake sacrifice has at least three causes: the curse of Kadrū is the more distant cause, the death of Parikṣit is the central cause, and Uttanka's inciting of Janamejaya is the proximate cause. We have seen the first link in the chain; let us now consider the second. Parikṣit's birth conjures up Aśvatthāman's ghastly slaughter of the unborn children, setting in motion the final doomsday machine. Parikṣit is a symbol of survival, but a grim symbol indeed. The text seems most concerned here with ways in which Parikṣit's curse might have been averted but wasn't—just as the *Mahābhārata* as a whole is concerned with ways that the war might have been averted but wasn't. Parikṣit's complicity in his own death is quite clear: he was wrong to mock the Brahmin in the first place and wrong to mock the Brahmin's curse later by laughing at the tiny worm. The encounter between Takṣaka and a descendant of Kaśyapa (the husband of Kadrū and Vinatā, who was given the power to avert snake-bite right after Kadrū was given the power to curse her sons to be burnt in Janamejaya's sacrifice) is the turning point for the fate of Parikṣit. The burning and revival of the tree that stands for Parikṣit and his tree-house is a recapitulation of the circumstances of Parikṣit's birth and revival, but not, as Kāśyapa intends it to be, a prediction of Parikṣit's death and revival:

revived/stillborn ≡ killed/unrevived

The bribery of Kāśyapa by Takṣaka is a sticky point; when the story of Parikṣit's death is retold to Janamejaya, Janamejaya says, "I would like to know exactly what was said between Takṣaka and Kāśyapa. Surely the forest was empty; were there any eye-witnesses? If I can hear the exact conversation, I will set out to kill all the snakes" [1.46.26–27]. The ministers then tell him, "There just happened to be a man who had climbed up into a tree, looking for kindling wood; that was the tree that Takṣaka burnt and Kāśyapa revived, and the man was burnt and revived along with them. Unseen by them, he heard them talk, and then he came and told it all here in the city." This final bit of evidence infuriates Janamejaya, the more so as in the eye-witness account Kāśyapa does not even justify himself with the thought that the king is fated to die anyway; he just accepts the bribe, which makes both him and Takṣaka more culpable and direct factors in the death of Parikṣit than they are in the earlier version.

EXCURSUS: RURU'S SNAKE-BITTEN BRIDE
(1.8–12; see story 4 in the Appendix)

The story of Ruru, a multiform of the tale of Parikṣit, is told as part of the extended preface to that story. As usual, there is a rather loose official thread to tie the story to the central theme: at the end of the episode, we discover that the tale of Ruru is part (a nonessential part) of the story of the telling of the *Mahābhārata*. But the tale of Ruru is more closely related to the tale of Parikṣit through its symbolic themes: the death and resurrection from snake-bite, the fight between a snake and someone named "Bird," the artificial snake that leads to the creation of a real snake (just as the harmless worm turned into Takṣaka and Nala's tiny snake turned into the great Karkoṭaka), the auspicious meeting between two people with the same name, and the inauspicious presence of a snake at a fire offering.

The lizard's sermon is reminiscent of the sermon of the sage upon whom Parikṣit drapes the snake: it is all right for kings (but not Brahmins) to commit certain violent acts. Finally, there is the liminality of the lizard, who is a reptile but not a snake, as he himself eloquently points out; he is a mediator between good reptiles and bad reptiles. In this he is a heightened form of the snakes themselves, who are, as we have seen, liminally attached/detached to the categories of gods, demons, and men. Like the snakes who refuse to commit the dishonest act of dyeing the horse's tail black, the lizard is unjustly punished at first but ultimately rescued from that punishment. In light of the tremendous importance that deserved and undeserved curses have played throughout the Epic (and, indeed, throughout Hindu mythology in general), this adds an important dimension to our understanding:

Brahmin/Kṣatriya ≡ lizard/noxious snake ≡
just punishment/unjust punishment ≡ curse/revenge

THE BIRTH OF ĀSTIKA
(1.13, 1.34–35, 1.42–45; see story 5 in the Appendix)

The story of the snake sacrifice begins, in the *Mahābhārata*, not with the circumstances that led to the attempt to kill the snakes, but with the circumstances that led to the rescue of the snakes. Indeed, the story as a whole is known formally as the Tale of Āstika [1.13–53], not the story of Janamejaya, though that tale actually begins after the narration of the birth of Āstika (a story that is retold in three different places).

Jaratkāru's unwillingness to marry leads him to suggest a condition that he assumes will in fact prove insuperable (just as demons often choose conditions for their death that they hope cannot possibly be met): he wants to marry a mirror image of himself, a girl with his name. When he finds that Vāsuki's sister just happens to be named Jaratkāru, he is forced to keep his promise. (We have already seen a similarly striking coincidence in the prediction that someone named Ruru will be released from his curse by someone named Ruru.) The unlikelihood of finding such a girl is mocked in the Epic; when the bard Ugraśravas tells Śaunaka that the girl was named Jaratkāru, Śaunaka bursts out laughing and says, "How fitting!" [1.36.5]. To get out of his promise, Jaratkāru places his wife in a no-win situation and then uses this as an excuse to leave her. But he has already done both of his duties: he has provided an heir for his ancestors and a savior for the snakes.

EXCURSUS (?): THE CURSE OF THE DOGS (1.3.1–18; see story 6 in the Appendix)

It must have been some time before the snake sacrifice of Janamejaya that there occurred the first event of the series that is narrated in the Epic: the curse of the son of Saramā by the brothers of Janamejaya. On the narrative level, this episode merely tells how it came to pass that Janamejaya employed a sage very much like Āstika and how that sage performed a sacrifice on behalf of Janamejaya. But the sage, named Somaśravas, is a slightly distorted twin or mirror image of Āstika, as is evident from the peculiarities of his birth: like Āstika, he was born of the seed of a sage shed in the womb of a snake woman. Unlike Āstika, however, who thwarts Janamejaya's sacrifice, this sage is engaged by Janamejaya and successfully completes a sacrifice for him—a sacrifice that is not described here, but that may well have been a horse sacrifice, an expiatory ritual for which Janamejaya was already famous in the Brāhmaṇas[17] and in the Epic itself [1.90.11]. The "unseen evil" from which this sacrifice saves Janamejaya is specified neither in the *Brāhmaṇas* nor in the *Mahābhārata*, but why could it not have been the evil of the death of his father from snake-bite, or indeed the evil of the subsequent snake sacrifice?

Less obvious, but equally important, is the offense for which the dog was originally cursed: he is wrongly accused of wrongly eating something; that is, his accusers sin in thinking that he has sinned by eating a forbidden food. The dog did *not* lick the oblation (perhaps an echo of the Soma that the snakes tried to lick up) and so he produces a dangerous curse, while the snake woman eats the seed of the sage (an unusual but not unprecedented act) and produces the child who will end the curse. Like Ruru the lizard, a liminal reptile who is unfairly confounded with a noxious snake, the dog as an individual is wrongly blamed for the sins of the larger category of which he is a part.

For dogs are notorious scavengers in India, and the *Brāhmaṇas* abound in tales of dogs who defile the sacrificial offerings[18]—of whom by far the most important is Saramā herself, the mother of the dog in this episode. Dogs and birds are here, as in Homer, the creatures who devour carrion, particularly the bodies of unfortunate heroes who fall in battle and are denied the proper funeral rites. It was a dog, too (or, rather, the god Dharma in the form of a dog) who accompanied Yudhiṣṭhira to heaven [17.3]. Dogs thus foreshadow the final battle and the death of the heroes. We might therefore say that dogs and birds in their negative aspect as carrion eaters are to be contrasted with snakes and horses as sacrificial animals:

bird/snake ≡ dog/horse

or that birds and snakes as wild animals are to be contrasted with dogs and horses as domesticated animals:

bird/dog ≡ snake/horse

or that birds and horses as solar, heavenly animals are to be contrasted with dogs and snakes as lower, earthly animals:

bird/snake ≡ horse/dog

This last formulation seems to be the pattern emphasized by our text. But however one chooses to draw lines between these charismatic animals, it is clear that the episode of the dogs and the sacrificial food is not an accidental interpolation but an essential link in the chain of threatened sacrifices.

THE UNCLEAN FOOD OF UTTANKA
(1.3.85–95; see story 7 in the Appendix)

The story of Saramā's son and the sacrificial food is immediately followed by a sequence of apparently unrelated stories about pupils whose teachers cause them to eat improper food—or, more precisely, food that *seems* to be improper but is in fact proper. The central figure in these episodes, Uttanka, reappears later in the Epic at a crucial moment—right before Yudhiṣṭhira's horse sacrifice in Book Fourteen. Moreover, it is to Uttanka that Kṛṣṇa gives a vision (and a sermon) like the one that he gives Arjuna in the *Bhagavad Gītā* (this one is much longer and is called the *Anugītā* [14.16–51]), and it is Uttanka to whom Kṛṣṇa makes his famous justification and apology for having allowed the war to take place [14.53.11–22]. Even today, the bards who narrate the Epic in South India say that the Uttanka story is the beginning of the *Mahābhārata*.[19] The Uttanka stories are not, therefore, casual interpolations—though, as we shall see, they may once have been interpolations.

The passage in the *Ādi Parvan* begins with the story of the young pupil Upamanyu, who is so starved by his teacher that he drinks the froth spat out by the calves that he is tending (the same substance that nourished the sage mocked by Parikṣit); the Aśvins rescue him and tell him, *en passant*, that his own teacher had once improperly eaten a cake given him by the Aśvins, without offering it first to *his* teacher [1.3.34–78]. Upamanyu's fellow pupil, named Veda, later has a pupil named Uttanka, who becomes the preceptor of two kings: Janamejaya and Pauṣya. Uttanka then becomes the victim of a more bizarre series of culinary challenges, including bull's dung and the fiery farts of a magic horse. In terms of the narrative, this story explains why Janamejaya decided to undertake the snake sacrifice. Uttanka's arrival at Janamejaya's palace mediates between Janamejaya's encounters with two other Brahmins: Somaśravas (who performs a horse sacrifice for him) and Āstika (who prevents his snake sacrifice). The information about Parikṣit that Uttanka gives Janamejaya is quite superfluous, since any of his ministers could have told him the same thing, nor does Janamejaya really need the knowledge of Takṣaka's relatively minor offense against Uttanka to drive him (Hamlet-like) to avenge Takṣaka's murder of his own father. We can best understand the role of this encounter as yet another instance of the narrative that is told in order to explain the *telling* of the *Mahābhārata* war rather than the *doing* of that war.

But the Uttanka story is also told to reinforce the symbolism of the story of the war. The strange meals offered to Uttanka are part of the topsy-turvey world of the snake sacrifice and the chaos that precedes doomsday. The purity or impurity of dung generally varies according to the nature of the creature that produces it: cow dung is a source of purification (when eaten as part of the pañcagāvya or five cow-products) but snake-dung, for instance, is highly impure: when the snakes hear of Janamejaya's intention to kill them in a sacrifice, some of them suggest that they dirty his sacrifice with their dung and urine, in order to defile all the food [1.33.24]. The bull's dung is an unusual food, and disgusting, but probably more pure than impure; it was, moreover, like the cakes of the Aśvins, eaten by the teacher in previous times. In any case, it turns out to be the most wonderful of all foods, the Soma, while the feast fit for a king turns out to be defiled. Though Uttanka does drink the Soma when it is presented in this unlikely form, he loses it symbolically when he loses the earrings by setting them down on the ground, a clear echo of the fate of the snakes who lost the Soma when Garuḍa tricked them by putting it down on the ground. Uttanka is polluted twice: by eating without cleansing himself and by seeing a "beggar" (Takṣaka); the first causes him to lose sight of the woman who will give him the earrings, and the second causes him to lose the earrings:

bull's dung/horse's ass ≡ Soma/king's food ≡
food pollution/caste pollution

Uttanka also "eats" by blowing into the horse's ass; this is not, literally, food; but it functions as food in two ways. Blowing *into* the ass of the horse is the inversion of eating the dung that comes *out* of the bull, and this noneating or reversal of eating protects the boy in the underworld, just as the refusal of magic food offered in the underworld protects other boys who journey to the kingdom of death.[20]

It is in the kingdom of death or in the underworld, too, that the young hero usually encounters the good and evil goddess (here transformed into the two fates—black and white, like Kadrū and Vinatā), the dangerously seductive woman (here transformed into the teacher's lustful wife, a notorious creature in Hindu mythology), the magic woman whom he can see only when he has been ritually prepared (here transformed into the wife of King Pauṣya), and the magic horse on which he rides away with his stolen treasure, the magic earrings.

The horse in this underworld is the god of fire, Agni, who is often depicted as a horse in the *Ṛg Veda*[21] and who appears as the underwater doomsday mare in later Hindu mythology;[22] Kadrū and Vinatā see the underwater mare deep in the ocean when they go to view Uccaiḥśravas [1.19.6–17]. Agni himself (though not in the shape of a horse) is cursed (and blessed) to be omnivorous—that is, to be able to eat anything without being defiled by it—in an episode that follows shortly after the story of Uttanka [1.5–7].

But what is significant for our purposes in the story of Uttanka is the fact that the horse is the *enemy of the snakes*. More specifically, the horse in the underworld is the fire into which the snakes will eventually be sacrificed. In light of the snake-symbolism of the tail of the stallion Uccaiḥśravas, it is not surprising that it should be the hind-quarters of the horse that Uttanka must deal with in the world of snakes. And where it was the head of the snake that produced fire at the time of the churning, it is the tail of the horse that produces fire here. This may be no more than an expression of the zoological truth that the danger of snakes comes from their mouths while the danger from horses comes from their hind-quarters, but it may mean something else as well: a reversal in keeping with the enmity between horses and snakes and the inversions generally characteristic of the underworld. Our normal expectations were reversed in the myth of the churning, where the head turned out to be worse than the tail, because one was dealing with the "wrong" animal, the snake; these reversals are maintained here even when one is dealing with the "right" animal, the horse, in the context of the "wrong" world. Indeed, we might further develop our set of contrasts:

horse/snake ≡ head/tail

That Indra should be mounted on a snake named Airāvata seems strange at first, since Airāvata is usually the name of the elephant that Indra rides upon; but since the Sanskrit word *nāga* means both snake and elephant (probably because of the serpentine trunk), it seems likely that the author chose the snakier of the two alternative meanings for this snakey story. That the snake (*ne* elephant) further masquerades as a bull makes sense too, since all of these snakes disguise themselves, and Indra normally rides on a bull (when he is not riding on an elephant). The serpentine identity of Airāvata is, in any case, confirmed a few lines later, when Uttanka, upon arriving in the underworld of snakes, sings a hymn of praise that begins with a flattering description of Airāvata as the lord of snakes [1.3.139–146] and only then goes on to praise Takṣaka.

The story of Uttanka is repeated, with variations, in the fourteenth book of the *Mahābhārata*, the *Āśvamedhika Parvan*, which tells of Yudhiṣṭhira's successful horse sacrifice. This version is longer than the one in the *Ādi Parvan* and makes better sense of some of the incongruities of that version, so much so that it seems likely that the version in the fourteenth book was the original version, later reintroduced into the *Ādi Parvan* (with certain revisions) *precisely because the redactors saw how very relevant it was to the introductory themes*. It is worth summarizing the *Āsvamedhika* version here:

Once when Uttanka was wandering in the desert, he saw a naked Untouchable surrounded by dogs; the Untouchable invited Uttanka to accept the copious fluids that were coming out of his penis. Uttanka refused and the Untouchable disappeared, whereupon Kṛṣṇa appeared and told Uttanka that the Untouchable was in fact Indra in disguise and that the fluids coming out of him were the Soma juice that would have made Uttanka immortal. In compensation for this lost opportunity, Kṛṣṇa promised Uttanka that whenever he was thirsty he could sumon rain clouds, named Uttanka clouds.

Uttanka had been the pupil of the sage Gautama for many years, and when he grew very old, Gautama made him into a young man again and gave him his young daughter in marriage. Gautama's wife, Ahalyā, asked Uttanka to bring her the earrings of Madayantī, the wife of the cannibal Saudāsa. Uttanka met Saudāsa, who was smeared with human blood, like the god of death himself. Saudāsa was hunting for food, and eager to eat Uttanka. But Uttanka persuaded Saudāsa to tell him where he would find Madayantī and to teach him the meaning of certain mystic signs. She gave him the earrings—which, she said, would protect him from hunger and thirst—but she warned him that the snakes would get them if he put them down on the ground, the Yaksas would get them if he was impure from eating, and the gods would get them if he fell asleep.

On the way back to Ahalyā, Uttanka got hungry and dropped the earrings; a serpent of the race of Airāvata carried them down into an anthill. Indra pierced the anthill with a thunderbolt, opening a way into the underworld, which Uttanka entered. There he saw a black horse with a white tail, who told Uttanka to blow into his ass; "don't be disgusted, just do it," he said; "You used to do it all the time in Gautama's hermitage in the old days." Uttanka blew, and from the horse—who was Agni, the god of fire—came smoke, which pervaded the world of the snakes. Vāsuki gave the earrings to Uttanka, who took them back to Ahalyā [14.55–57].

Here it is Indra himself, with no bull beside him, let alone a snake disguised as a bull, who offers Uttanka the Soma (in the form of a liquid, far more appropriate than dung); with complementary economy, the horse in the underworld is riderless and speaks for himself. Indra then reappears to drive a thunderbolt into the anthill to open a way to the underworld; the association between snakes, anthills, and lightning is well known in India.[23] It is not surprising that the earrings should have the property of staving off hunger and thirst, since they are assimilated to the Soma and to the Uttanka clouds; but it is both unfortunate and surprising that they fail to exhibit this property at the crucial moment, when it is hunger and thirst for water to drink (rather than the need for water at the sight of a beggar in disguise) that causes Uttanka to lose the earrings. This time he is warned that the snakes are not the only people after those magic earrings: the snakes are flanked by gods and demonic Yakṣas. King Pauṣya—who is, it may be recalled, one of Uttanka's two patrons, the other being Janamejaya—is here replaced by a cannibal, who looks like the god of the underworld. Now, a cannibal is the extreme instance of a person who eats forbidden food; Pauṣya's fastidious bickerings about hair in food thus appear to have been transformed from the far more straightforward statement that Saudāsa was smeared with human blood. (The hair in the food may have been suggested by the importance of the hairs of the tail of Uccaiḥśravas in another part of the same cycle.)

The villainous serpent in this version is first an anonymous member of the race of Airāvata (Airāvata being the source of the magic dung in the first version) and then Vāsuki, rather than Takṣaka; there is therefore no explicit connection with Janamejaya's snake sacrifice. It would have been simple enough, however, to change Vāsuki and the anonymous snake into Takṣaka in order to incorporate this story into the cycle of Parikṣit and Janamejaya. As in the *Ādi Parvan* version, Uttanka blows into the horse's ass, but this time the horse reminds him that this is an old habit long practiced in Gautama's hermitage. Precisely what is meant by this mind-boggling statement I would not care to say, though it is worth remarking that a man capable of eating bullshit is capable of sodomizing horses. But there is, unfortunately, a more sober explanation. The horse's remark is merely a twist on the usual statement made to persuade someone to eat unusual food (the cakes of the Aśvins, the dung of the bull): your *guru* used to do it. Moreover, the horse, as he explains to Uttanka, is fire, "your guru's guru," and so it is likely that Uttanka used to "blow' into it to fan its flames.

But there is one striking implicit connection between the horse in the underworld in the *Āśvamedhika* version of the Uttanka story and the horse/snake complex in the *Ādi Parvan* as a whole: the black horse has a white tail. (Here one must note that the bards of the *Mahābhārata* are bothered by this tail. One manuscript says that it is a white horse with a black tail, and the version selected by the Critical Edition could also mean that it is a horse with a black-and-white tail. One way or another, however, it is a horse of another color.) The hairs of this tail make the horse the very inverse of Uccaiḥśravas, the white horse with a black tail, who is the source of the enmity between the birds and the snakes:

Janamejaya/cannibal ≡ human hair/human flesh ≡
white/black ≡ [black/white ≡ horse-head/horse-tail]

JANAMEJAYA'S SNAKE SACRIFICE
(1.47–53; see story 8 in the Appendix)

We come at last to the central myth in the cycle, the story of Janamejaya's snake sacrifice. Janamejaya decides to avenge his father, just as the son of the sage mocked by Parikṣit decided to avenge *his* father—and as Paraśurāma decided to avenge *his* father, by wiping out the race of the Kṣatriyas altogether. And just as Parikṣit failed to carry out his "ritual" (of protection from snake-bite) because he jumped the gun, relaxing before the day was completely over, so Janamejaya fails to complete his ritual because he offers a boon to Āstika before the last and most important snake—Takṣaka—has been killed. Takṣaka hovers in mid-air, caught between the black magic of the snake ritual and the white magic of Āstika; in this he is the very embodiment of the liminality of the snakes.[24] The contrast between the two paradigmatic sacrifices is made clear at the end, when Janamejaya asks Āstika to come for the *other* sacrifice, the horse sacrifice; as Āstika disapproved of the snake sacrifice, so he approves of the horse sacrifice. Finally, the story of the happening of the snake sacrifice gives way to the telling of the snake sacrifice, an act which in its turn becomes a deed: the telling is a way of doing what Parikṣit and Janamejaya could not do: it protects you from snakes:

completed ritual/incomplete ritual ≡
horse sacrifice/snake sacrifice ≡ telling/doing

This function of the story may also provide us with a more specific clue about the origins of these putatively "interpolated" snakey passages. The story of Parikṣit bears a striking resemblance to many folk tales, of which perhaps the most famous is the tale of Behulā, which Ed Dimock has so well translated.[25] So, too, other folk stories about people saved from snake-bite are often used as charms to save the listeners from snake-bite. It may well be that stories of this type, which surely must have been current in the oral literature of India from a time long before the recension of the *Mahābhārata*, are the source of some of the episodes in the *Ādi Parvan.*[26] But the snakes are not dragged in "by the hairs" (*an den Haarn*), like Draupadī. It took the vision of the Epic poet to see why and how these stories were relevant to the great battle of the Bhāratas, and to insert them, like so many snakey hairs, in the tale of the sacrificial horse.

THE BURNING OF THE KHĀṆḌAVA FOREST
(1.215–225; see story 9 in the Appendix)

The final episode in the *Ādi Parvan* is the burning of the Khāṇḍava Forest, an episode tied to the central story of the Epic ritual battle by the snake/ropes of the mythology of Janamejaya's sacrifice. It is evident that the burning of the Khāṇḍava forest is a multiform not only of the great *Mahābhārata* battle itself but of the snake sacrifice that is an already transformed variant of the ritual battle. The theme of unclean food, reflected in the curse that Agni would be omnivorous (together with the boon that he would remain undefiled by all food), here culminates in Agni's insatiable hunger (an incidental mockery of the hunger of a Brahmin) that drives him to devour not only the trees in the forest (his proper food, an expanded form of the kindling sticks of the Vedic fire) but all of the living creatures in the forest (improper food, not a usual component of the Vedic oblation). The torment of the creatures in their death throes in the forest fire echoes the torment of the snakes in Janamejaya's fire.

The horror inspired by the vivid descriptions of these two scenes of suffering is a vision of the shadow side of the Vedic ritual and the ritual of battle. But more than that: Agni functions in the Khāṇḍava forest as the doomsday fire that sweeps all before him. The death of the creatures in the great forest fire is an inversion of their birth in the churning of the ocean, with which the conflagration is explicitly contrasted. Aśvasena's mother swallows his head and then his tail just as the demons and gods grab first Vāsuki's head and then his tail, and she is beheaded when she has swallowed him, just as Rāhu is beheaded when he has swallowed the Soma.

The episode of the little birds introduces a bit of unexpected comic relief into otherwise grim tragedy. The birth of the birds, fathered by Mandapāla, parallels the birth of Āstika, fathered by Jaratkāru: here, a bird mother replaces the snake mother. The fight between Mandapāla's two wives—one maternal, the nonmaternal—further recapitulates the quarrel between Kaśyapa's two wives, Kadrū and Vinatā. (So, too, Aśvasena's mother is good in her intention to save her child but evil in her act of devouring him; fittingly, she is cut in half.) Moreover, the fact that the little birds regard rats and cats as greater enemies than fire (or snakes) introduces further subtlety into our attempts to draw up ranks in the animal kingdom.

This myth diverges from the Janamejaya cycle in several interesting ways. Here, at first, horses are ranged against horses—Agni's fiery Gandharva steeds against Indra's stormy bays—and snakes are no longer pitted against birds; as doomsday draws near, the lion lies down with the lamb, and together they fight in vain against Agni and his allies. Our simple categories have been subdivided and confused, giving us something like this:

animals/gods ≡ Indra/Agni ≡ water/fire ≡
Varuṇa/Kṛṣṇa + Arjuna ≡ bay horse/white horse ≡
birds + snakes/rats + cats ≡ good mother/evil mother

But this unstable situation cannot last. Takṣaka is a key figure in both the sacrifice and the conflagration: at first, Indra protects him from the fire, as he protects him from Janamejaya (and as he protects the snakes from the heat of the sun when Garuḍa is carrying them to Ramaṇīyaka). Then, however, there is a new twist: Takṣaka turns out not to be in the forest at all; he has gone to that other scene of doomsday—the field of the Kurus, where the great battle has taken place. His absence releases and resolves the tension between Agni and Indra. Indra and the gods leave the field to Agni and the Pāṇḍavas, and almost everyone else is killed.

gods/animals ≡ fire/water ≡ horses/snakes + birds ≡ victory/doomsday

Only a tiny miscellaneous group survives: the demon of illusion (Maya), a snake named after a horse, and a small family of birds. These happy few are the bare bones of our paradigmatic symbolic structure: demonic snake, bird, and horse.

THE FINAL HORSE SACRIFICE AND THE SURVIVAL OF PARIKṢIT

The fourteenth book of the *Mahābhārata* is devoted to the great horse sacrifice of Yudhiṣṭhira, which should be a triumphant event. And to a certain extent it is: the consecrated stallion is set free to roam for a year, guarded by Arjuna (who has several exciting adventures in the course of his wanderings), and Yudhiṣṭhira, the Dharma King, ascends his throne. But the triumph is bitterly undercut by the fruition of several tragic events, the seeds of which were sown in the very first book of the Epic.

One striking echo from the first book to the fourteenth is the episode of the mongoose, who comes to the horse sacrifice and tells his life story to Yudhiṣṭhira. He tells of a time of famine, when Dharma wandered the earth disguised as a Brahmin until he found a devout family that gave him their last food; the mongoose, who witnessed this extreme of generosity, scorns the official munificence of Yudhiṣṭhira's horse sacrifice. Moreover, as he says, he himself is Anger (Krodha), who became incarnate as the result of a curse: in order to test Jamadāgni's equanimity, he had defiled the milk offering made by Jamadāgni to the ancestors; Jamadāgni passed the test, but the ancestors cursed Anger to become incarnate as a mongoose. To modify the curse, they gave him the power of human speech and promised that he would be released from his mongoose form when he would scorn Yudhiṣṭhira's sacrifice [14.96]. The polluted food, the famine, and the appearance of the god in disguise might suggest themes from the Uttanka episodes (though the themes appear in many other texts as well). The story about Jamadāgni reminds us of the slaughter of Kṣatriyas that his son, Paraśurāma, perpetrated to avenge his death, an episode that began the whole *Ādi Parvan*. More particularly, the mongoose is the traditional enemy of snakes, an enemy more tenacious and bloodthirsty than any bird. (The word for mongoose, *nakula*, is also the name of one of the twin heroes born of the *equine* Aśvins.) This mongoose is a welcome, albeit critical, visitor at the horse sacrifice—perhaps because he keeps the snakes away.

By the time the horse sacrifice is completed, almost everyone is dead; the Pāṇḍava brothers alone remain alive, Pyrhhic victors, to rule their decimated kingdom. And even they will soon die; as they themselves foresee, only their descendant Parikṣit—the man who is doomed to die of Takṣaka's bite—will remain to carry on the family line. Indeed, right before the sacrifice, Parikṣit is stillborn—an inauspicious beginning, though Kṛṣṇa quickly revives him. (Parikṣit's name is glossed to mean that he was born when all the rest of the Bhārata race was defunct [parikṣīna; 10.16.3].) When the Pāṇḍavas leave this world, Parikṣit is installed as king in Hāstinapura [17.1–7]. And though Parikṣit dies an unnatural and early death, at least he is not cut off before begetting a son—Janamejaya, who persuades Vyāsa to grant him a final vision of his dead father [15.43].

When all were in despair at the death of the newborn Parikṣit, suddenly the death was reversed into life; and when Parikṣit laughed at Takṣaka's threat to his life, the life was reversed into death. So the auspicious horse sacrifice is directly preceded by the death and revival of the man whose death will supply the final spark to ignite the inauspicious snake sacrifice. In a sense, Parikṣit's appearance in the fourteenth book casts upon the triumphant horse sacrifice the chill of the black sacrifice of snakes that is to take place in the future, though we have read of it in the past. The circularity of doomsday could not be better expressed.

My purposes in laying out the structures of the snake/horse myths of the *Ādi Parvan* in this way have been several. I have wanted to show the unification of the first book, which has so often been seen as a pointless and irrelevant miscellany. I have wanted to show how the subtle repetitions, never quite the same, reveal a point that is never stated outright.[27] And I have wanted to show that the relentless volume of those repetitions testifies to the great importance that the author of the great Epic placed upon that complex of perceptions which saw a snake behind every horse, a doomsday behind every victory, an uncompleted ritual behind every completed sacrifice, and the survival only of the telling when all the doing was over.

Though the underlying structure that unifies the tales in the *Ādi Parvan* cannot be stated baldly, it can, I think, be suggested by a chart compounded of all the charts that we have sketched as we moved through the myths [segments that are reversals of the basic pattern will be bracketed]:

gods/demons ≡ gods/animals ≡
Brahmin/Kṣatriya ≡ Brahmin/Niṣāda ≡ man/woman ≡
Janamejaya/cannibal ≡ good mother/evil mother ≡
sun/moon ≡ fire/water ≡ white/black ≡ [black/white ≡]
head/tail ≡ [tail/head ≡] bull's dung/horse's ass ≡
bird/snake ≡ horse/dog ≡ horse/snake ≡ horses/snakes + birds ≡
[golden horse/white horse ≡] lizard/noxious snake ≡
[birds + snakes/rats + cats ≡]
horse sacrifice/snake sacrifice ≡
permitted food/forbidden food ≡
Soma/king's food ≡ human hair/human flesh ≡
food pollution/caste pollution ≡
just punishment/unjust punishment ≡ curse/revenge ≡

immortality/death ≡ revived/stillborn ≡ killed/unrevived ≡ victory/doomsday ≡ completed ritual/incomplete ritual ≡ telling/doing

APPENDIX
SUMMARY OF EPISODES FROM THE *MAHĀBHĀRATA*

1. Once upon a time, the gods and demons decided to churn the ocean in order to obtain the Soma, the elixir of immortality. They used Mount Mandara for the churn and the snake Vāsuki as the churning rope: the gods took hold of Vāsuki's tail and the demons took Vāsuki's head, and they began to churn. Vāsuki belched forth fire and smoke from his mouth, but the clouds of smoke became rain to cool the gods in their labors. Eventually there emerged from the ocean the sun, the moon, the goddess Śrī, the goddess of wine, and the white horse; and finally the elixir came forth. The gods and demons fought for possession of the Soma, and the demons managed to steal it for a while; a demon named Rāhu swallowed the Soma, but when it had reached his neck, Viṣṇu beheaded him; Rāhu's head remained immortal (periodically swallowing the sun and moon in eclipses), but his body perished. Finally, the gods won the Soma for themselves [1.15–17].

2. Kadrū and Vinatā, two sisters, were the wives of Kaśyapa. Kadrū chose to give birth to a thousand snakes, and Vinatā chose to have two sons. When Kadrū had hatched her eggs, Vinatā worried that hers were still unhatched; she broke open the first too soon and produced a deformed son, Aruṇa (the dawn), stunted from the waist down. But her second son was Garuḍa, king of the birds, who blazed like fire.

One day the two women saw the stallion Uccaiḥśravas; Vinatā claimed that he was entirely white, but Kadrū said he had a black tail. They made a wager, the loser to be the slave of the winner. Then Kadrū ordered her sons to become like black hairs and to insert themselves in the horse's tail; at first they refused, and so she cursed them to be burnt in the fire at the snake sacrifice of King Janamejaya. Brahma endorsed this curse, and in addition gave Kaśyapa the power of curing anyone poisoned by snake-bite. When Vinatā saw the many black hairs in the horse's tail, she agreed to become the slave of Kadrū.

One day, Kadrū commanded Vinatā to take her and the snakes to the island of Ramaṇīyaka; Vinatā asked Garuḍa to help her. So Garuḍa carried Kadrū and the other snakes toward Ramaṇīyaka; as they flew near the sun, the snakes fainted with the heat, but Kadrū prayed to Indra, who sent rain that refreshed the snakes. After they had arrived on Ramaṇīyaka and enjoyed themselves on that island, Kadrū asked Garuḍa to take them to another island.

Then Garuḍa asked his mother why he and she were the slaves of the snakes, and she told him the story of the wager about the horse. Kadrū told Garuḍa that she would set the snakes free if he brought them the Soma, the elixir of immortality. When he asked for food to sustain him on his flight, she told him that he could eat the outcaste Niṣādas, but never a Brahmin. Garuḍa feasted on Niṣādas; when he accidentally ate a Brahmin who had a Niṣāda wife, he quickly regurgitated them both. Still hungry, he was given permission to eat a tortoise and an elephant who were forever quarreling, the reincarnations of two quarrelsome brothers. Garuḍa carried off the Soma, having conquered the two snakes who guarded it; challenged by Indra, Garuḍa promised that Indra could take the Soma back if Garuḍa ever put it down, and in return Indra promised Garuḍa that he could have the snakes for his food. Garuḍa then presented the Soma to the snakes; he placed it on the sacred *kuśa* grass and advised them to bathe before drinking it. The snakes set Vinatā free from slavery, and Indra scooped up the Soma and took it back to heaven. When the snakes returned from their bath, they found that the Soma had been stolen; they licked the sharp *kuśa* grass but got only split tongues for their pains [1.14–30].

3. King Parikṣit was born in the lineage of the Kurus. His birth was an ominous foreshadowing of his death: Aśvatthāman had cast a magic weapon that destroyed all the embryos in the wombs of the Pāṇḍava women [10.15.32], and Parikṣit was stillborn. Kṛṣṇa had promised to revive the child, however [10.16.1–5], and he carried out his promise immediately before Yudhiṣṭhira's horse sacrifice [14.66–70].

One day Parikṣit went hunting and wounded a deer; as he followed the wounded deer deep into the forest, he came upon a sage sitting in a cow pasture, where he fed upon the froth from the mouths of suckling calves. Parikṣit asked the sage if he had seen the deer go by, but the sage was under a vow of silence; infuriated, Parikṣit picked up a dead snake with the end of his bow, draped it around the hermit's neck, and returned to the city. The sage thought nothing of this insult, but his son, Śṛngin, uttered a curse that within seven days Parikṣit would be bitten by the great snake Takṣaka and die. His father chastised him for this curse, reminding him that it is the duty of kings to commit crimes in the course of protecting *dharma*, and sent a messenger to warn Parikṣit to take measures to protect himself against Takṣaka.

Parikṣit built himself a platform, carefully guarded by doctors and Brahmins with magic spells, and on the seventh day Kāśyapa, a descendant of Kaśyapa, came there to cure the king if he were bitten. Takṣaka took the form of a Brahmin and met Kāśyapa upon the road; he identified himself as Takṣaka and demonstrated his power to reduce a tree to ashes, whereupon Kāśyapa demonstrated his own power to bring the tree back to life. Then Takṣaka promised that, if Kāśyapa turned back and did not cure the king, he would give him more money than the king would give him if he did cure him. Kāśyapa was impressed by this, and, telling himself that the king was fated to die that day in any case, he turned back.

Takṣaka then had some of his snakes, disguised as ascetics, bring Parikṣit a basket of fruit; as Parikṣit was about to eat a piece of this fruit, he saw a small worm there. Laughing, Parikṣit picked it up and placed it on his neck and said, "The sun has set and I am no longer in danger from snake poison; let this worm stand for Takṣaka and bite me, so that the Brahmin who cursed me will not prove a liar!" He was still laughing when Takṣaka coiled around him and killed him. As the ministers fled, they saw Takṣaka streak away through the sky and the tree-house go up in flames from the virulent poison. Janamejaya, still a child, was anointed as king [1.36–40].

4. The sage Ruru fell in love with a beautiful girl named Pramadvarā and asked her father for her hand in marriage. A few days before the wedding, Pramadvarā was bitten by a snake and died of the venom. Ruru begged the gods to revive her, and they agreed to do so if Ruru would give her half of his own life-span. He did this, but he also swore an oath to destroy all the snakes. Whenever he saw a snake he would grab a club and beat it to death.

One day he came across an old lizard and began to strike it, but the lizard pointed out that, though he was a reptile, he did not bite people: "Lizards share the shortcomings of snakes but have separate uses; we share their sorrows, but we have our own joys." Ruru was frightened, thinking that the lizard was a seer, and he asked him who he was. The lizard replied, "I was once a seer named Ruru, and I had a Brahmin friend named Khagama ('Bird'). One day when I was still a child and was playing with him, I made a snake out of straw and frightened him with it when he was performing a fire sacrifice. He fainted, and when he regained consciousness he cursed me to become a reptile, but to regain my true form when I met a man named Ruru. Now, let me tell you that it is not right for a Brahmin like you to kill. Killing is the job of a king, like Janamejaya, who destroyed the snakes at his snake sacrifice, while it was a Brahmin, named Āstika, who rescued the frightened snakes." Intrigued by this story, Ruru went home and asked his father to tell him the story of Janamejaya's snake sacrifice [1.8–12].

5. Long ago, when Vāsuki had first discovered that the snakes were cursed to be sacrificed, he had learned from Brahmā that the one who would put an end to the sacrifice would be a son born to Jaratkāru and to Vāsuki's sister, who was also named Jaratkāru. Therefore Vāsuki

guarded his sister and kept her safe for the sage Jaratkāru [1.34–35].

Jaratkāru had vowed never to marry, but he had been persuaded, against his better judgment, by his dead ancestors, who needed the oblations that the descendants of Jaratkāru would offer to them. So he promised to marry only if he met a virgin with the same name, Jaratkāru. One day he met the serpent Vāsuki, who offered him his sister, who happened to be named Jaratkāru [1.13.9–45]. Shortly after the woman Jaratkāru had conceived a child by the sage Jaratkāru, he picked a quarrel with her and threw her out; she ran back to her brother, Vāsuki, and gave birth to her child there. The child was Āstika [1.42–45].

6. When Janamejaya and his brothers were performing a sacrifice, a dog, a son of the bitch Saramā, came near. The brothers beat the dog, who ran howling back to his mother and told her that they had beaten him though he had neither looked at nor licked the offerings. Saramā then went to the sacrificial grounds and said to Janamejaya, "Since you beat my son when he had not done anything wrong, you will suffer an unseen danger."

Janamejaya then sought a priest who could avert the evil that he had incurred, and one day while he was hunting he came upon the sage Śrutaśravas and his son Somaśravas, and he chose Somaśravas for his priest. Śrutaśravas then told Janamejaya how Somaśravas had been born: he had grown in the womb of a snake woman who had drunk Srutaśravas's seed. Janamejaya then brought Somaśravas back to his brothers and told them to do whatever he asked them to do to avert the evil of the curse [1.3.1–81].

7. One day when the sage Veda was absent, his wife asked his pupil Uttanka to sleep with her during her fertile period; Uttanka refused, and though Veda praised him for this when he returned, the wife set him a difficult task: she asked him to bring her the earrings that belonged to King Pauṣya. Uttanka set out to do this, but on the way he met a man mounted on an enormous bull; the man said, "Uttanka, eat the dung of my bull. Your own teacher ate it in his day." Uttanka ate the bull's dung and drank the bull's urine and went on his way.

But he forgot to clean himself properly after eating, and so he arrived at Pauṣya's palace in a state of pollution. This pollution prevented him from seeing Pauṣya's queen until Pauṣya pointed out the cause and Uttanka remedied it by washing himself properly. When Uttanka asked the queen for her earrings, she gave them to him willingly, but she warned him that Takṣaka, king of the snakes, wanted the earrings too. Uttanka assured her that Takṣaka could not overcome him, and then he returned to Pauṣya.

Pauṣya asked him to stay for a meal, to which Uttanka consented unwillingly, as he was in a hurry; and Pauṣya fed him hastily with cold food that had a woman's hair in it. Uttanka then cursed Pauṣya to go blind for serving him unclean food, and Pauṣya cursed Uttanka to remain barren; but they regained their tempers and modified their curses. Uttanka set out with the earrings, but on the way he saw a naked beggar, a polluting sight; hastily Uttanka put the earrings down and went for water to purify himself, at which the beggar took the earrings and ran away; when Uttanka grabbed him, the beggar assumed his true form, Takṣaka, and entered a chasm that had suddenly opened up in the ground.

Uttanka followed him down into the realm of the snakes. There he saw two women weaving with black and white threads, and he saw a handsome man with an enormous horse; he asked the man to help him overcome the snake. The man said, "Blow into the ass of this horse," and Uttanka did so. Then flames shot out from all the openings in the horse's body, and these flames smoked out the world of the snakes; Takṣaka gave the earrings to Uttanka. The man gave the horse to Uttanka to ride back to his teacher's wife, and Uttanka arrived just in time to avoid *her* curse.

Then he asked his teacher the meaning of what he had seen, and his teacher told him that the two women were the fates, the handsome man was the god of rain and his horse was the god of fire; that the bull was Airāvata, the king of snakes, and the man who rode him was Indra. It was because Uttanka had eaten the bull's dung, which was Soma, the elixir of immortality, that he had not been overcome in the land of the snakes. The teacher then dismissed Uttanka.

But Uttanka was still furious with Takṣaka, and he went to Hāstinapura, where he met Janamejaya. He told Janamejaya that it was Takṣaka who had killed his father, Parikṣit, and that it was therefore the duty of Janamejaya to burn Takṣaka as an offering at a great snake sacrifice in order to avenge the death of Parikṣit—and also, incidentally, to do a favor for Uttanka, giving him revenge for having been robbed by Takṣaka [1.3.85–195].

8. When Janamejaya heard the story of his father's death, he vowed to undertake a great snake sacrifice. Even before the sacrifice began, there was an evil omen portending that it would not be concluded; therefore the king ordered that no one who was not known to him should be allowed to enter. The priests put on their black robes and began to drop the terrified snakes into the fire; the snakes darted and hissed and wildly coiled about, screaming horribly. Some were as small as mice, some as big as bull elephants; all of them died powerless, punished by their mother's curse.

As soon as Takṣaka learned of the sacrifice, he sought protection with Indra, who granted him refuge. But Vāsuki told his sister Jaratkāru to summon her son Āstika; at his request, she told him the story of the quarrel between Kadrū and Vinatā, and Āstika promised Vāsuki that he would save him and the other snakes. Āstika went to Janamejaya's sacrificial ground, but the guards did not let him enter. Then he recited a long poem in praise of Janamejaya, and Janamejaya was so pleased that he not only let him in but was about to offer him a boon. The priests, however, reminded him that, though the sacrifice was almost over, Takṣaka had not yet been sacrificed; he was still lurking in Indra's palace.

The priests increased their incantations, and just as Takṣaka was about to fall into the fire, Āstika demanded his boon: that the sacrifice be stopped. "Stay there," he said to Takṣaka, who hovered in the air, caught between the incantations of the priests and the incantations of Āstika, until Janamejaya said, "Let the sacrifice end." The king gave Āstika many gifts and sent him home, saying, "You must come back when I have my horse sacrifice." Āstika agreed to this, and as he went home he was greeted by the delighted snakes, who also offered him a boon. He asked them to grant that anyone who recited his story would never be in danger from snakes. And, indeed, whoever recites this Epic of Āstika is never in danger from snakes [1.47–53].

9. One day Agni, the god of fire, took the form of a Brahmin and came to Arjuna and Kṛṣṇa. He told them that he was insatiably hungry and wished to devour the Khāṇḍava Forest, but Indra quenched the fire with rain, in order to protect his friend Takṣaka, who lived there. Agni, abetted by Kṛṣṇa and Arjuna, proceeded to burn the forest. Creatures by the thousands screamed in terror and were scorched; some embraced their sons or mothers or fathers, unable to leave them. Everywhere creatures writhed on the ground, with burning wings, eyes, and paws. The noise of the forest animals was like the noise made by the ocean when it was churned.

Then Indra sought to quench the fire, and a great battle ensued, in which all the gods and demons took sides. Agni drove a chariot yoked with silvery Gandharva horses, that Varuṇa gave him, and Indra drove a chariot yoked with his bright bay horses. All the flocks of birds, descended from Garuḍa, together with all the swarms of snakes fought against Arjuna and Kṛṣṇa, but in vain: they all fell back into the fire and died. Aśvasena, the son of Takṣaka, sought to escape; to save him, his mother swallowed him. She began by swallowing his head; but as she stretched upward to swallow his tail, Arjuna cut off her head. Aśvasena escaped, but Arjuna, Kṛṣṇa, and Agni cursed him: "You will never find a safe shelter." As the holocaust continued to blaze, a disembodied voice told Indra that Takṣaka was not in the forest; he had gone to the Field of the Kurus. Hearing this, Indra went away, and Agni continued to burn the forest unopposed.

Now, in this forest there lived a family of birds who had been born when the ascetic Mandapāla had been persuaded by his dead ancestors to marry so that they might have descendants. Mandapāla had become a bird and married a bird named Jaritā; later he ran away with another bird named Lapitā. As the forest fire spread, Jaritā tried in vain to persuade her fledglings to hide in an empty rat hole; she assured them that a kite had carried away the rat, but they refused to believe her. Finally, she flew away, and the four fledglings begged Agni for mercy. He spared their lives and also granted their request that they should always be safe from cats. As Mandapāla feared for the safety of his sons in the forest, Lapitā became jealous and accused him of wanting to return to Jaritā. She left him and he returned to Jaritā and his sons; though Jaritā spoke bitterly to him at first, they became reconciled and went away together with their four sons.

Only six creatures survived the fire: Aśvasena, Maya (the architect of the demons, granted safe-conduct by Arjuna), and the four little birds. Finally Agni was sated [1.215–225].

NOTES

1. Edward C. Dimock has made his indelible mark on our understanding of the literature of Bengal, a very snakey literature (from a very snakey part of the world). I hope, therefore, that he will find acceptable this snake/horse offering from an equine Sanskritist who has learned most of her snake lore from him.
2. *Tāṇḍya* (*Pañcaviṃśa*) *Brāhmaṇa* 25.15.1-4.
3. This and all subsequent unspecified numerical references are from the critical (Poona) edition of the *Mahābhārata* (1933-1960).
4. *The Mahābhārata*, translated and edited by J.A.B. van Buitenen. *Book 1: The Book of the Beginning* (Chicago, 1973). p. 4.
5. *Ṛg Veda* 1.163; *The Rig Veda, An Anthology Translated from the Sanskrit*, by Wendy Doniger O'Flaherty (Harmondsworth, 1981), pp. 87-88.
6. Madeleine Biardeau, *Études de Mythologie Hindoue* (Paris, 1968-1969); Alf Hiltebeitel, *The Ritual of Battle: Krishna in the Mahābhārata* (Cornell, 1976).
7. Van Buitenen, *The Mahābhārata*, p.12.
8. Ibid., p.439.
9. Robert P. Goldman, *Gods, Priests and Warriors: The Bhṛgus of the Mahābhārata* (New York, 1977).
10. Wendy Doniger O'Flaherty, "The Origins of Heresy in Hindu Mythology," *History of Religions* 1:4 (May 1971), 271-333.
11. Wendy Doniger O'Flaherty, *The Origins of Evil in Hindu Mythology* (Berkeley and Los Angeles, 1976), pp. 212-247; cf. pp. 248-271.
12. *Ibid.*, pp. 94-138.
13. *Ibid.*, pp. 118-120; and Wendy Doniger O'Flaherty, *Tales of Sex and Violence: Folklore, Sacrifice, and Danger in the Jaiminīya Brāhmaṇa* (Chicago, 1985), pp. 86-93 (*Jaiminīya Brāhmaṇa* 1.154-155; 1.125-127 and 2.126; *Aitareya Brāhmaṇa 3.21-22*).
14. Cf. Georges Dumézil, *La problème des centaures* (Paris, 1929).

15. See the stunting of the sun, the bird-child of Aditi, in the *Brāhmaṇas: Śatapatha Brāhmaṇa* 3.1.3-5; Wendy Doniger O'Flaherty, *Women, Androgynes and Other Mythical Beasts* (Chicago, 1980), pp. 174-175.
16. *Bhāgavata Purāṇa* 10.15-17; Wendy Doniger O'Flaherty, *Hindu Myths* (Harmondsworth, 1975), pp. 221-228.
17. *Śatapatha Brāhmaṇa* 13.5.4.1.
18. *Jaiminīya Brāhmaṇa* 2.440-442; O'Flaherty, *Tales of Sex and Violence*, pp. 97-100.
19. Personal communication from Alf Hiltebeitel, August 4, 1985.
20. Cf. Bhṛgu in the *Jaiminīya Brāhmaṇa* 1.42-44; O'Flaherty, *Tales of Sex and Violence*, pp. 32-49. The symbolism of this text is strikingly like that of the Uttanka episode, and Uttanka in the *Mahābhārata* is explicitly called "descendant of Bhṛgu" when he is in the underworld (14.57.37). See too the adventures of Naciketas in the *Kaṭha Upaniṣad*.
21. *Ṛg Veda* 1.164.2-3, 10.5.2, 10.51.6, etc.
22. O'Flaherty, *Women*, pp. 213-237.
23. John Irwin, "The Sacred Anthill," *History of Religions* 21:4 (May 1982).
24. Similarly, Triśanku, suspended between heaven and earth, embodies the liminality of his conflicting aspirations (see Wendy Doniger O'Flaherty, *Dreams, Illusion, and Other Realities* [Chicago, 1984], pp. 103-108. Henry Wadsworth Longfellow wrote a poem about "King Triśanku":

    Viswamitra the Magician
    By his spells and incantations,
    Up to Indra's realms elysian
    Raised Trisanku, king of nations.

    Indra and the gods offended
    Hurled him downward, and descending
    In the air he hung suspended,
    With these equal powers contending.

    Thus by aspirations lifted,
    By misgivings downward driven,
    Human hearts are tossed and drifted
    Midway between earth and heaven.

25. Edward Cameron Dimock, *The Thief of Love: Bengali Tales from Court and Village* (Chicago, 1963), pp. 195-294.
26. S.A. Dange, *Legends in the Mahābhārata* (Delhi, 1969), p. 354.
27. *Claude Lévi-Strauss, "The Story of Asdiwal," pp. 1-48 of The Structural Study of Myth and Totemism*, edited by Edmund Leach (London, 1967).

Echoes of Love and Creation in the Poetry of Sūr Dās

JOHN STRATTON HAWLEY

Close to the center of the scholarly work of Edward C. Dimock, Jr., lies the intense microcosm of the *nikuñj*—the thicket, the bower where Krishna and his beloved consummate their love, or where one waits painfully for the other to appear. This *nikuñj* is the center of Brindavan, that simple but magical forest playground that became Krishna's home on earth and is now—in its earthly aspect, at least—the principal magnet for pilgrimage to Krishna in all India. Of course, Brindavan is no longer a forest; there are temples and stores and pilgrim houses and the rest. But at its heart, behind a high wall and somewhat removed from the rich din that fills the town during its active seasons, lies the grove that makes Brindavan what it is. This happy preserve of monkeys and peacocks is *sevā kuñj*, "the thicket of devotion," the place where Krishna is supposed to have been most intensely enveloped in love.

All worshipers of Krishna hold his *nikuñj* central, but certain among them—the Nimbārka and Rādhāvallabha communities—insist that any proper talk of Krishna must be contained within its borders. They feel that anything that is not love in this purest, most refined sense must be excluded from Krishna's discourse. Hence the poetry and hymnody generated by these communities restricts itself to endless elaborations of this theme, and the dramatic troupes allied with them, who present the events of Krishna's life in musical plays called *rās līlās*, refuse to enact any vignette that does not take place in or around the enchanted bower. The theological thrust in this is that God can only be experienced in intimacy—a radically immanentist position.

This, however, is not the only point of view that exists in regard to dogma of drama or poetry, and our concern in this essay will be to see how a broader cosmos can make its way into the thicket of love. Our text—in truth, a collection of independent poems—will be the *Sūr Sāgar* attributed to the sixteenth-century poet Sūr Dās, and we will begin by taking note of several poems in which the larger, rougher, natural world makes an entry into Krishna's delicate, supernal arena. Then we will turn to compositions in which Sūr sets his eye more directly upon the broader canvas—creation with all its karmic realities—yet does so in such a way that it sheds light upon the other, more intense world of love. The hope is that by considering poems that touch on these two realms we can see how, at least for Sūr, the one seems to need the other to realize its own true shape.

The *Sūr Sāgar* ("Sūr's Ocean") is a collection of freely formed, rhymed lyrics of various lengths called *pads* that constitute the central monument of poetry to Krishna composed in Braj Bhāṣā, the dialect associated with the Braj region not far to the south of Delhi. It was here that Krishna is supposed to have herded his cows, played his flute, and made love to his women, and it is here that Sūr Dās is said to have spent the greater part of his life. In actuality we know virtually nothing about the poet's life, but the language of the *Sūr Sāgar* is clearly Braj Bhāṣā, and the poetry that constitutes its oldest core—only 241 poems in the earliest extant manuscript—is of such a uniformly high quality that it is hard not to attribute it to a single talented individual we call Sūr. Here we will restrict ourselves to the poems that occur in that venerable manuscript.[1]

GLIMPSES OF THE CREATION FROM THE THICKET OF LOVE

The *Sūr Sāgar* holds the unusual honor of being accepted and embraced by all the religious communities that look to Braj as their homeland. Though the Vallabha Sampradāya has laid special claim to Sūr, it has only with difficulty manged to cast him as one of its sectarian fold, and little in Sūr's poetry has compelled other communities to accept the claim.[2] Most of what is in the *Sūr Sāgar* is as congenial to theologians of the *nikuñj*—Nimbārkīs and Rādhāvallabhīs—as to those who are willing to admit the value of meditating on other aspects of Krishna's (or even Rām's) activity.

All of that finds a place in the *Sūr Sāgar*, but Krishna's interactions with his milkmaid loves (*gopīs*) are at the center. One expression of this fact is the conviction that the earth of Brindavan is blessed in a measure that makes any other place unworthy of comparison. This is a way of saying that no other field of activity, even that which traditionally passes for religion, can approach the realm where love finds its fulfilment. In the following composition (NPS 1107) Sūr explores this pastoral perfection from the point of view of the gods who have been excluded from it:

If only we'd been fashioned as the dust of Brindavan!—
The dust that is raised by Nandanandan's feet
when he goes grove to grove to herd the cows.
What have we gained by being born as gods?
what's the point in gaining some elevated place
When the Merciful One, out of mercy for all beings,
can inundate the world in a flash, with just a sign?
How much more blessed are the trees and blades of grass,
the children and calves, the flutes and the horns,
For Sūr says, he laughs, talks, and plays with all of them,
roams around and churns and drinks the foam.[3]

Or one may see the enchanted groves of Brindavan from closer up, and with a clearer focus on the love to which they so naturally play host, as in the following poem (NPS 1744). Here Sūr depicts the condition of Krishna's favorite *gopī*, Rādhā, as she waits for Krishna, "the Joy of the Yadus," to manifest himself in the *nikuñj* again:

Rādhā is lost to the onslaught of love.
She weeps from tree to tree and finally collapses,
searching through the forests and groves.
Her braid—a peacock grasps it, thinking it a snake;
her lotus feet attract the bees;
The honey of her voice makes the crow in the *kadamb* tree
caw, caw to mimic its cuckoo;
Her hands—the tender leaves of blossom–bringing Spring:
the parrot, when he sees, comes near to taste;
And the full moon in her face inspires the *cakor* bird
to drink the water washing from the eyes.
Her despair, her desperation—the Joy of the Yadus sees it
and appears at her side in the nick of time:
Sūr Dās's Lord takes that seedbud of new birth
and cradles it like a baby in his arms.[4]

In the earlier poem, it was the gods who were drawn to the magical realm defined by the groves of Brindavan; here we find a redoubling of that centripetal movement as the forest creatures themselves are drawn toward the center of the *nikuñj*, pulled into the vortex of love. No longer serving as material for the static similes with which Rādhā's beauty is so often described, they actively come to her side, each one attracted to the aspect of her person that it resembles. The final figure to be so attracted, of course, is the one who is implied not by some external feature of her character but by the center of her emotion, namely, Krishna himself.

A similar momentum finds expression in other compositions. In the one that follows (NPS 1806), for instance, the clouds and the forest reshape themselves in response to what is happening in their midst as Krishna and his mate (perhaps Rādhā, once again) move toward the consummation of love. Trees and vines tangle around them in an ever thickening grove. The woman in the pair speaks to her love:

Black storm clouds have risen in the sky,
  and herons in an eerie row.
Please, Kānh, look—the beauty of a rainbow,
  bearer of all colors,
    bow for the arrows of the gods.
Lightning erupts into sparks here and there
  like an eager, restless woman
Whose husband, the rogue, is at every other house:
  now she has the chance to range about herself,
    singed by the God of Love.
Peacocks and cuckoos cry out in the woods
  and trees dispatch their messenger girls—
Vines—to find their loves, but it seems love's longing
  has also poisoned and angered them
Till they break their envoys' vows,
  what they promised to do,
    and lock themselves in embrace with every tree
      in a network of darkened groves.
Kāma, the expert, awakens to the wish
  of Sūr's dark Syām: he lifts his own hand
    to decorate a bower,
      a home.

Each of these poems seems at first glance to present the world of the *nikuñj* as a realm sufficient unto itself: no unruly voice from the outer world intrudes. But a second look reveals that even in these cozy lyrics the door to the wider universe is left slightly ajar. In the most recent, for example, we have a visit from Kāma, the god of erotic love. Now Kāma is admittedly a familiar, almost necessary presence in the realm of amorous sentiment. We already see traces of his power halfway through the poem as fitful, intermittent flashes of lightning are compared to a woman darting about town to avenge her husband's unfaithfulness with liaisons of her own. At the conclusion of the poem, however, Kāma becomes more than a part of the metaphorical furniture of the *nikuñj*: he makes a personal appearance as if he were an independent, living being—at once an incursion from outside the discourse previously established by the poem and at the same time its fulfilment.

Similar stretchings of the boundary of the *nikuñj* are to be found in the other poems we have quoted. In "Rādhā is lost," the figure who materializes in the final verse to alter the dramatis personae is Krishna himself—no alien figure to the *nikuñj* and indeed the very thing that Rādhā has "lost." Krishna completes the poem as announced; he makes the *nikuñj* what it is meant to be. But the poet introduces this familiar, expected figure in such a way that when he comes, he brings with him not only the answer the poem expects but a slightly foreign element that casts the grove of love in a more vivid chiaroscuro than it would have had if it were depicted entirely by means of its own palette. When Krishna comes, he takes Rādhā in his arms as if she were a baby, a "seedbud of new birth" (*janma kai aṅkur*). The seed that is sown is love itself—*anurāg*, "new love," the name of the genre to which the poem belongs—but the mention of birth in the realm of a love that is held by theologians to be entirely separate from any possibility of progeny is a stroke of enlivening disquietude.

One has a similar brush with the outside world in "The Dust of Brindavan." It is not just that the evident format of the poem causes us to see the charmed forest realm from the perspective of those it excludes—the gods, of all people! Rather, the way in which they explain why they wish they could trade in their exalted rank to become bits of dust in this other medium conjures up the image of how the entire world as now constituted could be destroyed in an instant if the God of all gods, "the Merciful One," so desired (NPS 1107:3–4). They refer to the primal dissolution (*pralaya*) that stands, in Hindu thinking, at the beginning and end of all created reality. It is the prospect of such dissolution, from which the world is safe at no point because of the God's unlimited prerogative to do precisely what he wants, that makes them see why order as they and we now know it has no ultimate value. Thus a tremor from the world of creation, the world superintended by the gods, adds resonance to the greater value of the world of love that surrounds the *nikuñj*.

In another group of poems this contrast is exploited even more directly. These are compositions that expound the power of Muralī, who appears to be but a simple bamboo flute, but who, once Krishna sets his lips to her, becomes the agent that gives animus to everything that happens in and about the *nikuñj*. She is the voice of love and nothing can resist her call. Often, however, the force of that call is best illustrated not by the motion it generates, the rhythms of love, but by the natural rhythms that it brings to a halt, as in the following example (NPS 1276):

Muralı, adorning his lips, conquers all.
Just one sound and the women are transfixed;
  the clothes slip from their breasts.
Birds close their eyes, motionless as yogis
  intent on a night of meditation.
No vine rustles or sways on its tree—
  so weary and sluggish the breeze—
And cows and deer have abandoned their grass;
  calves disdain their milk.
Sūr says, on hearing that mind-beguiling sound
  the Jumna waters tire and cease to flow.

In India, the movement of rivers is the lifeblood of the land, hence rivers are the most potent symbols of the forces of creation and are themselves worshiped as manifestations and embodiments of that power (*Śakti*).[5] For the Jumna to stop in her course, then, is an event of earth-shaking magnitude, though she seems at first blush merely to constitute the border of the forestland where Krishna roams.

Another poem makes it even more explicit that Muralī's piercing call of love is sufficient to upset the structure of creation. Here are mentioned not only the Jumna, and not only the superintending gods we have already met, but the Creator (*vidhātā*) himself. In this poem, as in many others of the genre, the voice that speaks belongs to one of the milkmaids of Braj. She complains to a friend about the intimacy that Muralī, whom she personifies as a woman, has achieved in relation to Krishna, and points out that Muralī's status has evidently gone to her head (NPS 1271):

These days Muralī's become so proud
  she refuses to speak to a soul,
As if she'd found in the land of his lotus mouth
  a kingdom to supply her every joy.
Insolent girl—his hands are her throne,
  his lips her parasol,
His hair her whisk as she reigns, my friend,
  over a court of sweet perfume.
There she decrees that the waters of the Jumna
  stop on their course to the sea,
And as for the gods in the city of the gods,
  she summons them down to earth.
Stable things move and moving things are still—
  both are triumphs for her
As she cancels the way the Creator set things up
  to institute her own design.

That bamboo flute rules all, says Sūr—
god, sage, man, and snake;
Even Śrī's Lord—he forgets his Śrī,
obsessed with his newfound love.

The culminating instance in this testament to Muralī's power is her effect on Krishna himself, for the double visions of her world, the *nikuñj*, and the natural world ultimately converge in him. On the one hand he is the soul of love, whose music attracts all to his bower, but on the other hand he sits enthroned at the apex of creation, the universe whose three tiers are ruled, respectively, by gods, humans, and snakes (*nāg*, NPS 1271:9). In this role, as superintendent of creation, Krishna (who is also Vishnu, Hari) is wed to the goddess Śrī ("auspiciousness"). Together, and in their relation to one another, they cause what is to be. The final evidence of Muralī's power, then, is that she has displaced Śrī from her throne, and with that the world of music and love is shown to be more powerful than the facts of creation upon which it seems—falsely—to depend.

In another poem, this observation is made in an even more pointed form by comparing Muralī not to Vishnu's eternal consort, Śrī, but to a form of Vishnu himself. Here (in NPS 1893) Muralī is represented as Mohinī, the female form that Vishnu projected from himself at the beginning of time to facilitate the process of creating order in the world. It was a situation in which the gods and their opponents, the demons, were struggling together to churn up from the primeval milk-ocean the precious liquid that would make them immortal (*amṛt*). Vishnu intervened on the side of the gods by manifesting himself as Mohinī, "the bewitching one," who appeared before the demons and distracted them from their otherwise single-minded pursuit of *amṛt*, with the result that the gods captured the prize and the chaotic struggle was resolved.

The *gopī* who utters the poem suggests, however, that when Muralī assumed the role of Mohinī all creation went berserk. It is true in a way, she says, that Muralī makes the liquid of immortality available to others, as Mohinī once did, by blanketing Braj with the nectar of Krishna's sweet sound, but it is also true that she adulterates it in the very same instant that she broadcasts it. For she herself is its first recipient; what comes to the *gopīs*' ears is merely leftovers from her table. Thus from the *gopīs*' point of view it is not really clear whether she has served the cause of right—their own—or whether she has become the enemy, a recrudescence of demonic force sufficiently powerful to cancel the principles and harmonies upon which the creation is established. Here is what the *gopī* says:

Muralī has become Mohinī:
You know what she did to the gods
  and anti-gods: she's done it again.
They churned the milk sea; we, a sea of vows,
  and from it a new immortal nectar arose:
An oceanic liquid, held in Hari's lunar face—
  that she stealthily snatches away
And quaffs down, making us drink octaves of sound
  that pour from her victory tour.
One single vessel—then it held elixir
  but now, says Sūr, intoxicating liquor.

Nowhere more vividly than in the Muralī poems are the rhythms of the *nikuñj* compared and contrasted with those of creation. Yet because this contrast was on its way to becoming a standard conceit in Sūr's time, it is perhaps less convincing as an expression of how Sūr personally measured the force of the *nikuñj* against that of the creation than less encompassing but more individual turns of phrase might be. For examples of these, let us consider yet a third trio of poems that appears in the Jaipur manuscript. Two of them are documents of love such as we have already heard, but the third, interesting for purposes of comparison, is a meditation on quite a different milieu: the world of war and battle.

In the two love poems the generic name of the Creator—*vidhātā*: "the maker," "the one who effects"—is once again sounded, and in both cases a lament is involved. The person who lodges the complaint, one of Krishna's women, alleges that the order of creation is inadequate to the demands of love (NPS 2402):

I've found something that the Creator failed to do.
I looked at Govind today; I looked and then
  I knew what was wrong and lamented it.
He had dressed my frame in a dazzling way,
  given brilliance to my intellect, and yet
He neglected to give eyes to each tiny body hair,
  and with that minor oversight he failed.
What am I to do? These poor strained eyes
  are overwhelmed; they overflow each moment.
And how, says Sūr, am I to fit great gold Mount Meru
  in some worn-out little change purse of a brain?[6]

It takes words of recrimination directed at the architect of creation to illustrate the strength of that other creative force, love. In the contest that develops between the two, the natural Creator tends to be cast as a sort of Gnostic demiurge, a being sometimes cruelly indifferent to the needs of his creatures, as above, and at other times positively inimical to their welfare. The poem that follows provides an instance of the latter, and once again the complaining voice is that of a woman who has been deprived of Krishna's presence (NPS 3886):

Thoughts of him stalk me, even in my dreams,
Now that he has gone; and oh, my friend, it hurts
  as hard as on the day that Nandanandan left.
Last night, in fact, that cowherd came to my house:
  he laughed his laugh and grasped me by the arm.
What am I do to? The night is now my foe.
  Will I ever know another wink of sleep?
I've become like a sheldrake who sees her own reflection,
  takes it as the gladdening image of her mate,
And then, says Sūr, that menacing Creator
  masquerades as wind and brings ripples to the lake.

Of course, the whole of the *Sūr Sāgar* is not couched in the vocabulary of complaint, nor does it exposit the world of the *nikuñj* alone. Hence it may be useful to quote just one poem from another genre to show how once again a reference to the Creator serves to underscore the earth-shaking effects that Krishna's presence has on the world of those who love him. The love, in this case, is quite different from the love the *gopīs* lavish on their youthful cowherd. It is the devotion shown to Krishna by Bhīṣma, the aged but ever-agile commander of the Kaurava forces in the great war depicted in the *Mahābhārata*. Krishna took part in that war too, but not as a combatant. He vowed instead that he would merely serve as the charioteer for his devotee Arjuna, who belonged to the opposite camp, the Pāṇḍavas.

This was not enough for Bhīṣma. Though Krishna's alliance with the Pāṇḍavas made Bhīṣma his enemy, yet the latter remained Krishna's devotee and as such desired to experience him in the most immediate way possible. For him, this meant confrontation in battle, so it was Bhīṣma's fondest wish that Krishna would abrogate his promise to keep aloof from the fighting and enter the fray. Bhīṣma attempted to provoke him to battle by raining countless arrows upon him and Arjuna; both sustained multiple wounds. Krishna was impervious, but when he sensed in Arjuna an unwillingness to retaliate against Bhīṣma, he feared for Arjuna's safety and sprang onto the battlefield himself, thus fulfilling Bhīṣma's desire and serving both devotees at once. Because Krishna was unarmed, he simply picked up what was at hand, the wheel of the chariot, and brandished it as if it were his very own divine weapon, the *sudarśan*

("Fine Vision") disc.[7] As Sūr Dās tells the story, we see what Bhīṣma saw at that point, but we see more as well (NPS 273):

Mādhav, in anger, took the wheel in his hand
In order to answer the wishes of his servant,
  abandoning his promise and thus the Vedic word.
He stepped from his chariot with a reckless lunge to earth,
  and the moment his foot touched the ground, he ran;
The earth could not endure the fearful weight she bore
  and shuddered as if utterly deranged.
His upper garment slipped part way down his limbs
  as he lifted his vast, strong arm and revealed
A torso absorbed in a sweat of brilliant blood—
  a thundercloud raining rubies, scarlet pearls.
Sūr says, when Brahmā saw that discus, called Fine Vision,
  and the warrior, just as fine, who held it in his arm
He fell into confusion, as if this were a new creation
  and he a baby lotus-born upon an umbilical stem.[8]

Once again it takes a look at how the creation falters and recoils before Krishna to make clear his devastating effect. In this case the Creator is not the generic entity *vidhātā* but quite definitely Brahmā (*birañci*, NPS 273:7), and he seems to make his appearance on the scene by stepping directly into the shoes of Bhīṣma. We assume that it is Bhīṣma who watches the dread fulfillment of his dreams—he is about to die in consequence of the epiphany for which he has been praying—but at the end it turns out that Brahmā has been put in his place.

The transposition is not an impossible one, for Bhīṣma and Brahmā share a number of qualities, chiefly their advanced age, and Bhīṣma is often compared to Brahmā.[9] Now metaphor turns to reality—Brahmā himself is present on the scene—and at the same moment the death of an old man is transformed into the birth of a baby. Brahmā sees the arm of Vishnu extended out toward him, adorned with its wheel, and senses not death but creation, as he returns to the moment when the chaotic fluidity of *pralaya* yields to order. It is the moment in which a lotus-stem umbilical cord emerges from the belly of Vishnu, recumbant upon the primeval waters, and Brahmā as a baby emerges on the flower of the lotus to give birth, in turn, to the rest of creation. Indeed, it takes the reference to Brahmā to illustrate the force of what is happening at this moment, for with the death of Bhīṣma the salvation of the Pāṇḍava brothers is proleptically assured. It may only be the five of them and one of their progeny who survive, but that is enough to rescue the world from total destruction as the old generations go down in conflict with one another.

Thus one world age (*yuga*) comes to an end, but another simultaneously begins—"a new creation" (*ān sṛṣṭi*, NPS 273:8), in the words of the poem at hand.

In this case, as in so many that we have already surveyed, Sūr seems to feel that it takes a glance at creation or its Creator to come to a full consciousness of what the presence of Krishna means in this world. Krishna is at the center of the narrative and at the focal point of the field of vision, but Sūr seems to be saying that until one adjusts one's focus and takes in the periphery, the whole creation, one scarcely knows what one is seeing. Often the two are made to appear competitors—the background blurs before the intensity of the divine presence at the center—but that blurring effect is required before one really has the foreground in focus. Until the world goes out of focus, Krishna cannot truly come into view.

GLIMPSES OF LOVE FROM THE WELTER OF CREATION

So far we have considered compositions in which the poet reflects upon the charmed world in which Krishna has made his appearance. Some moment in the narration of Krishna's life serves as the point of departure, and the natural, created cosmos provides a term of comparison capable of illustrating the special dynamics of his world.

There is another other series of poems in the *Sūr Sāgar*, however, in which things dispose themselves just the other way around. The poet begins with his feet firmly planted in this world and searches the horizon for the Lord's magical, healing presence. From this perspective, the creation looks quite different. It is seen from the point of view of one's own creation, one's own birth, and in a usage that is surprisingly close to notions prevalent in Judaism, Christianity, and Islam, Sūr often laments a parentage that he and other human beings have stupidly disowned. Far from echoing what the *gopīs* say about the cruel indifference displayed by the Creator toward his creatures, Sūr places the blame for the estrangement between Creator and creature squarely on the shoulders of the creature. The Creator, by contrast, is depicted as a concerned father whose ministrations have been ignored or refused. In the following poem (NPS 323), for instance, he speaks to his soul as a father might to his son, and urges that the soul look to another father, "the Father of the world" (*jagat pitā*, NPS 323:4), for its redemption:

No one aside from Govind, my son,
   can take away your pain;
Finance and fortune and finesse will ever wish
   they could, but they fail and fail again.

Śiva, Brahmā, the Sun, the Snake, the seers—
they sink their thoughts in Him,
For apart from the Father of the world, its Lord,
a person is an orphan—no master, no home.
Every other option on this earth I've examined:
they're like shadows of passing clouds,
like bits of straw near a fire.
Sūr Dās says, unless you sing the song of God,
you can try a million times,
but the pain will never go.

In other poems, Sūr extends the indictment from this life to the many preceding it. He points his finger at an anamnesis that has been in effect for ages now, a perversion of the creation whose repeated consequence—birth and birth again—vividly displays the heinousness of the sin that gives it rise. The Creator, the father, stands ready to help, but the soul goes on unawares, preferring a polluted creation of its own as expressed in countless mothers who deliver it into a life of continuing loss. Here is Sūr's sentiment on the matter (NPS 320):

Now that you've returned here, you've forgotten those days:
How you tasted the drug of mindless delusion,
wandered about with your hair all wild,
Settled again in the belly of some new mother
and once again your troubles began.
The terror, the trauma: cooked like an eggplant
and head-first thrust in filth!
Your mind was forceless, your body thin and weak,
every advantage was wrested from your hand.
Who was it, tell me, that stood beside you then,
providing you with food and drink?
Give it some thought: the Lord was your father,
the one who gives all living beings life.
But like the deer you prefer to meet the arrow, says Sūr,
when the huntsman of the senses sings his song.[10]

A number of poems of self-reproach like this are included in the Jaipur *Sūr Sāgar*, but the most extended meditation on the subject is a composition that has traditionally been called *sūr pacīsī*, "Sūr's twenty-five," because it contains twenty-five rhymed couplets in *dohā* meter accompanied by a refrain (NPS 325). In it one hears again of the horrors of rebirth to which the soul has sentenced itself, and of the care nonetheless showered on such a soul by the Lord, who is called the "companion" and "guardian" of living things.[11] This time, however, the description of the soul's fallen state and the sermon of repentence addressed to it are prefaced by an equally long exposition of what ought to have obviated any need for either. We are given example after example of what it means to love, and this extended encomium serves both as an indication of what is involved in the Lord's faithfulness to his creatures and as a measure of what creatures failed to do his response:

Pledge your love to Mādhav, oh my mind.
Put every opposite emotion aside—
  lust and rage, greed and pride.
Bees feast on love, so they wander through the wilderness
  in search of fragrance. Enough they never find:
They drain the nectar from every blossom
  until the lotus catches them inside.
Listen to the limit a lover's love can know:
  how the crested cuckoo trains its eye afar
And suffers every ill in hopes of a raincloud,
  never looking elsewhere for something to drink.
The moth, not knowing that a flame brings pain,
  lets itself be taken by the fire:
Its body is singed in the blaze for which it yearns,
  but nothing dries the nectar from its soul.
On robbery, good folk and the holy books agree—
  every eye, on seeing it abhors—
But thievery is something a thief will never leave,
  even at the cost of losing all.
A fish cannot suffer to be parted from its water,
  yet the water never thinks to miss the fish;
That, you see, is the way things work with love—
  the body may go, but the passion doesn't lift.
Remember the tenacious obsession of the deer,
  how its ear became enraptured with the hunter's sound
And it held its ground, its back to the path of flight,
  and faced the arrow destined for its breast.
Look at the fire that burns that lifeless woman
  alongside her ghostly mate:
Neither the pyre nor the heart burns in vain
  for they're kindled with the fuel of love.
It's love that propels the turtle dove
  as it soars aloft in the sky,
But even at the highest, if it sights its beloved
  it sighs and tumbles to her side.

Look at the way of the lotus,
  how it's bound by its love of the sun:
It may lose its life, but it never loses love,
  preferring to dry with the pond.
Love is the essence of every other essence,
  and the gambler has to throw the dice:
He may lose body and mind, wealth and youth,
  but never will he say he's lost the prize.
Now the jewel you've won is a jewel indeed,
  but you can't seem to care for it or mount it;
Love is a tale you've heard told every day,
  but somehow it simply doesn't take.
The one who always stays with you, the one who is your own,
  the one who breathes life into those who live—
That's the one you've so effortlessly forgotten:
  Hari, the Lord, the Blessed One.
Think of the stuff from which he shaped your awareness,
  from which he created all the elements of order,
Molding your feet, your hair, hands, and nails,
  your eyes and ears and nose:
What a fearful place, that womb where you were
  before any limb had taken form,
And listen, fool, the guardian of your life
  refused to leave you there alone.
Day by day he held you and fed you,
  wrapped you tight as betel in its leaf,
Then pulled you out of that unhappy place
  and gave you milk to grasp and drink.
Food and clothes and money he gave you
  whenever the need arose,
A mother and father and brothers to surround you—
  new tastes, new people to know;
Your fine friendships grew, your house and your kin,
  your sons and wife and wealth and home,
But the wiles of this world made a worldly man of you
  as your heart became fixed on desire.
Your happiness grew, your wealth grew too,
  but at every stage you wanted something else
Till in time, in the haze, as your eyesight slipped away
  you no longer knew who'd befriended you,
And now it's all gone: youth and life are spent
  in the tastes of food and drink and clothes,
Like a rogue who beds down with someone else's wife,

then at dawn begins to feel the chill of fear.
Death knows all about it. And the whole world has heard:
the glory of your name has grown to matchless infamy,
And no one is left to intervene
when the messengers of Death descend to strike you down.
Who knows how many deaths you'll have
for meeting death so badly, thinking such bad thoughts?
Oh low-minded one, you set Hari's love aside
to satisfy yourself with fun.
The Lord is the companion who fulfils and purifies;
the Lord is the guardian of everything that lives,
More merciful than any, a treasury of giving—
life he holds in his hands;
It is he who is magnified in Vedas and Purāṇas
and Smṛitis, and praised by gods and men:
But faced with the wiles of this world, and its folly,
why did you not tend your tie to him?
Now I have searched through every place I know,
thought about moths and fish and birds and deer,
Considered all the creatures on both land and sea:
tell me, what can I do more?
Even if I had no shame in saying things,
a hundred times again, what could I say?
Just this: not once did you sing of Hari, never.
You're wasted, Sūr. You're a fool.

Against the background of other poems in the *Sūr Sāgar* this juxtaposition of the ideals of love with the dreary realities of this life has a strange ring. We are accustomed to find the "moths and fish and birds and deer" (NPS 325:49) used as metaphors for the *gopīs*' unyielding attachment to Krishna, but here they are abstracted from that familiar realm and made to symbolize love pure and simple, as evident even in the created world. The acts of the lower species then become the standard by which the failings of the human beings are measured and found to be woefully lacking. Thus we hear the counterpoint of love and creation again, but now in an entirely new key. Instead of discovering how inadequate the creation is to the loving intensities of the *nikuñj*, we discover how inadequate the human self tends to be in relation to the love that sets the creation in motion and holds it together from birth to birth. This is no longer love measuring its glories in terms of the inadequacies of the creation but the creation seeing what it has become without love. The perspectives are decidedly different. In the one genre the alleged failings of the creation display the majesty of love, while in the other the greatness of love shows the poverty of a world in which love is forgotten. Yet the message is recognizably the same. It is love that makes the world go round, and when it doesn't, the world is a sorry place to be. Both ways of approaching the issue have their value, for in both cases it takes the one reality to cast the other in the light it deserves.

A CODA

For the most part, then, Sūr is eager to plunge his hearers into either the realities of this world of perverted creation or the glories of that supernal world that radiates from Krishna's *nikuñj*. The drama with which these two relate to each other sets the dialogue for much that animates Sūr's poetry. But there is a poem—so far as I know, a single poem—that seems to transcend or perhaps precede this dialogue, and with this poem we may close. It presents creation in its pristine form. Here Sūr is far from allowing some love-struck *gopī* to depict the creation as the act of an unfriendly demiurge, and equally far from seeing it through the eyes of a creature who has twisted it into a mechanism of torture that it was never meant to be. Instead, Sūr describes what the creation is to the Creator himself, and it is a remarkable vision (NPS 371):

Hari has fashioned on offering of lights
Created in so unusual a way
  that language can hardly give it measure.
A tortoise provides him with a throne unexcelled
  while Śeṣa the snake makes a long, hooded handle
For its vessel, Island Earth; the seven seas are the butter oil;
  and the wick has the thickness of a mountain.
The sun and the moon fill the world with their flame,
  vanquishing the darkness of night,
And sparks fly up as stars undarkened by a sky
  spread black with the collyrium of clouds.
Śiva and Brahmā, Sanak, Prajāpati,
  and all the host of gods and anti-gods and men—
They rise and dance their dance of many parts,
  each in a rhythm of its own.
The times, the deeds, the character
  of those who love the Lord
    are creatures of his wisdom and will,
For Sūr Dās's Lord has fashioned the world—
  substance and artifice—
    an offering unexcelled.

The "offering of lights" (NPS 371:1) that provides the metaphor upon which the poem turns is the *āratī* ceremony, performed with a cruse of oil or, as in this case, clarified butter (*ghī*) to illuminate an image of a deity. The person officiating—a priest in a temple, a householder at home—lifts the lamp with circular motions to bring light to the often dark recess in which the image is housed. Such images are typically installed on thrones, as specified in verse 3.

The novelty here is that the deity being illuminated is also the officiant—Hari or Krishna—and the ceremony is the creation itself. This accounts for the reference in verse 2 to the myth of the churning of the milk ocean, in which the Lord participates in creation by allowing himself to be used, in his tortoise avatar, as the base upon which the great world-churn can be mounted: Mount Mandara upended and pulled back and forth by a cosmic snake. This snake is customarily identified as Vāsuki, but here a more intimate connection with Hari (Vishnu or Krishna) is suggested, for the snake is Śeṣa, who served as the couch upon which Vishnu reclined at the moment of creation and who is, as his name "Remainder" suggests, an overflow of Vishnu himself. By assigning Śeṣa to Vāsuki's role, the poet strengthens the sense of the divine self-sufficiency.

"Island Earth" (NPS 371:4) translates the word *dīp*, which carries a double meaning. In the first instance it is, as the variant *mahi* in several manuscripts makes plain, the earth, conceived as the island-continent Jambudvīp (*dvīpa* = *dīp*). The second meaning, however, refers to the lamp itself (*dīpa* = *dīp*), which the earth also is, according to the metaphor that guides the poem. Mount Mandara or Meru, the axis of the world, then becomes the wick that is placed in the cruse, and the seven seas that surround Jambudvīp are the *ghī*. Once these connections have been made, the poet leaves the rest to our imagination. He merely comments that this is truly "an offering unexcelled" (NPS 371:10).

Or that is almost all he does. In the penultimate line he makes mention of "those who love the Lord" (*bhagatani*, NPS 371:9), which places us in the position of having to assess whether we belong in this group or not. If we qualify, we play a role in this great, reflexive cosmic ceremony. If not, then evidently not, and as in all of what we have heard Sūr say, love is the key.

For Sūr, thus, the creation is not some great affidavit proclaiming, as do the heavens in Haydn's oratorio, the glory of God. Instead it is an offering that the Creator makes to himself, an act of worship. Sūr's affirmation is that only by taking part—by worshiping, by loving—can one know what it is to be genuinely alive. And if that original completeness is obscured or deflected, one is left with a seemingly ever-unresolved dialogue of love and creation in which neither can quite find its way back into the act of worship that set the whole in motion. It is a horrifying thought that even Krishna's *nikuñj*, then, is perhaps but a retreat.

NOTES

1. The manuscript, dated *vikram saṁvat* 1639 (A.D. 1582), is preserved in the City Palace in Jaipur, and has recently been published in a facsimile edition under the patronage of the House of Jaipur (Gopāl Nārāyaṇ Bahurā, ed., *Pad Sūrdās jī kā / The Padas of Sūrdās*, Jaipur, 1982; with an introduction by Kenneth E. Bryant). The poems presented below, however, are based on critical editions made by consulting the full range of manuscripts predating about A.D. 1700 in which they occur. Kenneth E. Bryant, who was successful in encouraging the authorities in Jaipur to make their *Sūr Sāgar* available for wider inspection, is also ultimately responsible for editing the critical edition. I am grateful to him for permission to discuss these poems in advance of the forthcoming critical edition, translation, and commentary in which we are jointly engaged. The number assigned to each poem here is that in Jagannāth Dās "Ratnākar" et al., *Sūr Sāgar* (Varanasi, 1972, 1976), though the version of the poems appearing in that volume often differs considerably from the text translated here.
2. See J.S. Hawley, *Sūr Dās: Poet, Singer, Saint* (Seattle and Delhi, 1984), pp. 3-33.
3. Nandanandan (NPS 1107:2), "Nanda's Joy," is a title of Krishna. Nanda is his foster father. I am grateful to Mark Juergensmeyer for helping me render this and all other poems translated here into English verse.
4. The translation of verse 4 (*bāṇī madhur jāni pik bole kadam karārat kāg*) is somewhat problematical. The option chosen here follows the interpretation of Sītārām Caturvedī, ed., *Sūr-Granthāvalī*, vol. 2 (Varanasi, 1974), 762. An alternative possibility is that the koel (an Indian cuckoo) and the crow respond separately to the sound of Rādhā's voice. The cuckoo's call replicates the sound of a woman calling out for her beloved, and the cry of the crow is an omen that the lover is in fact approaching. The omen is fulfilled by time the poem reaches its conclusion.
5. See Diana L. Eck, "Gaṅgā: The Goddess in Hindu Sacred Geography," in J.S. Hawley and D.M. Wulff, eds., *The Divine Consort* (Berkeley, 1982), pp. 172-180.
6. Govind (NPS 2402:2) is a title of Krishna.
7. The story is told in *Bhāgavata Purāṇa* 1.9.37-39.
8. Mādhav (NPS 273:1) is a title of Krishna.
9. See Greg Bailey, *The Mythology of Brahmā* (Delhi, 1983), pp. 122-123.
10. The comparison of birth to cooking an eggplant refers to the way in which *bhurtā* or *bhartā* (cf. *bharat*, NPS 320:4), a favorite eggplant dish, is prepared in Braj. The vegetable is first suspended in a fire until it is shriveled and baked; sometimes it bursts with the heat. Then it is peeled, its inner contents are crushed, and again it is submitted to the fire, this time to be fried. The poet implies that birth is a process no less grueling.

    The final verse (NPS 320:8) refers to the fabled ability of Indian hunters to cause the deer they stalk to stand still by enchanting them with music. The same image is used in NPS 325:13-14, below.
11. *prabhu pūran pāvan saṣā prabhu prānani ke nāth* (NPS 325:45).

On Stone and Artistic Production

FREDERICK ASHER

A quest for the source of stone from which the Pāla period and earlier eastern Indian sculptures were carved led me to a group of artists settled at a place called Patharkatti, 28 km northeast of Gaya and 32 km east of Rajgir. The two, that is, stone and the artists, do have something in common and fruitfully can be examined together in this very preliminary report on my findings.[1]

My opening question, at the commencement of the research, related to the black or grey stone used for the eastern Indian sculptures. Called variously Rajmahal schist, black basalt, chlorite, and a host of other names,[2] I wondered whether the stone came from one or more quarries. Since the sculptures appear to my untrained eye to vary considerably in color and texture from light grey to dark black and from coarse-grained to very fine, it seemed likely that the stone came from several quarries. This would coincide with Susan Huntington's thesis that the dark stone comes from the Rajmahal hills located on the Bihar-Bengal border and the lighter grey stone from the vicinity of Gaya.[3] But this hypothesis and others relating to the source of the sculptures' stone, it seemed, only could be tested by a minerological comparison of samples from quarry sites with samples taken from sculptures themselves. To make the test meaningful, that is, to permit determination of which quarries probably served which sites or which — assuming that there was more than a single quarry — it seemed appropriate to take samples only from sculptures of known provenance, not the unprovenanced pieces that abound in Western museums.[4] Thus in certain quarries really did provide stone to sculptors only in rather limited areas, then this study's results might substantially aid the determination of the provenance of sculptures whose origin is unknown.

With trusting permission from several museum curators, samples from the sculptures were taken with a flat or pointed chisel from the back side of the tenon, an area that is customarily placed below the display base on which the sculpture is mounted. The samples then were made into thin sections for microscopic analysis. Sculptures selected for sampling were drawn from as wide an area as possible in eastern India, that is, from sites in all possible districts of Bihar and Bengal. But how to find the quarries? That, for an art historian, was a far more complicated task.

Road construction offered one entree to quarries, for the roads of India are generally repaired with crushed stone. Thus quite simply, whenever I saw roads being repaired with stone that seemed to resemble the grey to black stone used for Pala sculptures, I asked the foreman of the repair crew where he got it. I was thus led to several active quarries. Among them were some in the vicinity of Gaya, one in the city itself at the foot of Pretaśila Hill and another in the nearby Barabar Hills, as well as several in the Rajmahal Hills, mostly located between Sahibganj and Rajmahal town. Although I did not know it at the time, not one of these was the source of stone for the Pāla sculptors.

In the course of this quest for stone, I came upon a sculptor working in Gaya city, making the sort of objects that would probably best be described as souvenirs. I asked him about the source of his stone and was directed to his village, which he identified as Patharkatti, 28 kilometers northeast. There not only was his stone quarried but also, he said, many others sculptors worked.

Immediately upon arrival in the village, one recognizes sculptors at work, for the dominant sound is that of hammers hitting chisel. It is, in fact, a village comprised almost entirely of artists. Patharkatti, literally meaning the [place of] stone cutters, is located at the foot of a hill which is the source of these artists' stone. On this visit and two subsequent ones, I gained insights into the artists, many of them pertinent to understanding the artist in ancient India and thus supplementing the texts that provide our principal knowledge of the artists.[5]

Tradition among these artists holds that they came to Patharkatti from the Jaipur area when Ahalya Bai Holkar (1761–1795) brought them to construct the Viṣṇupad temple, the largest and most important monument at Gaya.[6] That tradition is probably true, for still in the village are pieces that they say were intended for the temple but that were improperly made and so never used; in both style and material, they correspond precisely with those on the temple. Why, then, did the artists settle so far from Gaya, surely a couple of days' walk when transporting heavy architectural members? I propose that they settled there because that is where the quarry was and because that is where artists traditionally had worked.[7] Still today, the tradition seems to be that artists work in established locations and send out the finished product. That is the way the artists of Patharkatti work, and so do other artists of the general region, such as, those of Tulsee and Company, stone contractors in Chunar, who recently completed a Śiva temple commissioned by a family in Faizabad, more than a hundred kilometers north. The temple components, even the *linga,* were fashioned in Chunar and sent by rail and truck to Faizabad. Might this present-day practice, then, be a model for the way artists worked traditionally, even as early as the Maurya period? It may not seem practical to send the finished product, where damage in transit would be more serious than damage simply to the unworked stone. More sensibly, artists might travel to the site of construction, working there until the project is completed and then moving on to the next project. Nevertheless, the artists are settled today and possibly were in ancient times as well.[8]

The Patharkatti artists know their stone extraordinarily well. They have names for almost a dozen different types from Patharkatti Hill itself, all varieties of the stone that we would loosely call Rajmahal schist.[9] They never sign their work, and no one artist of the village has achieved personal fame as an artist, but they all recognize individual styles and can quickly and easily identify the artist of any piece produced there — a task of some note, for there are more than seventy-five artists working in Patharkatti. In fact, they say they can even recognize the artist of a work produced ten years ago.

However, when pressed to identify the best sculptor or sculptors of the village, every one of them to whom I spoke demurred, insisting that quality is in the eyes of the beholder, a matter of personal taste. No matter how the question was rephrased, no matter who was asked, a similar answer was elicited.

They are not low-caste craftsmen, but brahmins, Gaur Brahmins. Their association with Gaur, the old capital of Bengal, is murky, but they acknowledge a Bengali heritage and believe that their ancestors were among the first Indian artists to work stone, at the time of Aśoka, they say.[10] How they came to Rajasthan, from which Ahalya Bai brought them to Patharkatti, they do not know, but still today they maintain close relations with relatives in Jaipur. Their sisters and daughters marry artists in Jaipur, those who work the white Makarana marble, and they in turn often take their wives from Jaipur families.[11] Although they value formal education and stress with pride that every boy *and girl* of Patharkatti is in school, the children learn their parents' craft from a very early age, about five or six. They then begin working in and subsequently move on to stone, from which they make small Śiva *lingas,* the sort that one sees ubiquitously in the souvenir shops of Gaya and Rajgir or at the entrance to the sites of Sārnāth and Nālandā, where the merchants all know that the images came from Patharkatti. In time, the young sculptors graduate to larger and larger pieces of stone.

The artists, especially when engaging in innovative work, follow published photographs or drawings that they have made, just as the Chunar artists followed a drawn plan of the temple they built and drawings for every component. The Patharkatti sculptors, in the course of their carving, make extensive use of drawing directly on the stone as they work out details. Generally one artist makes a work from start to finish. Only the final polishing is sometimes done by another person, usually a woman, as is the practice of their Jaipur relatives. They prepare their own tools, thus operating simultaneously as blacksmiths and sculptors. However, they purchase some chisels and files from Calcutta and polishing carborundum from Varanasi.

Only rarely are images made on commission. More commonly, the artists double as merchants, selling from what they call showrooms, a corner of their houses, to the very rare wholesaler who visits Patharkatti or, more commonly, travelling out across all north India, as far east as Calcutta and as far west as Rajasthan. Every one of the adult males had traveled rather widely to sell images. Indeed, something of the mercantile sensitivity is reflected in the following response to my oft-repeated question, "What is a good *mūrti?*" "Good art," one artist stated, "is good quality; if it sells, it is good!" This response, reflecting sensitivity to the marketplace, suggests parallels with the role of the patron in traditional Indian art. It is the patron's name, not the artist's, that is generally recorded in dedicatory inscriptions. The artist thus probably worked essentially at the behest of his patron, perhaps following his dictates but in any event producing works that conformed to his tastes. Is there any significant difference, then, between the influence of a patron who pays for the work before its commencement — if that is, in fact, the way the system worked in ancient India — and the patron who pays for the completed product? In both cases, commercial considerations have a significant effect on the artist and his product, as implied by the artist who correlated quality and marketability.

What does all this have to do with stone? Something, for now many samples of stone that the Patharkatti artists worked have been analyzed. Minerologically, some of them match precisely with stone used for images at Nālandā and at several other sites in both Gaya and Nalanda Districts. For that reason, it seems likely that stone from Patharkatti Hill was fashioned into images long before the current artists migrated to the place. Further, the stone at the hill's surface appears in large rocks that might be casually described as one Viṣṇu in size. That is, they are about 80 to 120 cm. in length, the size of a characteristic Pala image, so the artists may have worked natural boulders, not quarried blocks of stone.

The Patharkatti stone is, however, different from stone used for images in Bengal. As Richard Newman, working at the Center for Conservation and Technical Studies at Harvard, has stated, the stone for all eleventh- and twelfth-century sculptures from eastern India is "petrographically uniform enough to have come from a single quarry."[12] That is partly true, but not entirely, for generally Bihari sculptures of this late Pāla date are minerologically different from contemporary Bengali examples. Newman drew his conclusions because he tested examples from the Nallin collection, entirely comprised of sculptures from Bangladesh. Still, his conclusions, insofar as they pertain to Bengal, are correct. Testing examples of known provenance, largely from the Rajshahi and Bangladesh National Museums, I, too, found that all the late Pāla works of Bengal, regardless of the district from which they come, are carved from the same stone, as are some early works from Bengal. That stone, a very glassy basalt, probably came from either near Tinpahar or just west of Rampurhat, that is, just south of the Rajmahal Hills, but both close enough to the Ganga that the great river could have been the source of transport for the stone. It did not, however, come from the Rajmahal Hills, where today a black basalt, much more crystalline than that used for the sculptures, is extensively quarried for use in road construction and repair.

In any event, the parameters of a search for the source of stone used for eastern Indian sculptures have been narrowed; the ramifications of doing so are considerable, for example, adding a factor to supplement style in determining the provenance of a sculpture and certainly determining something about patterns of trade in the Pāla period. But the discovery of the Patharkatti artists in the course of this quest for stone, a kind of story within a story, was a special find of this search. Their work is intrinsically interesting; but more significant to the art historian, these artists may provide useful models for understanding artists in ancient India.

NOTES

[1]The research for this project was undertaken while in India on a grant from the Smithsonian Institution that was administered by the American Institute of Indian Studies.

[2]The stone used for sculptures in this and other parts of the subcontinent has been examined minerologically by Richard Newman, *The Stone Sculpture of India; A Study of the Materials Used by Indian Sculptors from ca. 2nd century B.C. to the 16th century* (Cambridge, Mass., 1984).

[3]Susan L. Huntington, *The "Pāla-Sena" Schools of Sculpture*, Leiden, 1984, p.2.

[4]The weakness of Newman's study, *Stone Sculpture*, is that he used largely unprovenanced sculptures and studied no samples from quarry sites; its art historical value is thus diminished.

[5]The texts, however, represent the ideal and provide little real insight into the artists and their mode of working. Inscriptions also provide significant data. See, for example, R.N.

Misra, *Ancient Artists and Art-Activity*, Simla, 1975.

[6]The Jaipur origin of these artists was repeated also to Francis Buchanan-Hamilton, *Journal of Francis Buchanan (Afterwards Hamilton); Patna and Gaya in 1811-1912.* Patna, 1925, p. 24.

[7]Buchanan-Hamilton, *ibid.*, records a mythical account of the quarry's early use, one possibly dating to the time of Aśoka.

[8]There were exceptions to this practice. Rock-cut sanctuaries required artists *in situ,* and several Orissan temples have unfinished areas, places where the sculpture had been outlined but not fully carved, indicating that the sculptures were fashioned after the stone blocks had been put in place.

[9]Among the names of stone are Pir Kasoti, Kala Kasoti, Danmahua, Hansraj, Hansraj Mangechha, Tamra, Motia and Urda.

[10]One artist told me, "In Aśoka's time, all Bengal, Bihar, and U.P. were one. Only here were stone images made [and our ancestors made them]." Then leaping over hundreds of years: "Under the Mughals, we went to Rajasthan, and then stone sculptures were made everywhere."

[11]For the Jaipur artists, see Sumahendra, "Marble Idols of Jaipur," *Arts of Asia,* XV: 4 (July-August 1985). pp. 75-81.

[12]Newman, *Stone Sculpture,* p. 63.

Keshub and Chaitanya: Brahmo Evangelism and the Indigenous Modernization of Vaishnavism in Bengal

DAVID KOPF

Brahmoism before Keshub Chandra Sen: Neo-Vedantism as Reformed Hinduism

Brahmoism was the earliest broadly inclusive ideology of socio-religious reform in modern India. Its history constitutes a vital episode in the intercivilizational encounter between India and the West. In content, it was neither purely Western nor Indian, but a syncretism of various redefined elements that ultimately became a new reintegrated tradition among the progressive middle-class Hindus of twentieth-century India.[1] Brahmoism was the foundation of what we today call Hindu modernism.

The first charismatic hero of the Indian Renaissance and Hindu Reformation was Rammohun Roy (1774–1833). Modern India owes much to the immense curiosity and restlessness of his intellect, the depth of his understanding about the major religions of the world, and his passion for ridding contemporary Hinduism of its many abuses—especially those facets of the system that tended to exploit and degrade women. Rammohun's greatest contribution, perhaps, was his ideology of salvation for India that he formulated as a response to Western intrusion, and that proved to be a model for subsequent generations of Hindu reformers. Because Rammohun refused to remain complacent about the inhumanity of quotidian Hinduism, but also refused to become a Christian convert, he has earned the title "Father of Modern India."[2]

In 1815, Rammohun settled permanently in Calcutta, an event of momentous importance to historians of the Bengal Renaissance.[3] That same year, he published his earliest translation of the Vedanta in abridged form. Though the book leaves much to be desired from a scholarly point of view, its impact on the Hindu Reformation cannot be denied.[4] Rammohun argued that Protestant missionaries were correct in their assertion that Hindus were idol worshipers, but that image worship as then practiced in India was an aberration from the authentic monotheistic tradition. In the manner of the British Orientalists, he divided Indian history into a Vedantic period that provided the authentic model for "the whole body of the Hindu theology, law, and literature" and was "highly revered by all the Hindus," and a later period of "Hindoo idolatry" with its "innumerable gods, godesses, and temples" which have since been destroying "the texture of society."[5]

In the next couple years, Rammohun continued to publish more translations of ancient texts to elaborate upon his renaissance view of history. For him, the Upanishads and the Vedanta were part of a "monotheistical system" that was akin to the Western notion of the "unity of the Supreme Being as sole Ruler of the Universe."[6] By 1820, with the publication of his *Precepts of Jesus*, Rammohun believed that Vedantism contained a purer form of monotheism than Christianity.[7] He savagely attacked such "fabricated fables" as the doctrine of the vicarious sacrifice of Jesus on the cross," which he felt were all designed to establish the "false identity of Christ with God."[8]

The more Rammohun debated trinitarian Christians, the more support he received from radical Unitarians in England and America. Rammohun actually converted a Baptist missionary named William Adam to Unitarianism, and the two of them organized a Calcutta Unitarian Committee in 1823.[9] Unitarian principles of monotheism, social reform in the name of religion, and universalism greatly influenced his developing idea of Hindu reformation. Then, in 1828, he founded the Brahmo Sabha, precursor of the later Brahmo Samaj (Society of God). He never achieved much with the Sabha, because he left for England shortly after its inception, never to return.[10]

In 1843, ten years after Rammohun's death in England, Debendranath Tagore established the Brahmo Samaj in Calcutta. Rammohun's works were reprinted, while the scriptual source upon which authentic Hinduism was based was reaffirmed as the Vedanta.[11] In 1845, Tagore collaborated with Rajnarian Bose in a publication against trinitarian Christian missionaries called *Vedantic Doctrines Vindicated*. Missionaries had questioned the assertion by Brahmos that the Vedanta expressed a notion of a personal god analogous to Jahoveh. In this defiantly nationlistic work, Tagore and Bose accused the Christians of "rushing headlong into the hideous errors of a reckless anthropomorphism." On the other hand, "the Vedanta, while it utterly rejects and condemns such degrading of the deity, conveys to our minds a far loftier, a more adequate, consistent, and ennobling idea of His attributes, by prescribing His worship as the Supreme Regulator of this boundless universe and as the glorious and beneficient originator of all earthly good."[12]

Throughout the 1840s, missionaries and other European observers of the Calcutta scene tended to view the Brahmo Samaj as a "Vedantic Sabha."[13] But in actual fact, during that very decade Brahmos were involved in a debate between Vedantists and universalists, the latter were repudiating sectarianism in religion along with sectarian scriptures, arguing instead that "all human beings are the children of God and the worshipers of God consider this earth to be his home and all human beings to be his brothers."[14] Akkhoy Kumar Dutt, a nontheistic Brahmo fellow-traveler who believed that natural religion had neither national origins nor a revealed source, persuaded Tagore in 1850 to drop the Vedanta as the book of the Brahmos.[15]

Nevertheless, Vedanta continued to be championed as the one revealed source in Hinduism comparable to the Bible and Koran. It can be said that a school of thought developed among younger philosophic Brahmos known as Neo-Vedantism, which included such luminaries as Vivekananda and Brahmobandhab Upadhyaya.[16] One Brahmo philosopher, Sitanath Tattvabhusan, actually believed that Tagore's decision to abandon the Vedanta did "a great deal of harm to the Brahmo Samaj" and had a disastrous impact on the new theological scholarship of the Hindu Reformation.[17]

BHAKTI INSPIRATION AND BRAHMO EVANGELISM UNDER KESHUB SEN

In an autobiographical sketch written later in life, Satyendranath Tagore, one Debendranath's more able and successful sons, admitted that in the mid-fifties "the progress of the Brahmo Samaj was slow." Then, when his father returned from Simla, "an epoch making event" took place and a "new chapter in the history of the Brahmo Samaj was opened." It was Keshub's coming into the Samaj that "created a new life" by giving the society a "new image." He recalled how "I also was swept by the tide of the new enthusiasm.[18]

Keshub Chandra Sen (1838–1884) was probably the most innovative, charismatic, and influential Hindu religious reformer in nineteenth-century India. Not only did he start the Brahmo Samaj mission movement that carried Hindu modernism across India but he provided the inspiration to other great Indian reformers such as Vivekananda, Dayananda, Dharmapala, and Sivanath Sastri. He was so conspicuous and controversial a figure that his one-time mentor, then archival, Debendranath Tagore, was compelled to admit in 1881 that "whether it be in praise of him or in blame, men cannot drink their daily drop of water without uttering Keshub's name.[19] And abroad, in England especially, of all the obituary notices of charismatic Indians known in the West, probably none gave more extensive coverage than that of Sen's death on January 8, 1884.[20]

Among those inclined to recall his achievements rather than his shortcomings, Keshub has been viewed as Rammohun Roy's successor, who sought to infuse progressive Western values into Hindu theism. Rabindranath Tagore, another of Debendranath's famous sons, saw Keshub as a profound scholar of world religions and a sincere believer in universal harmony.[21] Others, such as Bipin Chandra Pal, discovered in Keshub's writings the seeds of Indian nationalism.[22] There is also little doubt that Keshub was instrumental in initiating the Arya Samaj and the Maha Bodhi Society.[23]

These tributes to Keshub, when put side by side, which they seldom are, suggest a great adventure of the mind taking place in the Calcutta of the Bengal Renaissance. They suggest that the intellectual giants of the Renaissance, from Rammohun through Keshub to Rabindranath, were all philosophers of intercivilizational encounter between East and West at work formulating ideologies of salvation for India and the world of the nineteenth century.

But in the immediate socio-cultural context of contemporary Bengal, the intellectual concern for global synthesis gave way to the more pressing need to find indigenous solutions to the reformation of existing institutions and practices. On the provincial or parochial level, Keshub had little choice but to work within the sectarian atmosphere of Bengali religion during his own time. Interestingly enough, though he was attracted to Debendranath's Brahmo style in the 1850s, Keshub expressed little enthusiasm for Neo-Vedantism. Surprisingly, at least for a leader of the Renaissance, he began to lean in the direction of Vaishnavism or the Bhakti tradition of Chaitanya. Vaishnavism was looked upon by reformers as "the greatest obstacle to the promotion of the true religion." Tattvabhusan repudiated it for its lack of philosophic depth, its emotionalism, and above all, "its sensuality and disregard of ethical distinctions."[24]

Keshub's partisanship for the "medieval excrescence" of Vaishnavism was a radical departure for any Brahmo leader up to the mid-sixties. This Brahmo evangelism, as I have called it elsewhere, which Keshub began flirting with in the 1860s, was in fact a brilliant ploy to widen and deepen Brahmo appeal.[25] In part, Keshub was already responding to the religious orientation of new Brahmo recruits who were no longer the Calcutta-based, Western-educated intelligentsia but were the alienated youth of mofussil towns in north and east Bengal. Men such as Aghore Nath

Gupta, Troylokya Nath Sanyal, Dinanath Mozumdar, and Nanda Lal Banerji, among others, were part of a new generation who were anxious to reform Hinduism but knew very little English.[26] Their inspiration as Brahmos, though certainly intense and genuine, came less from British sources than from Keshub's new image of the sixteenth-century Vaishnava saint, Chaitanya.

The implications of incorporating bhakti into Brahmo ideology has not been seen as a key issue that divided Keshub from Debendranath and led to the schism of 1866. No doubt the lack of a progressive social activism by older Brahmos was a crucial factor, as was the lack of representative government within the Samaj. But equally important was Keshub's new vision of missionaries who might traverse the countryside and convert thousands to the Brahmo faith. Rammohun Roy's Unitarian-inspired rationalism and reinterpretation of the Upanishads were far too exotic and abstract for most Hindus outside the reach of Calcutta intellectual circles.[27] But there was great danger, as Keshub would soon learn, that unleashing bhakti emotionalism could lead to a betrayal of fundamental Brahmo principles as easily as it could lead to the revitalization of Vaishnavism to meet the challenge of modernization.

Keshub saw the great potential of transforming the Brahmo Samaj into a mass movement by means of what we today call indigenous modernization. Could he not open the hearts of countless Hindus by pouring the new wine of Brahmoism into the older containers of Vaishnava piety and devotionalism? Keshub turned his back on Vedanta, which had continued to remain circumscribed among intellectuals and philosophers as a thinking man's religion. Why was it necessary to go back to the Vedas or to the Upanishads for egalitarian and other modern values when Bengal had produced Chaitanya, a reformer who had already condemned caste inequality and religious intolerance in the sixteenth century?

It was at this point that Bijoy Krishna Goswami began to play his major role in Brahmo history as the most effective missionary of Neo-Vaishnavism or Brahmo evangelism. The circumstances of his birth, early development, and education indicate that Bijoy Krishna Goswami was, among all the Brahmos in the Adi Samaj, the least Anglicized. Born in 1841 in Santipur, Nadia district, in the vicinity of the sixteenth-century Vaishnava reformation, he was descended from the advaita preceptor in Chaitanya's movement. His father was a devout Vaishnava priest, his uncle a scholar who roamed about north Bengal offering mantras and collecting donations for the local Goswami temple dedicated to Lord Krishna.[28]

How Bijoy Krishna underwent a serious identity crisis that ended ultimately in Brahmo conversion is a fascinating story; suffice it to say here that Bijoy Krishna's new consciousness was a painful birth, and that he remained for many years deeply moved by the experience.[29] He never learned English well enough to write in it, but his understanding and defense of Western rationalism was beautifully articulated in Bengali prose.

In the 1860s, Bijoy Krishna supported Keshub against Debendranath.[30] Perhaps he even encouraged Keshub to launch his rebellion. After the schism of 1866, Bijoy collaborated with Keshub in the rather delicate operation of fusing elements of Vaishnavism with Brahmo ideology.[31] There was also an attempt to resurrect Chaitanya as a rebel against the Hindu establishment. Soon, with Chaitanya standing forth as a champion of Brahmoism, the two protests would merge into one.

After 1866, Keshub relied heavily on Bijoy, and it is not unlikely that the new emphasis on music and street processions in the Samaj was one important result. Possibly, it was Bijoy who suggested that Keshub model himself after Chaitanya, an incarnation of Vishnu. Bijoy was then a very strong rationalist and social reformer who saw in Chaitanya's image a marvelous opportunity to extend the Brahmo reformation and even reach the masses.[32]

By 1867, the Vaishnava emphasis seems to have changed Keshub's personality. In September of that year, he was described as "no longer being stern, ethical, and full of intellectual bitterness, but thawed into someone tender and full of humility and . . . trusting dependence which dissolved every heart it touched into kindred tears. The didactic devotions of the older Jorosanko pulpit were by an unseen process transformed into an all-piercing pathos, an inseparable sympathy with every form of sin, suffering, and desertion that made our daily services the veritable service of sorrow."[33]

By November 1867, the bhakti tradition had clearly won its way into the new Brahmo church. The sankirtan or Vaishnava devotional hymn was introduced, along with street processions characterized by "ecstatic devotion, rapture of the heart . . . zeal and emotional fervor." In the midst of the excitement, Keshub sang for the first time in public. According to Protap Majumdar, "He loudly sang, a thing which his natural shyness had never permitted him to do before; he had never been seen to weep, but now streams of tears ran down his handsome face. He was turned into a new man.[34]

Protap Chandra, who spent much of his life weathering the storms of Keshub's "religious aberrations," asked in one place "why did Brahmos borrow the old fashioned plebian forms of Vaishnava music and musical appurtenances?" Though Majumdar never answered the question, his comments are revealing. After all, he tells us, Vaishnavites were "neither high socially" nor "distinguished by modern education." Moreover, they "were noted for grotesque personal habits, intense wild devotional excitement leading sometimes to inconveniences." Majumdar, it should be stressed, was seeking to win over Keshub to Unitarian Christianity. On January 24, 1868, at the mandir consecration ceremony, the Vaishnava influence was never greater. Majumdar grimly reported that "Keshub held his Nagar Sankirtan with great flags inscribed with theistic mottoes. . . . Vaishnava kirtans had degenerated into mobbish assemblies and it required great moral courage and deep religious compulsion to be able to borrow and reform them.[35]

The success of Keshub's mission movement in the mid-sixties was largely due to Bijoy Krishna and the enthusiasm that Neo-Vaishnavism generated throughout rural Bengal. Neo-Vaishnavism in the guise of Brahmoism reached out to all young men feeling a sense of alienation or identity crisis generated largely by conflict between family obligations and new Western ideals imbibed in the classroom. Often, Brahmo conversion was the only way many young persons could resolve their conflicts and achieve a new identity.[36] Sivanath Sastri, for example, has recorded in his *Atmacharita* (autobiography) how he, a Shakto, joined Keshub in the face of ostracism and persecution at the very time when Vaishnava influence was at its height in the Brahmo Samaj.[37] Indeed, the years 1868 and 1869 were a kind of turning point in Sastri's life. In the former year, he identified himself with the Keshubites by joining them openly in their Vaishnava-inspired sankirtan procession. There he sang the Sanyal sangit, which proclaimed the equal rights of men and women while repudiating caste. In August 1869, Sastri was officially initiated as a Keshubite Brahmo at an impressive ceremony at the mandir.[38] His father was furious. Then, when the young man renounced his sacred thread, to the great satisfaction of the Brahmo community, his father grew abusively vindictive. Things went from bad to worse, until finally Sivanath broke off relations with his "tyrannical father," who drove his son out of his house and for the next nineteen years refused to see him.[39]

Vaishnavism was working well for Keshub. Though the masses remained outside the pale of Brahmo mission activity, the intelligentsia flocked to Bijoy and Keshub in great numbers. Would it not be a marvelous thing if the spirit of Chaitanya could be revived under the banner of the Brahmo Samaj? In June 1868, at the East India railway junction town of Monghyr in Bihar, Keshub publicly assumed the pose of a Brahmo Chaitanya, but with disastrous results. Protap Chandra Majumdar has described the event with obvious misgivings. Bengali railway clerks sympathetic to Keshub came to hear him. The congregation was convened weekly to be inspired by the Brahmo leader who spoke and acted like a Vaishnava saint. "They would often be moved to tears and sobs and ejaculations," wrote Majumdar, "that were well nigh hysterical." Keshub "had the whole town in ferment."[40] Then on June 7, as

Sivanath Sastri later wrote with regret, "People prostrated themselves at the feet of Mr. Sen (and each other) and prayers were offered to him for intercession on behalf of sinners."[41] The incident was relayed from Bihar across India from east to west. Keshub's old friend, Satyendranath Tagore, now a successful government official in Ahmedabad, wrote that "I see that Keshub has been made an avatar, but I doubt whether Keshub himself countenances the folly of his disciples."[42] Protap Chandra wrote: "Thus began a new apostolic organization. The abnormal excitement of emotions first began at Monghyr and understandably emasculated a good many unripe minds in Keshub's church."[43] The most interesting response was Bijoy Krishna's. Ironically, it was Goswami who was determined to pull Keshub away from "superstition" back to rational Brahmo principles. He was angry with Keshub and those so-called Brahmos "who consider Keshub a savior." In one local Bengali newspaper, he lashed out at people who tried to make Keshub "an incarnation of God." Wrote Bijoy: "It is against the principles of the Brahmos to call Keshub Babu the Savior, to pray to him for salvation, to kiss his feet, and to compose sacred songs in his name. It is the duty of Brahmos to revere Keshub as a human being. Brahmoism recognizes only God as Savior. We request Keshub Babu to dissuade other Brahmos from this dangerous course."[44]

In order to heal the rift between himself and Bijoy, Keshub made certain that he did not appear as a divinely inspired prophet of the mass mind. Bijoy wanted Keshub to purify Vaishnavism from such abuses through Brahmo rationalism; and certainly at this point in his life, he feared for the survival of rationalism if Brahmo leaders themselves succumbed to the temptation of becoming objects of mass hysteria. On June 4, 1869, approximately one year after Monghyr, Keshub wrote a piece on the prophet of Nadia in which he tried to vindicate himself from the charges of avatarism and man-worship. "The Brahmo Samaj," he said, "will forever be indebted to the spirit of Chaitanya . . . his creed and character. But in four short centuries, he went on to say, "we have witnessed the rise and decay of that . . . branch of Hinduism which is now in a degenerate condition." What follows, in view of Goswami's influence, is highly significant: "The Vaishnava church which had done wonders in its days will be renewed and reformed, and render valuable services to the course of Indian regeneration. While we sincerely regret that Chaitanya's spirit has so soon passed from the vast majority of his followers . . . we cannot but speak with the utmost reverence and gratitude of him who achieved some of the highest religious and social reforms on effete Hinduism and whose true-hearted disciples are an honor to Hindustan."[45]

CHAITANYA AMONG THE WORLD S SAINTS AND PROPHETS: KESHUB AND THE NEW DISPENSATION

In perspective, Neo-Vaishnavism proved simply an episode in Keshub Sen's quest for spiritual truth and an ideology of salvation. He was a restless intellectual continually itching to embrace new ideas, to form new organizations. In Darjeeling, two years before his death, while already weakened by diabetes, he reminisced about his youth to his disciple, Protap Chandra Majumdar: "To me, the state of being on fire is the state of salvation. ... It was death to me to awake from my slumber without the consciousness of being baptized anew in fire. ... From when I was young, I have always kept burning the fire of enthusiasm ... and to keep up the condition of heat I have always run after what is new, always wished for new achievements, new ideas. What is new is warm, what is old is cold."[46]

In 1870, he went to England, met Queen Victoria, whom he admired, lectured to Unitarian and other liberal religious groups, was wined and dined everywhere, and enhanced his image as a Hindu religious reformer by means of a favorable press written by journalists greatly enamored by his oratorical gift and mastery of the English tongue.[47] The experience made him an advocate of radical reform efforts among women, workers, and peasants. From his return to Calcutta in 1870 to 1873, he worked tirelessly through an institution he created called the Indian Reform Association to raise the educational and moral standard of all three penalized groupings by means of schools, night classes, and specially printed materials and newspapers.[48]

Then in the mid-seventies, he found himself, as Debendrnanath once had, despised by a new radical generation of Brahmos who suddenly found him authoritarian and hypocritical.[49] The real issue was female emancipation in church, college, and the professional world. Then, when Keshub married off his daughter at a tender age, against Brahmo principles, to the allegedly "idolatrous" king of Cooch Behar, the radicals exploded in defiance and in 1878 formed a new Brahmo Samaj. About the same time, a weary and battered Keshub turned his back on Western-inspired social reform, interacted with the Neo-Sakto saint, Ramakrishna, and began his final quest to separate the essential from the nonessential in the major religions of the world.[50]

By 1881, when Keshub inaugurated his new world religion, or New Dispensation, he had totally renounced his earlier sectarian concerns with a revitalized Vaishnavism in Bengal. For years he had staged elaborate seminars on the founders of the world faiths, focusing on the diversified periods of crises each was confronted with. The means by which a saint or prophet helped civilization overcome a breakdown and catastrophe was studied in preparation for the propagation of a new ideology of salvation for the modern world. Keshub spoke of a religion of science and saw himself as the Newton of that science.[51]

A study of the rites and rituals of the New Dispensation suggests, however, that Keshub had not entirely abandoned Chaitanya and the Vaishnava tradition. He sitll conducted processions through city streets, but alongside the customary Vaishnava khole, kartal, and ektara were the Salvation Army trumpets and bugles.[52] Chaitanya was still one of the saints celebrated for the reformation he inspired, though he was now one of many protestors who appeared in history to oppose evil. Each saint had taught Keshub his own system or path of moral transformation. Sati Kumar Chatterji has succinctly listed these alternative paths: "Moses represented God's intervention in all of man's worldly concerns—both great and trivial. Socrates represented the path to self-knowledge; Sakhya Muni . . . self-denial; the yogis . . . the power of rapt meditation; Jesus equated the love of man with the will of God; Mohummad . . . the brotherhood of man through rigid monotheism; Chaitanya represented the path of rapturous devotion to God."[53]

NOTES

1. See D. Kopf, *The Brahmo Samaj and the Shaping of the Modern Indian Mind* (Princeton, 1979) especially pp. 313–334, "The Brahmo Reformation Diffused: Bengal's Legacy to Twentieth Century India."
2. N. S. Bose, *The Indian Awakening and Bengal* (Calcutta, 1960), p. 10.
3. *Ibid.*, pp. 12–13.
4. D. Kopf, *British Orientalism and the Bengal Renaissance* (Berkeley and Los Angeles, 1969), pp. 199–200.
5. R. Roy, *Abridgement of the Vedant,* reprinted in T. de Bary, *Sources of Indian Tradition* (New York, 1958), pp. 573–575.
6. R. Roy, *Translation of the Cena Upanishad*, Vol. CLX of India Office Library Tracts (Calcutta, 1816), p. v.
7. R. Roy, *The Precepts of Jesus: The Guide to Peace and Happiness* (Calcutta, 1820), pp. 116–117.
8. R. Roy, *Second Appeal in Defense of the Precepts of Jesus* (Calcutta, 1821), pp. 156–157.
9. For more information on the Unitarians of Calcutta during the 1820s and William Adam's role in their activities, consult W. Adam, *The Principles and Objects of the Calcutta Unitarian Committee,* Vol. CCVI of India Office Library Tracts (Calcutta, 1827).
10. Rommohun died in September 1833, while a house guest of the British Unitarian Lant Carpenter, in Bristol, England.
11. Kopf, *Brahmo Samaj,* pp. 163–164.
12. *Vedantic Doctrines Vindicated*, quoted *ibid.*, pp. 169–170.
13. De Rozario, "Letter from Calcutta," *Calcutta Corresponding Committee of the Church Missionary Society, 27th Report, 1846,* quoted *ibid.*, p. 165.
14. A. K. Dutt, *Who is a Brahmo*, 1854, quoted *ibid.*, p. 51.
15. D. Tagore, *Atma Jibani* (Autobiography), 4th Ed. Edited by S. C. Chakrabarty (Calcutta, 1962), p. 4.

16. See Kopf, *Brahmo Samaj*, pp. 76–85.
17. S. Tattvabhusan, *Autobiography*, quoted *ibid.*, p. 82.
18. S. Tagore, *Amar Valya Katha o Amar Bombai Prabash* (My Youth and My Stay in Bombay) (Calcutta, 1915), p. 57.
19. Letter from Debendranath Tagore to Protap Chandra Majumdar, n.d., in *Calcutta Corresponding Committee of the Church Missionary Society*, 62nd Report, 1881, p. xiii.
20. See discussion in Kopf, *Brahmo Samaj*, pp. 249–250.
21. For a good discussion of Keshub's influence on Tagore along these lines, see S. N. Hay, *Asian Ideas of East and West* (Cambridge, Mass., 1970), p. 23.
22. B. C. Pal, *The Brahmo Samaj and the Battle of Swaraj in India* (Calcutta, 1926), pp. 34–67.
23. S. K. Chattopadhyay, *Samanvag Marga* (Paths of Synthesis) (Calcutta, 1961).
24. S. Tattvabhusan, *Autobiography* (Calcutta, n.d.), pp. 61, 106.
25. Kopf, *Brahmo Samaj*, pp. 217–248.
26. Biographical sketches of these men appear *ibid.*, pp. 227–240.
27. For what was done in Brahmo mission work before 1860, see *ibid.*, p. 318.
28. B.C. Pal, *Saint Bijaykrishna Goswami* (Calcutta, 1964), p. 15.
29. Kopf, *Brahmo Samaj*, pp. 219–221.
30. *Ibid.*, pp. 134–136.
31. For a good discussion of the relationship between Keshub and Bijoy, see P.K. Sen, *Biography of a New Faith* (Calcutta, 1933), II, pp. 1–14.
32. For examples of Bijoy's effectiveness as a missionary among the people, see Kopf, *Brahmo Samaj*, pp. 224–225.
33. B.K. Goswami, *Brahmo Samajer Bartaman Abastha Ebong Amar Jibane Brahmo Samajer Parikkhita Bisay* (The Present Condition of the Brahmo Samaj and Brahmo Experiments in My Life) (Calcutta, 1882), p. 12.
34. P.C. Mazoomdar, *The Life and Teachings of Keshub Chunder Sen* (Calcutta, 1887), pp. 189, 192.
35. P.C. Mazoomdar, *Faith and Progress of the Brahmo Samaj* (Calcutta: Central Press, 1882), p. 224.
36. For a discussion of identity crisis among the young persons of East Bengal, see Kopf, *Brahmo Samaj*, pp. 97–103.
37. S. Sastri, *Men I Have Seen: Reminiscences of Seven Great Bengalis* (Calcutta, 1919), p. 127.
38. H.C. Sarkar, *Sivanath Sastri* (Calcutta: Ram Mohan Roy Publication Society, 1929), p. 14.
39. S. Debi, *Sivanath* (Calcutta, 1966), pp. 51–52.
40. Mazoomdar, *Life and Teachings*, p. 193.
41. S. Sastri, *History of the Brahmo Samaj* (Calcutta, 1911), I, p. 227.
42. Letter from S.N. Tagore to G. Tagore (January 10, 1868), quoted in Kopf, *Brahmo Samaj*, p. 225.
43. P.C. Mazoomdar, *Life and Teachings*, p. 200.
44. Letter from B.K. Goswami to editor of *Somprakash*, November 1, 1868, quoted in Kopf, *Brahmo Samaj*, pp. 225–226.
45. Cutting dated June 4, 1869, "The Prophet of Nuddea," *Sadharan Brahmo Samaj Library, Sophia Dobson Collet Collection*.
46. K.C. Sen, *Jiban Veda* (Life Inspiration) (Calcutta, 1915), pp. 17–18.
47. D. Kopf, *Brahmo Samaj*, pp. 261–264.
48. P.K. Sen, *Biography of a New Faith*, II, pp. 276–294.
49. D. Kopf, *Brahmo Samaj*, p. 138.
50. *Ibid.*, pp. 36–41, 140–141, 266–268.
51. *Ibid.*, pp. 270–271.
52. *Ibid.*, p. 269.
53. *Ibid.*, p. 272.

Indian Renaissance beyond Bengal: The Awakening in Maharashtra

FRANK F. CONLON

The concept of "Indian renaissance" has become an influential, widely accepted feature in the historiography of modern India's colonial encounter.* In a time of political and economic change, a small yet influential Indian elite intellectually "caught fire," fueled by new-found knowledge of the West and by rediscovered wisdom of their own classical traditions. Conscious of the image of a people emerging into light from a dark age, Indians accepted the European parallel. Rammohan Roy is reported to have told the missionary Alexander Duff, "I begin to think that something similar to the European renaissance might have taken place here in India."[1] One later Indian historian, writing of "the revivifying touch" of the West, declared that this "was truly a Renaissance, wider, deeper and more revolutionary than that of Europe.[2]

New ideas, new critiques, new communications, new solutions, even new problems all heralded the birth of a new age of intellectual development.[3] One issue that will not be addressed directly in this essay, but that does require further consideration, lies in the degree to which the "renaissance" is identified by its content. If, to borrow Professor Joarder's terms, for example, reason, humanism, and worldliness are central features, may we then include in the "awakening" the negative responses of those who did not readily embrace all of the new knowledge? Surely the "renaissance" did occur as new ideas gained currency and in the process stimulated the growth of public interest and communication and formation of opinions within the society. However, in the process defenders of tradition were also brought into the new public discourse and thereby were also a part of the story.

The pattern of "renaissance" did not appear simultaneously throughout India. It was in the region of Bengal, particularly in the new city of

Calcutta, where an early British presence produced a setting and circumstance for Indians to explore new paths of opportunity. It is, therefore, not surprising that subsequent generations would come to see the Bengal experience as a prototype that would later be manifested in some degree in the rest of the subcontinent. Nirad Chaudhuri captured this implication when he wrote of Bengalis as the "Torch Race of the Indian Renaissance."[4] Bengali historians have accepted the prototypical nature of their region's experience. "The evolution in Bengal formed a basic pattern for the rest of India," observed R.C. Majumdar, "so that a study of Bengal in the nineteenth century would not only facilitate a similar study of the regions, but seem to be a necessary precursor to it."[5] Sir Jadunath Sarkar would concur that Bengal was a "pathfinder and light-bringer." "If Periclean Athens was the school of Hellas, 'the eye of Greece, mother of arts and eloquence,' that was Bengal to the rest of India under British rule. . . . In this new Bengal originated every good and great thing of the modern world that passed on to the other provinces of India."[6]

The image of Bengal and its renaissance were important to all India, and Sarkar may be justified in claiming that new ideas, institutions, and manners spread like ripples from a central eddy. However, there follows from this a troubling sense that the rest of the subcontinent's history in terms of "renaissance" must be glimpsed only as a pale, imperfect shadow. Historians of other Indian regions, it seems to me, ought consciously to examine the Indian awakening within their regional contexts and try to specify the extent to which regional difference arose from the exhaustion of the energy of outward ripples, and to what degree geographical, historical, and institutional factors gave different shape, if not meaning, to the phenomena of renaissance outside Bengal.

This essay is concerned to explore the question of regional variation in the Indian renaissance within the context of the western Indian region of Maharashtra. In the course of identifying important figures and institutions of the "Maharashtra renaissance," several points of difference will be suggested by way of contrast with Bengal, including the geographic spread and nature of British rule, the comparative duration of contact with British influences, differing relations of city and hinterland, and variations of administrative and educational policy. Before exploring the manifestations of renaissance in Maharashtra, it will be helpful to sketch briefly the salient characteristics of the renaissance in Bengal, namely, certain geographical, cultural, economic, and political features against which the Maharashtrian experience may be compared.

The Bengal renaissance takes its name from the cultural region and former Mughal province that had undergone a transition during the early eighteenth century from imperial province to semi-autonomous polity, and thence to the domination of the English East India Company. In the view of a Maharashtrian observer, this transition had led to some admirable changes. Bal Shastri Jambhekar, writing in the first issue of the first Marathi periodical, stated:

> It is only sixty or seventy years that the province of Bengal has been in the possession of the English, but the changes which have taken place in the general condition of its inhabitants are truly astonishing. When we beheld the country that was but a century ago the scene of violence, oppression and misrule, enjoying security and freedom; and observe its inhabitants acquiring a superior knowledge of the Arts and Sciences of Europe, a bright example is presented to our minds.[7]

When Jambhekar wrote this paean in 1832, Bengal's awakening had matured substantially, most particularly in Calcutta. Possessed of a common cultural and political history, Bengal nonetheless was not fully integrated because of its deltaic geography, which limited internal communications and mobility. However, the *locus classicus* of the renaissance, Calcutta, built by the British to unite the functions of a colonial port and headquarters of administration, held the seeds of change. Not only did the city contain the principal offices of Company administration and trade, but here too there emerged institutions of education and the earliest monuments of British orientalist interest in Indian civilization, the Asiatic Society (1784) and for the College of Fort William (1800).[8] The orientalist scholars clustered in Calcutta not only sympathized with ancient Indian civilization, but assisted contemporary Indians in recapturing something of that culture's golden age of classical attainments. Here a figure like Sir William Jones (1746–1794) could sympathetically bring to Indian culture the rationalist and humanist universalism of the European enlightenment, even as in the adjacent Danish enclave of Serampore, Christian missionaries challenged Hindu tradition and launched, through the development of printing in Indian languages, a major innovation in the communication of ideas.[9]

Commerce created new wealth in Calcutta for Europeans and Indians. The city became an economic magnet for merchants, artisans, and clerks drawn by the burgeoning opportunities.[10] An unusually sympathetic contact between Calcutta's world of commerce and education produced a scintilating *timbre* of intellectual activity in the early nineteenth century. The elite of the new men of Bengal responded to Western values and recognized the elevated attainments of India's classical past. Although the most visible individual figure of this Bengal awakening, Rammohan Roy (1772–1833), was an active promoter of cultural, social, and religious reform, it would not be correct to think that all participants in the new debate over the public interest belonged solely to the cause of reform; there were equally influential and articulate conservative defenders of tradition such as Radha Kanta Deb (1794–1867).[11]

The wide range of ideology and expression was not matched in the social composition of the participants. The Bengal renaissance was primarily the realm of high-caste Hindus, drawn from among Brahmans, Kayasthas, and Vaidyas, known as the gentle-folk or *bhadralok,* whose situation was defined by a conjunction of tradition of high status and literacy, contact and appropriation of the new knowledge, and some accumulation of wealth in the new colonial economy.[12]

British administrative policy and structure provided another force that conditioned the changes in Bengal. The introduction of the permanent zamindari settlement of the land revenue under Governor-General Cornwallis in 1793 not only created a new basis for a rule of landed property, but also limited the government's requirements of administrative penetration in the countryside.[13]

The seedtime of the Bengal renaissance was thus a period of rapid and extensive change for those Indians who were its primary agents and beneficiaries. New men, linked by a new spirit of public affairs and education, profiting in the economic growth of Calcutta, generated a pattern of educational and public endeavor that spread from the city throughout virtually the entire cultural region of Bengal and beyond.

If one seeks to examine the phenomena of renaissance in Maharashtra, a rather different picture emerges. Although a clear sense of an awakening is to be found among an educated elite of Maharashtra in the years following the British annexation of the western Deccan in 1818, that elite's response to external ideas and values was tempered.[14] The Maharashtra renaissance produced a spectrum of thought, including vivid Vedic revivalism, critical social reform sentiments, and a revolutionary critique of Brahmanical religious and social traditions. However, the overall flavor of the mid-nineteenth century was of social and economic change that appears to be less intense than that experienced in Bengal. Whether this reflected a more deeply ingrained conservatism in Maharashtra's society or was the artifact of the comparatively short span of British rule, I cannot conclusively say. It is tempting to suggest that within the region there was a broad concern among the educated elites to integrate the Marathi-speaking people in a consistent, organic whole that was neither overtly reactionary nor radical, but as yet I have found no substantive basis for accepting this view.[15]

Maharashtra's historical experience prior to and during the expansion of British rule differed considerably from that of Bengal. Whereas eighteenth-century Bengal had existed at the administrative frontier of the Mughal empire, first integrated by the demi-independent nawabs and later dominated by the East India Company, Maharashtra had in that same period been the heartland of the Maratha state centering upon Poona, the capital of its hereditary chief minister, the *peshwa.* Although the *peshwas* did not control the entire Marathi-speaking region, the reality of Maratha power was the dominant strategic fact of western India.

The European presence in the region, which dated as far back as the Portuguese seizure of Goa in 1510, had nonetheless been extremely circumscribed in geographical extent, limited to coastal enclaves. Although the English had held Bombay island since the 1660s, the rising Maratha power had kept the Company in a position of strategic weakness throughout the eighteenth century. The Bombay Presidency's one major excursion into Maratha affairs in 1775 had proved to be utterly disasterous. As a result, Bombay's world tended to remain on the margins of India, in the realm of coastal commerce.[16] The *peshwa's* political fortunes did fall when, in 1802, he had to negotiate a subsidiary alliance with the Company in order to gain protection from the wrath of Holkar, yet still the semblance and sometimes the reality of independent rule was sustained for another generation.

Maharashtra never fell, as a unified political-administrative unit, under colonial rule. The East India Company rule over the southern Konkan and Deccan districts of the *peshwa* commenced only in 1817–1818. Even 1818 may seem a symbolic date, for Governor Mountstuart Elphinstone continued to attempt the administrative isolation of the new territories from Bombay under a commissionership that lasted until 1826. Furthermore, substantial portions of the old Maratha territory were confirmed in the rule of the Maratha rajas of Kolhapur and Satara and other members of the nobility of the old regime.[17] Eastern Maharashtra remained under Indian administration for at least another generation. The assignment of Berar to the Company by the Nizam of Hyderabad in 1853 and the Company's annexation of Nagpur in 1854 did extend British control, but under an administration separate from that of Bombay. The Marathwada districts of the Nizam's dominions remained under princely rule until 1948.[18]

Bal Gangadhar Shastri Jambhekar, sometimes called the first major actor of the Maharashtra renaissance, commented on the relative rawness of the region, attributing this not to a lack of administrative unity but simply to the fact that Maharashtrians had been exposed to a British presence for a time that was "comparatively short."[19] He nevertheless perceived that "the gloom of ignorance which has long prevailed over . . . this quarter of India . . . is beginning to vanish." He looked forward to a not too distant time "when we shall be able to view with our Eastern

Brethren [the Bengalis who had the benefits of] . . . long and intimate intercourse with Europeans."[20] That Bal Shastri was making this remark in the first number of the first Marathi newspaper, which he was launching in 1832, underscores the time lag in the origins of the Maharashtra renaissance. Jambhekar's comment also establishes that he was aware of the intellectual and cultural flowering of Bengal. Even so, the sequel did not produce an overt, conscious imitation.[21]

Along with the fact that Maharashtra was not uniformly subjected to one British administrative rule, there were other features that provided a contrast with the circumstance of Bengal. The relationship of Bombay and Calcutta to their respective hinterlands was not strictly comparable, nor, as we shall see, were the administrative structures, educational policies, missionary activities, or social order.

Calcutta and Bombay were both creations of British initiatives — classical examples of colonial ports of trade that became administrative centers, as well. Their social histories, however, were rather different. British Bombay's strategic and commercial interests had a long-term orientation to coastal trade hinterlands in Gujarat, the Konkan, and Malabar. Similarly, Bombay's social composition reflected its geographical situation. The city was, is effect, marginal to two linguistic cultural regions, Gujarat and Maharashtra. Its population majority may be said to have been Maharashtrian, but drawn primarily from the adjacent northern Konkan and not the western Deccan plateau. Within this Marathi population most elite positions were occupied by members of castes whose rural roots lay primarily in the Konkan littoral. Pathare Prabhus, Daivadnya Sonars, Gaud Saraswat Brahmans, and Palshikars had, for the most part, few significant social ties to the Deccan. Their members had risen in economic and social precedence within a relatively marginal situation of the Konkan or Bombay itself.[22] Collectively they enjoyed somewhat higher social status within Bombay and the Konkan than within the Marathi-speaking region as a whole. Although there were a few prominent Maharashtrian merchant princes, such as Jagannath Shankershet (1802–1865), the bulk of Bombay's Maharashtrians who were not laborers found employment in clerical service or the professions.[23] Those Bombay Maharashtrians who played any role in the influential strata of Indians in the city were drawn almost entirely from among the castes of coastal heritage and longer residence.

Although the annexation of the *peshwa's* territories in 1818 and the consequent expansion of British administration might reasonably have been expected to open new opportunities for the Bombay Maharashtrian communities, in the event, the fall of the *peshwa* resulted not so much in an "opening" of the Deccan to Bombay, as in an "opening" of Bombay to the Deccan. Subordinate British officers certainly expected that this should occur, and raised objections to Elphinstone's plan to launch a Sanskrit college in Poona. That city was "altogether a Mahratta country," too full of traditional brahmanical values. "On the other hand," a Maharashtrian,

> especially if young, can hardly visit Bombay without feeling his mind enlarged. He sees customs different from his own, he sees the wonders produced by wealth and trade and our busy harbours, our warehouses, our docks, our carriages and public roads, the appearance of ease, industry and comfort diffused over our large population, he can hardly help comparing the scene in which he is placed with that which he has left and his education is begun before he has opened a book.[24]

It might have been expected that "caste prejudice" could stand in the way of young men going to Bombay. One Gangadhar Dikshit Phadke of Poona went to the city to serve as a Marathi tutor in the Marine Department; six years later, on his return to Poona, he was treated as if he had undertaken the forbidden sea-voyage and had to undergo purificatory penances.[25] Despite this apparent impediment, there was no end of volunteers who came forward in Poona to go to Bombay to study at the English school that opened in 1824. The 1820s and 1830s saw a growing stream of migration for education and/or employment into the city by residents of the Deccan, including a number of members of Maharashtra brahman castes. Bombay was perceived to offer opportunities available nowhere else, at least up until 1833, when an English school was opened in Poona.[26]

The situation of brahmans in the Deccan was also conditioned by the impact of Mountstuart Elphinstone's administrative isolation policy, which was intended to insulate the Deccan society from the dynamics of rapid changes arising from Bombay. Thus the impact of conquest was to be cushioned for the old elites of the now vanquished Maratha raj. The old nobility, *inamdars, jagirdars,* and other rural notables were, wherever possible, continued in their positions of prestige and privilege. The downfall of the *peshwa* was not intended by Elphinstone to be an occasion for social revolution. The special place of brahmans within the state and society was to be protected and, to a large measure, continued.[27] Some modification of tradition was inevitable. The *Dakshina* awards to learned brahmans were reduced and a proportion dedicated to establishment of the above-mentioned Sanskrit college in Poona, where traditional brahmanical learning would be continued under East India Company patronage. In deference to the sensibilities of the brahmans, only members of that *varna* were to be admitted as students.[28]

Other educational initiatives in Maharashtra linked a growing Indian demand for entry into administrative employment to an official concern for training a suitable pool of native talent to aid in staffing the subordinate service. The Bombay Native School Book and School Society (later the Bombay Native Education Society) was begun in 1822, and soon gave support to the expansion of both English and Marathi instruction, first within Bombay city and subsequently in the countryside towns.[29]

The evolution of a new *ryotvari* land revenue settlement policy, commencing in 1826-27, with its expectation of careful measurement of individual cultivated plots, created further demand for trained Indian subordinates who would be required for the operations of the revenue survey, settlement, and collection. Unlike the Bengal Presidency's *zamindari* permanent settlement, the Bombay revenue system as it evolved required a significant penetration of the countryside. The Government of Bombay chose to recruit candidates from a growing framework of vernacular schools within the rural districts rather than rely upon relocation of individuals from the urban center at Bombay.[30] By 1840 there were fifty-seven government-supported Marathi schools scattered through the districts of British Maharashtra, reflecting in part the considerable enthusiasm for Marathi-medium education by one British officer, Captain Thomas Candy, the superintendent of the Poona Sanskrit College and supervisor of Marathi schools.[31]

English education was introduced into the districts in 1833, when a government district school was opened in Poona. This development reinforced an already visible tendency to generate an English-knowing cluster of scholars with the *desh* itself rather than remain dependent upon the products of the English schools at Bombay, primarily members of the city's older Maharashtrian communities. The Poona location not only put English education in proximity to a center of the old elite of the Maratha raj, but also enabled scholars from rural areas to enter the new education. Narayan Sheshadri, who would later gain prominence as a Christian convert and minister in Bombay, first came to study at Poona when he left his home at Parali in the Nizam's dominions. We cannot establish why he went to Poona instead of Bombay, but it may be speculated that Poona held out several advantages. It was nearer, less costly, and perhaps for a Deshastha Brahman more congenial and convenient. The availability of advanced education in the new schools drew an increasing proportion of pupils from among the Deshastha, Chitpavan, and Karhada Brahman castes of the Deccan and Southern Konkan. Thus these communities would supply a large share of the subordinate government service of the new Company raj. One important qualification must be entered here. These new intending scholars appear to have been rarely the scions of the old landed notables, the *sardars* whose interests Elphinstone had hoped to protect. Instead, the candidates came from among the poorer strata of their respective castes, who had held subordinate positions under the Maratha regime as well. These represented the *laukik* or secular as against the *vaidik* or priestly part of their communities.

The government vernacular schools did promote a deepening of Marathi literacy within this secular brahman stratum of Western India. Although the process was slow, the schools were also vehicles for the development of a standard literary language, which came to fruition in the era of great growth of printing and publishing after about 1840. Marathi had been the language of administration under the Marathas, and thus in some respects it was more current and adaptable within Maharashtra than was Bengali within Bengal, where the Mughal use of Persian remained into the nineteenth century. Nevertheless, the Bombay Native School Book and School Society was told in 1823 that there was little basis for an educational curriculum in local Indian languages: "the Maratha and Goojrathee languages have always been restricted to the purposes of conversation and business and have never been applied to the cultivation and extension of literature, even in its humblest form."[32]

The revitalization of Marathi was to play an essential part in the spread of education and the growth of a reawakened Maharashtra. The Bombay Government played a significant role in the standardization of Marathi. After several false starts, it sanctioned, in 1824, the compilation of a Marathi-English dictionary by Captain J. T. Molesworth. This work was finally published in 1831.[33] Molesworth also supervised a board of *pandits* in the creation of a Marathi-Marathi dictionary, the *Maharashtra Bhaseca Kosa* (or *Panditakosa*), published in 1829.[34] It is notable that Colonel Vans Kennedy, a soldier-scholar of some standing in Bombay, objected to the size of Molesworth's project, complaining that there were too many words that weren't really Marathi, but rather were simply borrowed from Arabic, Persian, or Sanskrit. Kennedy thought Marathi to be only a spoken language and of no potential value for development. His views were contradicted by another Bombay scholar, Robert C. Money, who insisted that the dictionary should be viewed from the point of view of students who would soon put the expanded vocabulary to constructive use.[35]

One of Molesworth's assistants was Thomas Candy, who having served as superintendent of the Native Schools in the Deccan, was in 1847 appointed as Marathi translator to the government, partly in light of his completion with Molesworth of a massive English-Marathi dictionary.[36] In his new position he, in the words of N.H. Kulkarnee, "soon became the sole and supreme arbiter for Marathi language and literature."[37]

Though apparently lacking any notable felicity of style, Candy worked diligently to root out nonstandard usages and railed against written work containing what he termed "concanisms," that is, usages of a subregional dialect. Candy and Molesworth both relied upon Poona Sanskrit College shastris, and hence clearly favored the brahman speech of western Maharashtra around Poona as a standard against which all other Marathi would be judged. They also made a decision to employ the *balbodh* or *devanagari* script for use in printing rather than attempting to adapt the common cursive *modi* writing system.

The migrations for schooling or employment from the Deccan into Bombay also furthered the process of language standardization. R.X. Murphy, sometime headmaster of the Bombay Native Education Society's school at Bombay, observed in 1936:

> The influx of the Brahmans from the Deccan and Konkan [into Bombay], the publications and Mahratha schools of the Native Education Society which have established a correct standard of language, and pride of caste . . . has led all the educated classes [of the city] to throw aside their barbarous idiom and ape the purest brahmanical dialects.[38]

Murphy's comment does not address the language usage of the vast majority of the population who had no access to the new educational order.

Clearly, in the middle of the nineteenth century there would remain a strong vernacular bias in the spread of knowledge, whether new or old. Although later in the 1860s prominent graduates of the new Bombay University would begin to make their mark in English discourse, their elders had already launched a burgeoning endeavor of communication in their mother tongue. This not only eventually promoted the percolation of new knowledge to strata other than the urban and brahmanical in western Maharashtra, it also eased the transit of new ideas and values from Bombay into the non-British territories, the princely states, *sardars'* enclaves, the Nizam's dominions, and Berar and Nagpur.

The educational initiatives of the Bombay government were paralleled by protestant Christian missionary activities. Although Calcutta had possessed in Danish Serampore a well-established mission station, famed for the work of Carey, Ward, and Marshman, Bombay did not receive a sustained Protestant Christian mission until 1813, and it was another ten years before a single missionary invaded the Deccan. Serampore, of course, had some impact on Maharashtra, for the Baptist missionaries there had developed Marathi-script type, *modi* and *balbodh,* and as early as 1802 had brought out Marathi editions of the New Testament as well as a Marathi grammar. The missionaries quickly discovered that technology is blind to theology. The type fonts that had formed the Gospel of

Matthew could now as easily form stanzas of the *Bhagavad Gita* or the *abhangs* of Sant Tukaram. In Maharashtra the coming of the new missions in the second decade of the nineteenth century opened up a new arena of confrontation in the form of challenges brought against religious orthodoxy and its social and cultural norms.[40]

If "renaissance" in India was constituted in part by the orientalist rediscovery of a classical past, it nevertheless was true that when that scholarship was conducted by missionaries, the intent seemed only to throw into high relief the presumed shortcomings of contemporary Hindu belief and practice. In western India, this situation was typified by the Reverend John Wilson (1804–1875), a Scottish missionary who served in Bombay from 1829 until 1875. Although he was a major critic of orthodox Indian beliefs, he was nevertheless a significant contributor to the spread of knowledge and a stimulator of religious revitalization.[41] Wilson challenged Indian religion primarily on ideological grounds, asking questions in terms of what it was that distinguished Indian religions from Christianity. Implicitly he believed in the ideological superiority of Christian teachings, and assumed that proof of this would yield conversions. In the process, however, his confrontations produced greater awareness and introspection among the practitioners of other faiths concerning their distinctive beliefs and values. The most prominent examples of this are somewhat marginal to the Hindu Maharashtrian majority. Wilson confronted the Parsis on the basis of his considerable training and Zend Avestan scholarship, much to the discomfiture of the Parsi *dasturs,* but he thereby stimulated a reaction among Parsis leading to a reformulation and validation of Zoroastrian theology, and reform.[42] Similarly, Wilson deserves credit for recognizing the Shaniwar Teli (Saturday oilmen) as being in fact Jews, and assisting in reintroducing these "Bene Israeli" to the orthodox tenets of their ancestral faith.[43]

The missionary challenge to Hinduism was of necessity broader, yet it also produced reactions that represented a vigorous defense of dharma. In May 1830, John Wilson engaged in a series of debates concerning the respective validity of Christianity and Hinduism. The following year Morobhat Dandekar adopted the missionary's own style and debated Wilson, subsequently publishing his case as *Hindu Dharma Sthapana.*[44] Another Marathi publication, *Paramadharmatattva,* was published by S.V. Junnarkar in the following year. The interplay of Christian critique and Hindu defense continued through the decade of the mid-nineteenth century, initially culminating in the radical anti-brahmanical critiques of Mahatma Jotirao Phule and in the Hindu revivalist speeches, debates, and books of Vishnu Bhikaji Gokhale, known better as Vishnubawa Brahmachari.[45] It may be submitted that the Christian challenge also stimulated, particularly among the educated young men of Maharashtra, a searching reexamination of Hindu social practices in light of external ethical criticism. The emergence of the Paramahamsa Sabha in 1849 may in part reflect a need to reduce dissonance between precept and practice on the part of "Young Bombay," although the fact that the society remained a secret one suggests the limitations of the age.[46]

Another critical element in the Bengal renaissance has been identified as the activities of British orientalist scholars. If Calcutta's focus of orientalist endeavor played a positive role in Bengali's awakening, it might be expected that similar activities and results would be found in Bombay and Maharashtra. Here, as in other factors discussed above, there is a considerable time-lag in western India when compared to Bengal. In 1784, a time when Sir William Jones was inaugurating the Asiatic Society in Calcutta, Bombay's energies were tied to an unsuccessful effort to seize territory in Kanara from Mysore's ruler, Tipu Sultan. In the first decade of the nineteenth century, most of Bombay's attention concentrated on the commercial profits to be realized in the extensions of Company rule in Gujarat. It was in 1804 that seventeen Europeans under the leadership of Sir James Mackintosh, a man of letters and judge of the Recorder's Court, founded the Literary Society of Bombay.[48] Under its aegis members contributed oriental and antiquarian scholarship, launched a small museum and library, and promoted the study of Hindu antiquities. In 1830 the Literary Society affiliated with the Royal Asiatic Society of Great Britain and Ireland, becoming its Bombay Branch, and in 1841 it launched a regular journal.[49] The literary productions of the society's European members were generally sympathetic to Indian culture and sought to preserve the content of Sanskrit texts and traditions.

Membership remained limited to Europeans until 1840. Bal Shastri Jambhekar had wished in 1836 that more Indians were "as much interested in the antiquities of India as the strangers who have come to sojourn among us and whose curiosity, industry and research are worthy of the highest commendation." He was confident that membership in the society ought not be denied to "any intelligent and well-instructed natives," suggesting that some of these might "make it a matter of solicitation."[50] The first Indian member, a Parsi, was admitted in 1840, and in 1845 the first Maharashtrian member, the wealthy and influential Daivadnya Sonar merchant, Jagannath Shankershet.[51] It would not be until the next generation that Indians would be encouraged to join as scholars, such as Dr. Bhau Daji Lad or Kashinath Trimbak Telang.

Manifestations of the Maharashtra renaissance continued to flourish into the late nineteenth century. The foundations rested on an amalgam of geographical, administrative, economic, and social policies of the East India Company supplemented by the efforts and institutions of Christian missionaries and orientalist scholars. As Ravinder Kumar emphasized in his well-known essay, "The New Brahmans of Maharashtra," it appeared that ultimately the British in western India had attempted to control social change "through deliberate acts of policy." Thus Elphinstone's policies in the newly annexed Deccan attempted at once the seemingly contradictory goals of protecting the old order while also trying to "disseminate values in the community which would reconcile it to the new order."[52] The calculated policy, in Kumar's view, sought to create a "new brahman" elite, inspired by Western values, that would mediate between government and its subjects. To some degree, the old order and the new could meet within the brahmanical communities, as traditions of literacy and government service served as a stimulus to new opportunities. New knowledge did become a prized possession, distributed most unevenly across the Bombay Presidency, but invariably with brahmans enjoying a predominant representation. Administrative policies within the colonial government and consequent structures of opportunities furthered an impulse to an educational system that was not centered upon the Presidency at Bombay, but that held out access, however unevenly, to the new knowledge through the districts of Western Maharashtra, and that with a strong vernacular bias.

It must be observed that the representativeness of these new "elites" may have been more apparent than real. The prominence of Konkanastha Chitpavan brahmans in the old regime could not fully obscure status differentiations applied to them by the Deshastha brahmans. There were, in effect, new brahmans and newer brahmans. And if Bombay and its environs are added to the account, the factor of claims to social status becomes even more pronounced an issue. The coastal elites who had flourished in Bombay had advanced claims to socio-religious standing and rights to ritual not readily recognized in the Deccan. Pathare Prabhus, Gaud Sarasvat Brahmans, Daivadnya Sonars, and Palshikars of the coastal tract had all sought to enhance their corporate status vis-ā-vis access to Vedic rites and recognition as brahmans.[53] In Poona, such claims could not be sustained by traditional brahmanical authority; in the marketplace of Bombay, such matters might be open questions. As the Deccan and Konkan were brought increasingly into contact, and as administrative service and education produced an intermingling of elites, a new regional arena of communication was coming into being.

Many of the most significant events in the early years of the Maharashtra renaissance — publications, institutions, individual teachers and reformers — arose in Bombay, yet for the most part the authors and founders of these were members of Maharashtrian brahman castes with ties to the Deccan or southern Konkan. With the establishment of new Marathi-language publications, newspapers (1832), magazines (1840), and books promoting a wide range of western information as well as Indian tradition from about 1830 onward, the renaissance may be said to have fairly begun. The variety of ideals and expressions that followed may be seen in the creative, sometimes contradictory, efforts of a series of notable figures to utilize the new channels of communication to generate a public interest in the very nature and shape of Maharashtra's society and culture.

Bal Gangadhar Shastri Jambhekar (1812–1846), Govind "Bhau" Mahajan (1815–1890), Vishnubawa Brahmachari (1825–1871), and Gopal Hari Deshmukh (1823–1892) ("Lokahitawadi") put forward diverging visions of the proper reform of Indian society.[54] Dadoba Pandurang Tarkhadkar (1818–1882) brought together the members of the Paramahamsa Sabha to move actively beyond orthodox religious beliefs and customs, providing a seedbed for the later social reform movements of Bombay and Maharashtra.[55] Finally, in this same generation of leaders is found the source of what would be the most radical critique of the old order, Mahatma Jotirao Phule (1890). Phule's reinterpretations of Indian tradition and his enlistment of western values and ideas on behalf of the claims of the majority of Maharashtrians marked a critical transition through which the renaissance became significant to a far wider population.[56]

A complete survey of the Maharashtra renaissance requires a lengthier essay than is possible here. I hope that what does appear here establishes the utility of the concept of "renaissance" in its Maharashtrian incarnation. India's modern history will be enriched and strengthened by the recognition of how the many regions of the subcontinent shared in its experience. Certainly in Maharashtra the flowering of educational and cultural activities and the burgeoning of literary production, particularly in Marathi, during the middle decades of the nineteenth century all point to the renaissance phenomenon of a people "catching fire." Historians should recognize that the diversity of responses to the new age and its opportunities cannot be explained only in terms of marginality or time-lag It is necessary to identify differences in geography, colonial administration, economic development, and social organization. Viewed from this perspective, the significance of the Maharashtra renaissance lies not in its response or similarity to a Bengal model, but in the role it played in subsequent development of public affairs and a conscious concern with a public interest in the Maharashtra region, preserving a flavor of social thought and action that would remain a distinctive thread in the tapestry of modern India.

NOTES

*This essay grew out of a discussion with Ed Dimock in a late-hour seminar at an A.I.I.S. meeting, and was offered in another version at the Western Conference of the Association for Asian Studies, November 9, 1984, at Santa Fe, New Mexico. I am grateful to Professor Michael Fisher for useful critical comments that do not relieve me of responsibility for errors of fact or interpretation that remain.

1. George Smith, *Life of Alexander Duff* (New York, 1879) 1: 118, quoted in David Kopf and Saifuddin Joarder, eds., *Reflections on the Bengal Renaissance* (Rajshahi, 1977), p. 4.
2. Jadunath Sarkar, *History of Bengal, Volume 2* (Decca, 1948), p. 498.
3. There are many variations in the meanings of "renaissance," especially as it has been applied in non-European settings. See Professor Saifuddin Joarder's concept as a sense of the acceptance of the primacy of reason, humanism, worldliness, individuality, and freedom; S. Joarder, "The Bengal Renaissance and the Bengali Muslims: Some Reflections" in Kopf and Joarder, *Reflections*, pp. 42-43.
4. Nirad C. Chaudhuri, *Autobiography of an Unknown Indian* (Berkeley and Los Angeles, 1968), p. 179. Note well that Chaudhuri is himself dubious about comparisons to the European Renaissance, "but in early life I accepted it without question as also did every other educated Indian."
5. R.C. Majumdar, *Glimpses of Bengal in the Nineteenth Century* (Calcutta, 1960), p. 3.
6. Sarkar, *History of Bengal*, 2: 498.
7. *Bombay Durpan* 1: i (6 January 1832) quoted in G.G. Jambhekar, ed., *Memoirs and Writings of Acharya Bal Shastri Jambhekar* (Poona, 1950), 2: 4.
8. David Kopf, *British Orientalism and the Bengal Renaissance: The Dynamics of Indian Modernization, 1773-1835* (Berkeley and Los Angeles, 1969), pp. 11-49.
9. S.N. Mukherjee, *Sir William Jones* (Cambridge, 1968), pp. 35-141; Eli Daniel Potts, *British Baptist Missionaries in India, 1793-1837: The History of Serampore and Its Missions* (Cambridge, 1967).
10. Peter J. Marshall, *East India Fortunes: The British in Bengal in the 18th Century* (Oxford, 1976); Pradip Sinha, "Social Change," pp. 384-426 in Narendra Krishna Sinha, ed., *History of Bengal (1757-1905)* (Calcutta, 1967), see esp. pp. 387-393.
11. Nemai Sadhan Bose, *Indian Awakening and Bengal*, 3rd ed., (Calcutta, 1976), pp. 62-68.
12. Sinha, "Social Change," *passim;* S.N. Mukherjee, "Class, Caste and Politics in Calcutta, 1815-1839," pp. 33-78 in Edmund Leach and S. N. Mukherjee, eds., *Elites in South Asia* (Cambridge, 1970).
13. Cf. S. Gopal, *The Permanent Settlement and Its Effect on Bengal* (London, 1949); Ranajit Guha, *A Rule of Property for Bengal: An Essay on the Idea of Permanent Settlement* (Paris, 1963).
14. It must be noted that at least one Maratha historian has termed the seventeenth century the "Maratha Renaissance," N.K. Behere, *The Background of Maratha Renaissance in the 17th Century* (Bangalore, 1946).
15. See Ravinder Kumar, *Western India in the Nineteenth Century: A Social History of Maharashtra* (London, 1968) for a clear presentation of the consensual interpretation.
16. Pamela Nightengale, *Trade and Empire in Western India* (Cambridge, 1969), pp. 1-72, contains a lucid account of the problems of the East India Company's Bombay Presidency at the end of the eighteenth century. For earlier development, see M.D. David, *History of Bombay, 1661-1704* (Bombay, 1973).

17. Kenneth Ballhatchet. *Social Policy and Social Change in Western India, 1817-1830* (London. 1957). pp. 52-76.
18. It is worth noting that in the early decades of British rule in Berar and Nagpur, officials found it necessary to recruit men from western Maharashtra to fill subordinate service positions. thus opening channels of movement and communications that transcended administrative frontiers.
19. *Bombay Durpan*. 1: i (6 January 1832) in Jambhekar, *Memoirs*, 2: 4.
20. *Ibid.*
21. By the 1850s some observers in Bombay had come to apply the term "Young Bombay" to a growing educated interest group in the city, with a slightly sardonic reference to "Young Bengal" of the more radical days of the Derozians in Calcutta two decades earlier. J.C. Masselos, *Towards Nationalism: Group Affiliations and the Politics of Public Associations in Nineteenth Century Western India* (Bombay, 1974), pp. 28-33.
22. Of course, the marginality of the Konkan had not prevented the rise of Chitpavan Brahmans in the Deccan as one of their number became *peshwa*, yet marginality of status was dramatically demonstrated when Peshwa Baji Rao II was denied access to a ghat at Nasik by the Deshastha priests; James Cunningham Grant Duff, *A History of the Mahrattas*, revised ed., revised by S.M. Edwardes (London, 1921), 1: 371n.
23. Purushottam Balkrishna Kulkarni, *Na. Nana Shankarshet yance caritra (Kal va Kamgiri)* (Marathi) (Bombay, 1959), cf. Christine Dobbin, *Urban Leadership in Western India: Politics and Communities in Bombay City 1840-1885* (London, 1972).
24. Minute of the College Committee to the Chief Secretary to Government, 18 May 1821, quoted in R.V. Parulekar, ed., *Selections from the Records of the Government of Bombay: Education, Part I, 1819-1852* (Bombay, 1953), pp. 97-98. M. Elphinstone did not dispute the value of bringing students to Bombay, but noted that the promise of a Sanskrit College at Poona was necessary compensation to brahmans whose fortunes had suffered with the fall of the *peshwa*. *Ibid.*, p. 100.
25. Dwarkanath Govind Vaidya, *Narayan Ganeś Candavarkar* (Marathi) (Bombay, c. 1937), p. 61.
26. R.V. Parulekar, ed., *Selections from Educational Records (Bombay), Part III: 1826-1840* (Bombay, 1957), pp. xix, 108-120.
27. Cf. Ballhatchet, *Social Policy*, pp. 30ff.
28. Parulekar, *Selections, Part I*, pp. xiii-xxx.
29. Idem., *Selections from Educational Records (Bombay), Part II: 1815-1840* (Bombay, 1955), pp. xvi-xxx.
30. In 1835-1836, the Government of Bombay considered a proposal for direct training of young men in the Revenue Department, but decided not to commence such a progam. Parulekar, *Selections, Part III*, pp. xxiv-xxvi.
31. Candy was also not as diffident as Elphinstone about brahmanical privilege. In his report of 1 May 1839, he related that at Akola (in Ahmadnagar district) he urged the headman "the advantage that would result to Koonbees from sending their children to school, upon which a Brahmun in the company cried out that this would be the ruin of their livelihood." Candy added, "I have no doubt that jealousy often instigates Brahmans to discourage the education of Konnabees." *Ibid.*, p. 203.
32. George Jervis to Committee, Bombay Native School Book and School Society, 13 September 1823, quoted in Parulekar, *Selections, Part II*, p. 50.
33. J.T. Molesworth, *A Dictionary, Marathi and English* (Bombay, 1831).
34. N.G. Kalelkar, "Preface to the Reprint," p. 10, in Molesworth's *Marathi-English Dictionary: Corrected Reprint* (of second edition) (Poona, 1975).
35. Sharad Gogate, *ibid.*, p. 17. A recent essay emphasizing the importance of "useful

knowledge" is Anil Samarth, "Awakening in Maharashtra (1818-1874): A Note on 'Enculturalisation' of Pragmatism," *Boletim do Insitut to Menezes Braganca*, No. 134 (1982), 41-76; No. 135 (1982), 43-61.

36. T. Candy and J.T. Molesworth. *A Dictionary: English and Marathi* (Bombay, 1847).
37. Narayan H. Kulkarnee, "Impact of British Colonial Policy on Marathi Literature, Religion and Culture," pp. 418-454 in N.R. Ray, ed., *Western Colonial Policy (A Study on Its Impact on Indian Society)*, 2 vols. (Calcutta, 1981-1982), 1: 425.
38. Robert X. Murphy, "Remarks on Some of the Oldest Races Settled in Bombay," *Transactions of the Bombay Geographical Society*, 1 (1838-1839), 128-129.
39. It would seem that the tradition of Marathi as an administrative language in many parts of Maharashtra would mean that the initial impact of of decision regarding English as language of higher education and administration arising from Macaullay's Minute of 1835 would have been less than in Bengal or Upper India.
40. Elizabeth G.K. Hewat, *Christ and Western India*, 2nd ed., (Bombay, 1953), pp. 43-105. For a succinct synthesis of the critical impact of Christian critiques of Hindu society and values, see Rosalind O'Hanlon, *Caste, Conflict and Ideology: Mahatma Jotirao Phule and Low Caste Protest in Nineteenth-Century Western India* (Cambridge, 1985), pp. 80-85.
41. George Smith, *Life of John Wilson* (London, 1879), *passim*. M.D. David, *John Wilson and His Institution* (Bombay, 1975), pp. 44-48.
42. Smith, *John Wilson*, pp. 120-140; Eckehard Kulke, *The Parsees in India: A Minority as Agent of Social Change* (Munich, 1974), pp. 92-101.
43. Smith, *John Wilson*, p. 71. Haeem Samuel Kehimkar, *The History of the Bene Israel of India* (Tel Aviv, 1937), puts greater emphasis on the influence of other external Jewish communities and on the 1819 American Marathi mission translation of the Book of Genesis. A new synthesis of the history of the Bombay Jews by Dr. Joan Roland is soon to be published.
44. Cf. Richard Fox Young, *Resistant Hinduism: Sanskrit Sources on Anti-Christian Apologetics in Early Nineteenth Century India* (Publications of the De Nobili Research Library, Volume 8) (Vienna, 1981), pp. 25-31.
45. Matthew Lederle, *Philosophical Trends in Modern Maharashtra* (Bombay, 1976), pp. 124-131; O'Hanlon, *Caste, Conflict and Ideology*, pp. 135-186; Frank F. Conlon, "Revival and Reform in Nineteenth Century Maharashtra: Vishnubawa Brahmachari," paper delivered at Association for Asian Studies Conference, Philadelphia, March 23, 1985, to be published in a forthcoming volume edited by N. G. Barrier and Kenneth Jones on religious polemics in nineteenth-century India.
46. Anant Kakba Priyolkar, *Rav Bahadur Dadoba pandurang* (Marathi) (Bombay, 1947), pp. 241-262.
47. Nightengale, *Trade*, pp. 175-235; Neil Rabitoy, "System v. Expediency: The Reality of Land Revenue Administration in the Bombay Presidency, 1812-1820," *Modern Asian Studies* 9 (1975), 529-546.
48. *Transactions of the Literary Society of Bombay* 1 (1819), vii-xli.
49. *Gazetteer of Bombay City and Island*, 3 vols. (Bombay, 1909), 3: 330-333.
50. *Bombay Durpan*, 5(7 May 1836) in Jambhekar, *Memoirs*, 2: 124.
51. Kulkarni, *Shankarshet*, p. 126.
52. Ravinder Kumar, "The New Brahmans of Maharashtra," pp. 95-130 in D.A. Low, ed., *Soundings in Modern South Asian History* (London, 1968) at p. 95.
53. On specific issues, see N.K. Wagle, "The History and Social Organisation of the Gaud Saraswat Brahmans of West India," *Journal of Indian History* 48 (1973), 21-24; idem., "A Dispute between the Pancal Devajna Sonars and the Brahmans of Pune regarding Social Rank and Ritual Privileges," pp. 129-152 in N.K. Wagle, ed., *Images of*

Maharashtra: A Regional Profile of India (London, 1980); V.D. Rao, "The Pathare Prabhus: Traditional Origins and History," *Journals of the University of Bombay* 38 (1969), 135–169.

54. Cf. Jambhekar, *Memoirs, passim.* On Lokahitawadi see Vasant K. Kshire, *Lokahitawadi's Thought: A Critical Study* (Poona, 1977); Gangadhar Balkrishna Sardar, *Maharastrace Upeksita Mankari* (Marathi), (Poona, 1941).
55. Priyolkar, *Dadoba Pandurang,* pp. 241–262.
56. O'Hanlon, *Caste, Conflict and Ideology,* pp. 193ff.

From Patronage to Partisanship: The Beginnings of the Women's Movement in India

GERALDINE FORBES

When India became independent of British rule in 1947, there was a well-established and vocal women's movement. By 1947 the All-India Women's Conference, having just absorbed the Women's Indian Association, claimed that it spoke for 30,000 women who belonged to 41 branches and 200 constituent branches. The National Council of Women in India also claimed an extensive membership through its affiliated associations. These three organizations, the All India Women's Conference, the Women's Indian Association, and the National Council of Women in India, had articulated women's opinion on a number of social and political issues and successfully insured that women be included on most of the decision-making bodies concerned with the future of India.

To understand how this movement began, it is necessary to look back at the nineteenth century and the first women's clubs. When the national women's organizations were formed, betwen 1917 and 1927, they superseded local organizations as the representatives of and spokespersons for women. But they neither replaced them completely nor took over all their concerns and interests. The earliest women's organizations — ladies' clubs, women's association, and *Mahila Samities* — were the first to articulate the demands of women as a group. They took the first steps to chart a public role for women. Their leaders, ideologies, strategies, and tactics were truly the forerunners of what was later to become the women's movement.

These first women's organizations were a result of nineteenth-century efforts to improve women's status by promoting female education. Education, the reformers believed, would produce women who would contribute to the progress of the nation. Because women as nurturers held the key to future generations, both reformers and conservatives agreed that some type of education was necessary. While the reformers argued with one another about the ideal curriculum for women, the conservatives contented themselves with schools that imparted literacy, religious instruction, and some needlework. The various schemes for female education created a small but significant number of literate women capable of understanding the new literature available to them. Furthermore, many of them were encouraged by members of their families to become friends with other educated women. Before the end of the century, India had its first women graduates. Women were awarded B.A.s and M.S.s, and completed their professional training to qualify as doctors and lawyers. For the first time in India's modern history there was a class of women who shared a common language. While these highly educated women were able to meet and discuss social issues with educated wome from other regions of India, their less-educated sisters had mastered the vernacular and were equally eager to participate in the first associations formed to improve women's position.

The first organizations for women were begun by male reformers who belonged to the new religious reform societies such as the *Brahmo Samaj* of Bengal. Keshub Chunder Sen, a charismatic young Brahmo leader, had demonstrated his willingness to take a strong stand on the "woman question" when he took his young wife to the ceremony where he was accepted into the *Brahmo Samaj*. Ostracized by his family for encouraging his wife to break purdah, he continued to champion the cause of women and developed schemes for female education, a journal for women, special prayer meetings for women, women's gatherings, and the *Bharat Ashram,* where families lived together and emulated the life style of the English middle class. The first organization for women was founded in 1865. Keshub began with a religious service for women, followed by sewing classes. Assisted in these projects by young reformers whose zeal frequently outran his own, Keshub and his followers pushed ahead with efforts to make their wives companions and partners. In the new Brahmo marriage ceremony, the bride was no longer a "gift" to her groom. Instead, the bride and the groom made promises to each other. Under Keshub and his followers, schools, journals, and social organizations formed an integrated set of institutions that provided female education, reading material, and a supportive network of women with similar experiences. The Brahmo-supported schools hired some of their own graduates as teachers, further consolidating the network. With time, a number of Keshub's associates argued that his views on female emancipation were too conservative, and they broke with him to form the *Sadharan Brahmo Samaj.*[1] They formed similar institutions but were motivated by the ideal of male-female equality, whereas Keshub's group aimed at developing more competent nurturers. Despite differences in ideology, the Brahmo sects developed institutions that educated women and made it possible for them to participate in the first organizations for women.

Whereas the Brahmo organizations were among the earliest associations for women, the *Prarthana Samaj* did similar work in Bombay. Keshub visited Bombay Presidency in 1864 and 1868 to urge the establishment of a prayer society. The *Prarthana Samaj* was established following these visits, and although it was modeled on the *Brahmo Samaj,* the founders were concerned that its members remain involved in Hindu society.[2]

Those men who were closely involved with the samaj from the beginning, especially the "famous elitist Prarthana trio" — G.R. Bandavarkar, Narayan Ganesh Chandavarker, and M.G. Ranade — were concerned with social reform and particularly with the uplift of women in the 1870s. When Pandita Ramabai Saraswati reached western India in 1882, she had already become famous for her extraordinary facility in Sanskrit (she had been awarded two titles — "Pandita" and "Saraswati" — by Sanskrit scholars in Calcutta) and for her statement in favor of female education, made before the Hunter Commission. With her arrival in Bombay Presidency the reformers agreed that "the cause of women's education had gained in her a supreme treasure."[3] Justice Ranade and his young wife Ramabai welcomed her into their home and invited her to give a "Purana," thus publicly recognizing her attainments as a Sanskrit scholar.[4] Soon after, Justice Ranade and Ramabai, Mrs. Gargabai Bhandare, and Dr. Radknabai helped Pandita Ramabai set up the *Arya Mahila Samaj* for the general uplift and enlightenment of women.[5]

The *Arya Mahila Samaj* had two aims: to help eradicate those customs which kept women in ignorance (such as child marriage and the conventions surrounding widowhood) and to work for the uplift of women. The organization, it was hoped, would be at the center of a movement to agitate for the emancipation of women. Pandita Ramabai traveled throughout Bombay Presidency seeking support for this concept, and eventually branches were established in Bombay, Sholapur, and Ahmednagar. But it was frustrating work. In *Stri Dharma Neeti* (Morals for Women, 1882) Pandita Ramabai argued that women's progress depended on women's own efforts.[6] Nevertheless, she acknowledged the difficulty of urging women to act independently when distrust and suspicion of them, part of Hindusim since the sixth century B.C., had been incorporated into law, custom, and behavior.[7] In order to effect change in the system, Ramabai argued that women would have to gain access to the colonial government and they could only do this only if they knew English. Chagrined at her own inability to communicate directly with members of the Hunter Commission (Ramabai delivered her report to them in Sanskrit), she traveled to England, where she had been appointed Professor of Sanskrit at Cheltenham College, and began to study English.[8]

Pandita Ramabai was far ahead of many of the women of her times in her mastery of India's classical language, Sanskrit; her independence (she was orphaned as a child and was a widow); and her daring. Few of her contemporaries had either educational opportunities or friends and relatives who would encourage them in their efforts. Ramabai Ranade, in her autobiography entitled *Himself,* has described the abuse heaped upon her by her mother-in-law and sisters-in-law when she studied the lessons assigned by her husband. Although these women were educated (Justice Ranade's father believed in female education), they would tease Ramabai when she entered the kitchen to perform her household duties. And they became angry when Pandita Ramabai came to Poona and the little women's group that Ramabai Ranade belonged to became the *Arya Mahila Samaj.* They taunted her, teased her, and generally made her life miserable. Ramabai has recorded an oft-repeated encounter between her and her mother-in-law and sister-in-law:

> They urged me not to go to the Sabha; and if Panditabai should come to our house that I should not touch her even to please Himself. When they reminded me that the women in my father's house were not educated, I would be almost persuaded that I might drop my studies.[9]

But it was women like Ramabai Ranade who became the backbone of the *Arya Mahila Samaj* and who continued to see women's problems as directly related to prohibitions on female education. In the early years, the weekly lectures and "at homes" provided opportunities for women to meet and come to know each other. As these women became more sure of themselves, they began to define the role of the educated woman. She was to continue to run her household, more efficiently and thoughtfully, of course, and in time of emergency (floods, famine, plague), she would come out of her home to help in relief activities.[10] In the view of this organization, women were given a role to play in the world beyond the household, but only in times of disaster.

Another category of women's organizations were the women's auxiliaries of general reform associations. The most notable of these was the *Bharata Mahila Parishad* (Ladies Social Conference) of the National Social Conference. The conference had been formed at the third meeting of the Indian National Congress (1887) to provide a forum for the discussion of social issues; but it was several years before the *Mahila Parisad* was inaugurated in 1905. Women had taken part in the general meetings but they seemed to feel that their problems were not taken seriously by men. When Mrs. Kamalakar, a medical student from Bombay, spoke about women's education at the 1904 meeting, she spoke of specific problems: the need for practical training and the difficulty of stimulating women to want an education; and of a general problem: men's indifference to the whole issue of educating women.[11]

When the first meeting of the *Bharata Mahila Parisad* was held, the hall was packed. The meeting had been arranged entirely by women and no men were allowed to attend. It was the largest gathering of women Bombay had ever seen. First came prayers in Marathi and Gujarati. Then Lady Bhalchandra, the president, declared the meeting open. One of the first speakers was the the newly widowed Ramabai Ranade, who urged women to work side by side with men for the regeneration of the nation. She asked women to devote their energies to teaching orphans, inspecting schools for girls, and helping widows find respectable employment.[12] This was followed by a paper read by Mrs. Abbas Tyabji on Muslim women's education, and lectures on philanthropic and charitable work. The discussion focused on a number of issues, including medical relief, domestic life, early marriage, and child welfare. From the accounts that exist, it appears that between two and three hundred women attended this meeting. Press accounts include only the names of the socially prominent, but these lists make it clear that the meeting was attended by women from various communities and religions.[13]

At subsequent meetings, there were usually as many as three hundred women, and sometimes over seven hundred were present. The president was chosen from the titled and wealthy, and those in attendance were wives of social reformers, generally well educated and well off financially. Speeches by the officers of the organization were followed by the reading of papers on topics of general concern and discussion of social reforms. The women who organized these meetings were anxious to have women meet to discuss social problems of particular interest to women and suggest solutions. It was clear they felt that sex segregation would benefit women although the topics they discussed, the speeches delivered, and even the resolutions passed were not unlike those of the male reformers meeting at the same time. The main issues continued to be the need for female education and the need to abolish "evil" social customs. The social customs that attracted the most attention were child marriage, dowry, and the degraded position of widows. These were the customs that made the social status of even wealthy and titled women precarious. But the discussions of what role women might play in changing the situation were just beginning. By and large, those who attended these meetings still believed that they needed to educate themselves about the issues.[14]

The women attending these early meetings had not yet moved beyond those sets of issues handed down to them from their husbands and fathers. Although there is no evidence to suggest that they rationally calculated the merits of supporting a platform similar to that of the National Social Conference as compared with striking out on their own, their organization existed because the conference met at that time, and most of them attended because they accompanied male members of their families. They did not deviate from the parent body, and their separate meeting place was as much a concession to the norms of female seclusion as it was an effort to have the women act in concert. Despite the limitations on independent action, this was a women's forum and it brought together educated and articulate women from all over India. And it was in an annual meeting of this body that Saraladevi Chaudhurani announced that women were planning to organize their own association for the discussion of social issues of concern to women.[15]

Women's organizations were also formed within communities by men in these communities. Two such examples in Bombay were the *Stri Zarthosthi Mandal,* formed by the Parsis, and the *Gujarati Hindu Stree Mahamandal* for Gujarati Hindus. Both of these organizations occasionally helped other women, but membership was restricted, and their main work was among their own communities. These organizations used vernacular languages for their meetings, record keeping, and transactions. Like caste organizations, their main aim was improving conditions within their community. The existence of a separate organization for women was based on assumptions about women's proper roles and their capacity for public work in light of their nature.

The *Stri Zarthosthi Mandal* grew out of work done during the 1896 plague by Mr. Naroji Patuck and his family. Mr. Patuck was deeply touched by the hardships suffered by women, and decided that he, his wife, and his daughters must do something. The family decided to set up a work class that would give women a chance to leave their distressing surroundings and work in a cheerful environment. By 1899 they had established a regular work class with six Parsi women in attendance. By 1903 there were over fifty women in the class, and it was at this time that they decided to form an organization. Mrs. Shirinbai Naroji called the first meeting. At the first meeting, those present made clear their aim of assisting poor women to learn skills in order to earn a living. Miss Serenmai M. Cursetjee became the first president and remained at the helm of the mandal for the next fifty-six years. As the organization's clientele expanded, it became clear that it would have to offer additional services beyond vocational training. Little by little the mandal began to offer medical care, convalescent facilities, and education. Sir Ratan Tata, the wealthy Parsi philanthropist, came to their aid with money for school fees. When they recognized that the women being trained were too hungry to attend to their lessons, they asked Sir Rattan Tata for money to provide school lunches. When they were unable to place the graduates of their training institution, Sir Ratan Tata again came to the rescue with the Industrial Institute, which provided employment for those newly trained.[16]

As pointed out earlier, the founders of this organization defined its role as helping "less fortunate" women. The founders were educated women, accustomed to meeting and entertaining both men and women from a variety of communities and countries. That they began their work in the public sphere with this particular act of charity may well have been an accidental result of the plague of 1896. These attempts to help families devastated by the plague, and particularly the women of those families, attracted a core of twenty-five well-educated young women. As they worked to improve the situation, they were led to an awareness of other social problems, and gradually began to expand the activities undertaken by the mandal. Within a decade they were overseeing a chain of institutions that not only identified women in need but attempted to rehabilitate them through education and training coupled with medical and nutritional care.

This organization proved a training ground for women who became active in a wide range of activities and organizations in the 1920s and 1930s. Their concerns with the lives of poor Parsi women led them, eventually, to agitate against the high rents these women had to pay. Fortunate in their connections with wealthy philanthropists, their action led to the construction of low-cost housing for the women involved in training schemes. Expanding from a single-issue base, the mandal took the lead in educating women about the franchise and, later, enrolling them as voters. When the Parsi Panchayat began discussions of legal change, members of the mandal held meetings, presented papers, formulated resolutions, and finally presented these to the panchayat as women's proposals for legal change. Members also played active roles in the Bombay Provincial Women's Council, the efforts to gain women's franchise, the agitation against child marriage, and the nationalist movement. The Parsi women who worked with the mandal pointed out that work within their own community had been educational and had given them an opportunity to gain experience in engineering social change.[17]

But not all communal organizations followed the same pattern of development. The *Gujarati Hindu Stree Mandal* was begun in 1903 by Mrs. Jamnabai Sakkai and Smt. Kalavatiben Motiwalla with the help of Mr. B.N. Motiwalla, a well-known pleader and social reformer. The purpose of the association was to help Gujarati women "develop themselves" mentally, morally, economically, physically, and spiritually. It was a tall order! In practice this meant encouraging female education, particularly establishing classes for married women and setting up social clubs where the newly educated women could meet and socialize. A number of prominent women associated with the *Gujarati Hindu Stree Mandal*, such as Lady Laxmiben Jagmohandas, helped found the *Bhagini Samaj*, an important organization for the nationalist movement. But the mandal never became a training organization for the political and social organizations for women that emerged in the 1920s and 1930s. The *Bhagini Samaj* and the mandal shared some members, but the samaj was open to all communities whereas the mandal continued to limit its membership to Gujaratis and its efforts to education. However, by limiting its aims and membership, the mandal was able to open branches in several neighborhoods and influence the lives of women who otherwise would not have been educated.[18] Personal accounts by women involved in nationalist protests underline the importance of neighborhood organizations. The education they imparted made it possible for women to read newspapers and journals, while informal networks spread information about nationalist leaders and goals and encouraged women's participation in the protest activities.[19]

Knowledge of these fledgling associations for women often encouraged male reformers to organize women in their own families. Begum Shahnawaz, later a prominent and influential member of national women's organizations, has recounted her first experience with a women's society. In 1902 her uncle, Shah Din, learned about a Sikh Conference in Lahore that included 2,000 women who had collected enough money to begin the *Maha Vidayala School*. Anxious that Muslim women begin to catch up, Shah Din decreed that henceforth women of his own (Mian) family would meet twice a month to discuss topics connected with female education and social reform. Women of the family were instructed to write articles on these topics, present them at meetings for discussion, and begin "social work" with poor women in surrounding villages. The experience gained from working within the family led the women to initiate a larger organization, and Begum Shahnawaz's mother, Amir-un-Nisa (called the Mrs. Pankhurst of the Mian family), became a founder-member of the Muslim Women's Association *(Anjuman-e Khawatin-e-Islam)* in the Punjab. By 1915, women of the Mian family were playing a leading role in the All-Indian Muslim Women's Conference.[20]

Although male-inspired and guided organizations for women did invaluable work in educating women and providing their first experience with public work, they imposed limitations when it came to expanding the issues under consideration and the articulation of a feminist consciousness. The religious-reform and communal associations dealt with women's problems as defined by male leaders. If the leaders believed that female education, concern for widows, and autonomy for women were important for the community, the women's organization would find support for activities that tackled these issues. However, support would not necessarily extend to problems the women identified independently. For example, the women of the *Stri Zarthosthi Mandal* received financial support when they extended the services offered to poor Parsi women. Yet Mrs. Herabai Tata and her daughter Mithan (who became India's first woman lawyer) received no support when they traveled to England to lobby for female franchise.[21] Similarly, the Panchayat welcomed the views of Parsi women on family law but soundly defeated Bai Dinhai F. S. Patuck's proposal that sex differences be eliminated from the laws of inheritance.[22] The advantages of having the full support of males were obvious; projects and schemes were fully supported and membership encouraged. The disadvantages only became evident as the women gained more experience and began to formulate their own solutions to women's problems.

It was the general associations begun by women themselves and composed of women from different religious groups and communities that made it possible for women to define their own interests, propose solutions, and take action. In the late nineteenth century and particularly in the early twenteeth century, these organizations — called variously Ladies Clubs, Women's Associations, and *Mahila Samities* — sprang up all over India. Most were limited to a specific geographic area, and identified specific needs of the locale. What they shared was a desire to bring together women of diverse backgrounds and similar problems.

One of the earliest general associations for women was established in Bengal by Swarnakumari Devi in 1886. The *Sakhi Samity* (Friend's Association) was organized to promote communication between women, provide education and training, and exhibit women's work.[23] Swarnakumari Devi (1885–1932) is best known for her novels in Bengali and work as editor of the journal *Bharati,* but she was also one of the first female delegates to the Indian National Congress, and was extremely active in social and intellectual circles of the late nineteenth century. She envisioned the *Sakhi Samity* as promoting understanding between women belonging to different social and religious groups, training helpless widows to become teachers of those women who were confined to their homes by the custom of purdah, appointing pleaders and barristers to argue women's cases in the *mofussil,* arranging *melas* (fairs) where women's handiwork could be exhibited, and running a primary school.[24]

The women who formed the nucleus of this organization had previously met to study Theosophy, very popular in Calcutta following a visit of the founders Madame Blavatsky and Colonel Olcott. Since we have no organizational records, it is difficult to assess the extent to which the

Samity was able to accomplish its goals. However, the records that exist confirm that the association educated women to become teachers, held exhibitions of women's work, and staged plays by women. They seem to have been less successful in providing other kinds of training, securing the assistance of attorneys to fight for women in the courts, and securing the services of those women they had trained as teachers.[25] One of the main concerns of the *Sakhi Samity* was money. They needed funds for scholarships and to pay the salaries of *zenana* teachers; they earned money from the sale of women's handicrafts and the staging of plays at their exhibitions, and from direct contributions. In 1888 the *Sakhi Samity* was able to collect Rs 2,405 from 162 members.[26] Despite its early successes, the *Sakhi Samity* had run out of steam in less than a decade, and had disappeared by the end of the century. It was, nevertheless, the first women's organization aimed at social welfare.

Women were slowly becoming aware that their perspective on social reform was somewhat different from that of male reformers. It seemed that male reformers, in pursuit of principles, were quite capable of riding roughshod over the interests of individual women. To give but one example, there is the case of Narmad, the famous Gujarati poet who advocated widow remarriage. Narmad was married and belong to a caste (Vadanagara Nagar Brahmin) that did not permit more than one wife. The British rulers recognized that customary law took precedence, and hence this caste was barred from polygamy. In 1870 the widow Narmadagauri fell in love with Narmad. He believed that he should stand by his principles and marry her even though to do so would mean defying his caste, breaking the law, and possibly subjecting his family to social ostracism. Before he decided on a course of action he discussed the matter with his wife and it has been reported that she, "like a true Hindu wife," told him to do what he liked as she had no intention of leaving him. Narmad decided to marry the widow.[27]

It must also have been clear to these early women reformers that they were at a disadvantage when others called the tune. Ordering the times and the frequency of meetings, choosing the topics for discussion, designating who would read papers, male sponsors of these organizations sometimes inhibited free expression. In 1872 Radharani Lahiri had read a paper at a ladies gathering organized and dominated by Keshub Chunder Sen. When she did so, she turned her back toward the audience and mumbled so badly Keshub asked her to "read it properly" a second time. Following her address, Keshub talked "a great deal" but solicited very few comments from women in the audience. In fact, the women present were described as "listless and inattentive."[28] Radharani later became a forceful public speaker within the confines of women's organizations.[29] Even though she had obviously gained by experience, the striking difference between her performance under Keshub and on subsequent occasions is very likely related to male sponsorship.

Women, as might have been expected, occasionally criticized reform efforts on their behalf. It was not that they were ungrateful; male reformers received considerable praise from the women who joined these early organizations. In fact, every history of the emancipation of Indian women, save those written by foreigners, pays homage to nineteenth- and twentieth-century male reformers from Rammohun Roy to Gandhi. Nevertheless, it seemed to many women that male reformers sometimes missed the point. In a somewhat humorous vein, one woman, who had been widowed at age ten, wrote about her "reformist" father:

> It is now four years since my father spoke in that memorable Social Reform meeting. He still speaks, thinks he is a reformer, adds to social reform literature and people admire and call him a great social reformer. He believes he has done a great deal in the cause of social reform and even scans the Birthday gazette. But I remain a widow still! Must men always talk and women weep![30]

This theme was to be repeated time and again until women had formed their own organizations and begun to articulate their solutions to the problems of child widowhood, child marriage, and polygamy.

Efforts to break away from male tutelage had occurred in the nineteenth century but became more common in the first two decades of the twentieth. There seemed to be a new spirit among educated women, wrote a British woman visiting India, and considerable evidence that they wanted to "own for themselves a share in the larger life."[31] As early as 1901, women in Bombay decided to form a social reform organization to commemorate Justice Ranade's death. Male reformers, having already formed such an organization, opposed this idea and suggested a merger. One of the women who had been present at the first women's meeting protested:

> Public spirited women are for the present in a minority and their individual efforts and eloquence would be submerged by the superior and voluminous activities of men, if a combination took place. The minority of their number and the recency of their experiences may prevent their influence from asserting itself.

She argued that segregated women could deal with their own problems in their own way, whereas men might not concede the rights that women wanted.[32]

Saraladevi Chaudhurani, the extraordinary daughter of Swarnakumari Devi, was critical of the women's meetings held in conjunction with the Indian National Social Conference. She used this forum, however, to pass a resolution calling for a permanent association of Indian women. The women at the conference voted in favor of such an organization. While Saraladevi was planning the first meeting, she encountered opposition from male colleagues. She, in turn, criticized her opponents for patronizing women. She wrote:

> They are the so-called social reformers. They advertise themselves as champions of the weaker sex; equal opportunities for women, female education and female emancipation are some of their pet subjects for oratory at the annual show. They even make honest efforts at object lessons in the above subjects by persuading educated ladies to come up on their platforms and speak for themselves. . . . 'Surely traditions die hard — even among social reformers of India. So they are not to blame if the shade of Manu still haunts them and actuates them in their want of faith in the capacities of Indian women and prompts them to follow the usage long established of keeping them under thralldom at every stage of their growth.[33]

Saraladevi persisted, and the *Bharat Stree Mahamandal* had its first meeting in 1910. This first all-Indian organization for women held its inaugural meeting at Allahabad, with her highness the Begum Saheba of Janjira presiding. The first meeting was attended by H.H. the Nawab Begum Saheba of Bhopal, the only woman ruler in India; Rani Saheba Partabgarh; Mrs. Motilal Nehru; Mrs. Leslie Porter, wife of the lieutenant governor of the U.P.; and Lady Stanley, wife of the chief justice. Her Highness the Maharani of Baroda and Sarojini Naidu sent telegrams of regret. Saraladevi's connections had served her well; she had attracted a number of powerful and respected women to attend the first meeting of this new organization.[34]

With its all-India pretensions and grand schemes for the promotion of female education, this organization became the prototype for the all-India women's associations begun in the next decade. Saraladevi's society developed branches in a number of Indian cities — Lahore, Allahabad, Delhi, Karachi, Amritsar, Hyderabad, Kanpur, Bankura, Hazaribagh, Midnapore, and Calcutta — and attempted to bring together "women of every race, creed, class and party in India ... on the basis of their common interest in the moral and material progress of the women of India."[35] Recognizing that purdah inhibited female education, the mahamandal sought to deliver zenana education. As well as basic literacy, the mahamandal's teachers offered instruction in music, sewing, and embroidery. The latter two were useful skills that the organization's founders thought might make it possible for widows and helpless women to earn a living.

The success of the *Bharat Stree Mahamandal* depended on the ability of women to run and support independently the educational schemes of the various branches. Saraladevi, dreaming of "a great sisterhood of purely Indian women extending over the whole of the motherland for self-services,"[36] enlisted the support of the begum of Bhopal and India's influential maharanis. Saraladevi had not asked male reformers to send their wives, but had attempted to form a women's association with women as patrons and contributors. The success of the various branches differed significantly. The Calcutta branch, supported by Saraladevi's mother and sister, and the Lahore branch, where Saraladevi resided, were the most active; branches in Karachi, Amritsar, and Allahabad accomplished very little. By 1911 the Calcutta Mandal had engaged six teachers to instruct eighteen young ladies in ten families. When Krishna Bhabini Das became the moving force of this branch, the number of females under instruction increased to three thousand in five hundred houses. The organization faltered in 1919, upon Krishna Bhabini's death, but revived somewhat in 1926, when the widowed Saraladevi returned to take charge. By this time zenana education had become prohibitively expensive, and the mahamandal opened a school for married women.[37] The fate of the society was similar in other cities. It had depended on the energy and skills of a few women committed to its goals and able to secure the funds necessary to carry out its program. After 1930, the organization seems to have disappeared.

The information about these early organizations begun by women is scattered and incomplete. Newspaper accounts, social reform journals, ladies' magazines, and biographies and autobiographies make it possible to compile long lists of women's associations and occasionally membership lists. What has not survived, assuming that they existed for at least some of these organizations, are records of their meetings. Equally rare are accounts of how they actually began. To date I have obtained two detailed accounts of how different women's associations or clubs were formed.

One account occurs in the memories of Shudha Mazumdar,[38] a Bengali woman who had first studied at St. Teresa's Convent and was then married, at age twelve, to a young man studying for the civil service examination. While he finished his studies she remained with his family. After her husband had passed the examination and received his first posting in the districts, the young couple began to live together. Enjoying the freedom of a nuclear family, they flaunted conventional rules of sex segregation and conducted cooking experiments, dined together, and continued Shudha's education with her husband as tutor. In 1916 they came to Suri and

> it was at this place I became interested in what is now called "social work," but I do not remember hearing this phrase in those days. Saroj Nalini Dutt, the wife of the District Magistrate, called on me and a few other officials' wives and proposed that we form a *Mahila Samity* [women's society]. She explained that this would be a social organization to provide an opportunity for the townswomen to come out of their homes and meet and know each other. This would help foster a better understanding between them and break the monotony of their secluded lives.[39]

Once Shudha had agreed to join her, the two set out on a series of social calls to the wives of the leading men of the town. Generally they were well received and their hostesses heard them out, but these women could not commit themselves without permission from their husbands. The husbands were quite in awe of Mrs. Dutt, the wife of the district magistrate, but this did not keep them from denying their wives permission to attend samity meetings. In response to Mrs. Dutt's further questioning, one individual answered that his wife's attendance would ruin his reputation. Another believed that it would mean "the death-knell of family life, and that it foretold nothing but discord and disruption." When the first meeting was held, the wives of these men were absent, and the samity was formed by the wives of government officers, junior pleaders, and others flattered by the visit of the district magistrate's wife.[40]

What this account and one by Kamalabai L. Rau, of the formation of the Ladies Recreation Club in Madras,[41] make clear is that women themselves were beginning to articulate their needs, take leadership roles in structuring organizations, and define the aims of their new societies. To a large extent their needs were for social skills that would equip them to assume new roles. Conscious that they were living in a world different from that of their mothers and grandmothers, they sought conversational and social skills that would make it possible for them to meet the demands that arose from their husbands' positions, the necessity of travel, and setting up households in new environments. Relationships with women belonging to their own family continued to be important, but they were not sufficient to sustain them in the face of rapid change and new demands.

The new organizations aimed at assisting these women to cope with the demands of modern life. Further education was seen as essential, since many of them had married young. Some of the mahila samities taught basic subjects such as mathematics and geography, while others offered only English. The necessity of understanding the world beyond the home was recognized and responded to by organizing lectures on domestic and international issues. Particularly popular were lectures and classes on health, child care, hygiene, and nutrition, as these women became aware that they were expected to introduce scientific nurturance into their homes. And they sought to learn social skills — how to converse politely, how to serve tea, how to speak in public gatherings, and how to remain at ease in new situations. Second-generation emancipated women (those whose mothers had been educated in the 1870s and 80s) had learned these skills as children, but for most of the women entering public life, their first encounter with tea and cake was something of an ordeal.[42]

These early women's associations were numerous, and they varied greatly in size, aims, and longevity. Some of them remained small local organizations for a number of years and simply died when their purpose was no longer relevant. Many of them began with one purpose and gradually expanded their concerns to include other issues. Still others modified their aims to suit the changing times. There were mergers galore, such as that described by Kamalabai Rau, and a number of small associations were absorbed by or affiliated with the larger all-India women's organizations. Still others changed, grew, and remain alive and active today.

In Suri, Mrs. Dutt's mahila samity began as a social gathering but during World War I took up war work: wrapping bandages, sewing garments, and feasting the new recruits. When Shudha Mazumdar's husband was transferred to Tamluk, she accompanied him and set up another *Mahila Samity*. This group began with social gatherings but soon expanded its activities to include lobbying for a lady doctor and collecting money to purchase a bed for the "women's wing" of the local hospital.[43]

Saroj Nalini Dutt continued to organize mahila samities as she accompanied her husband on his various work assignments. Following her premature death in 1925, these were brought together under the Saroj Nalini Dutt Memorial Association. Under the able leadership of Latika Basu, the number of samities grew until this became the major rural women's organization in Bengal.[44] In the beginning, Saroj Nalini had been concerned with bringing women together and making them more aware of the world. However, she later became equally concerned with their economic plight. The only training most women received was that provided by their mothers in traditional homemaking skills. This prepared them for their dependent role, but many customs, such as child marriage, an inability to inherit, polygamy, compulsory motherhood, and enforced widowhood, meant women that were often required to support themselves and their children. Before her death, Saroj Nalini began to shift the focus of her women's associations to industrial training.[45] It is possible to chart the shift in this organization's emphasis as it matured. Fifteen years after the first mahila samities were formed, the Saroj Nalini Dutt Memorial Association's main concern was teaching women marketable skills. The middle-class women for whom it was originally formed continued to belong, but their role had changed to that of assisting educational programs for "less fortunate" women. The transition happened rather quickly, which suggests that as these Indian women learned the social skills necessary to take part in public life they moved rapidly to take up questions of social reform.[46]

The movement to reform customs detrimental to women's status was begun by men. Their motives were clearly mixed. Many were conscious of injustices perpetrated on a daily basis; others were aware only of how an educated wife or daughter would reflect on their own status. Among the latter, some were anxious to respond to the critique of Hindu society by foreign missionaries, while others were concerned with career advancement. Not only were there differences in motivation, the reformers held different views of the causes of the problem, the solutions to it, and the actions required to carry out those solutions. What does seem clear is that there were a number of progressive men committed to social reforms focusing on women. And while the reformers sought the help of newly educated women, they had no intention of turning the entire problem over to them.

The earliest proponents of social reforms for women experienced the same dilemma as most social reformers: the recipients of their efforts did not seem particularly keen to take advantage of their new "rights." After *sati* was abolished, there were women who insisted on performing this rite[47] and the Widow Remarriage Act did not encourage large numbers of widows to remarry. The reformers soon became aware of the magnitude of the task before them; both women and men in general society needed to be educated. Women needed to learn more about the world and their place in it, and new institutions were required to educate women and help them adjust to the demands of new roles. In light of the dual problems of early marriage and restrictions on the physical movement of married women, schemes to bring women together so that they could continue to learn were essential. The first such organizations, actually akin to adult education classes, were established by the religious reform organizations — the Brahmo Samaj in Bengal and the Prarthana Samaj in Poona. Although religious activities played some part in these organizations, it was a small part; they were primarily concerned with providing educational opportunities. The organizations that limited their membership to one community were similar in many ways. Again, the primary concern was to provide an education — in this case for women of the community who had not had the same access to education as their elite sisters. The third type of organization, modeled on the new all-Indian organizations that men had set up for political action and social reform, was the general association General organizations began as ladies' auxiliaries, and although they were not able to throw off this derivative identity, they provided women with the experience and contacts to form new associations.

All three types of organization provided women with experience in organizing and running associations, acquainted them with the basic problems facing women, and gave them access to like-minded women. When they moved to form their own association, they used the general association as their model. And instead of focusing on issues that might be resolved with legal remedies, they focused on broader and more amorphous issues such as female education, child marriage, purdah, women's status in the family, and relationships with in-laws. Ghulam Murshid has entitled his chapter on Bengali women and social reform in the last decades of the nineteenth century "In Their Masters' Footsteps." According to Murshid, women had deserted social reform issues because their menfolk, increasingly concerned with political issues and less sanguine about reforming society with the help of alien rulers, were no longer interested in reform.[48] I would agree with Murshid that there was a shift in emphasis, not only in Bengal but all over India, as women moved from male-sponsored associations to associations they controlled. However, I do not see the shift as an indication that these women were afraid to express views different from those held by their husbands. Rather, they viewed the problems and the solutions differently.

Although Indian men did not have political power, they had access to those who did. That they might have sought remedies for social problems in legislation was not unusual. However, they soon realized the futility of expecting social change simply because a law had been changed. That women, newly educated and only recently introduced to the world outside the home, formed organizations with seemingly limited aims was what might have been expected. Women lacked mobility and were overwhelmingly dependent (physically, financially, and psychologically) on men. Clearly some of their new organizations had more limited aims than had the associations formed for them by their menfolk. But within the framework of the separate organizations, they were able to include a larger number of women. To a certain extent they were able to regain some of the power that had accrued to women who had remained inside the home: although the role of the housewife was certainly restricting, it was accorded respect. Once free of the day-to-day intervention of the parent body, these women learned how to conduct meetings, and began discussions of their perceptions of women's condition. Gradually they began to define women's issues and formulate solutions. Still without access to political power, they moved from discussions and the formulation of resolutions to attempts to ameliorate the worst situations. They set up new institutions, such as girls' schools, handicraft training centers, and widow's homes. In the short run they hoped to make things better for women; their long-range goal was to elevate women's status.

In the writings, speeches, and letters of these women we begin to find some signs of emergent feminism. They voiced their disgruntlement with their male patrons and sought to run things their own way, but found that they lacked both money and influence. When they formally presented petitions to the British on issues of social reform, they often found their petitions ignored while the government gave instructions that the males of all the important communities be solicited for comment. There were times when women's issues simply seemed another arena where the British and their colonial subjects fought for control.[49] In the 1920s, women began their efforts to secure the female franchise, and in subsequent years they worked to have women elected and appointed to as many public bodies as possible. When they formed all-India organizations for women they presented their resolutions as representing the will of the women of India. By the mid-1930s Indian social customs were being subjected to a feminist critique by women fully conscious of their dependent positions. They had moved slowly from the protection of their husbands and fathers to a cautious espousal of the cause of women.

NOTES

1. Sivanath Sastri, *History of the Brahmo Samaj,* (Calcutta, 1974), pp. 105–164. See also David Kopf, *The Brahmo Samaj and the Shaping of the Modern Indian Mind* (Princeton, 1979) and Meredith Borthwick, *The Changing Role of Women in Bengal, 1849–1905* (Princeton, 1984).
2. Charles H. Heimsath, *Indian Nationalism and Hindu Social Reform* (Princeton, 1964), pp. 230–232; Kopf, *Brahmo Samaj,* pp. 320–322.
3. Nicol Macnicol, *Pandita Ramabai* (Calcutta, 1926), p. 52; Rajas Krishnarao Dongre and Joseph F. Patterson, *Pandita Ramabai, A Life of Faith and Prayer* (Madras, 1969), pp. 10-11.
4. Macnicol, *Pandita Ramabai*, p. 53.
5. "Arya Mahila Samaj," in K.J. Chitalia, ed., *Director of Women's Institutions, Bombay Presidency,* vol. 1 (Bombay, 1936), p. 6. The earliest members of this samaj were Pandita Ramabai, Ramabai Ranade, Ramabai Bhandarkar, and Lady Shantabai Patkar.
6. Dongre and Patterson, *Pandita Ramabai,* p. 11.
7. Pandita Ramabai, "Women's Place in Hindu Religion and Society," *The Secularist,* no. 36 (November-December, 1975), p. 140.

8. Dongre and Patterson, *Pandita Ramabai,* p. 12; "Pandita Ramabai," *Men and Women of India, 1:6, 1905, p. 319;* Muriel Clark, *Pandita Ramabai* (London, 1920), p. 25.
9. Mrs. Ramabai Ranade, *Himself, The Autobiography of a Hindu Lady,* translated and adapted by Katherine Van Akin Gates (New York, 1938), pp. 25, 78.
10. "Arya Mahila Samaj," notes by Mrs. Leela Joshi, Bombay (from author); "Arya Mahila Samaj: An Appeal," cyclostyled sheet by Sarojini Pradhar; "Pandita Ramabai Saraswati," *Women's Forum,* March-April, 1972, n.p.
11. "The Indian Social Conference," *Indian Ladies Magazine* [hereafter I.L.M.], 3:8 (February, 1904), p. 225.
12. "Mrs. Ranade's Address," *ibid.*, p. 259.
13. "The Ladies' Gathering," *I.L.M.* 4:7 (January 1905), pp. 219-220.
14. "The Indian National Social Conference," *I.L.M.*, 5:7 (January 1906), pp. 230-232; "Ladies Gathering at Surat," *I.L.M.* 6:10 (April 1907), p. 380. "The Ladies Social Conference," *I.L.M.*, 8:7 (January 1908), pp. 227-228.
15. Saraladevi, "A Women's Movement," *Modern Review,* October 1911, p. 345.
16. *Golden Jubilee Stri Zarthosthi Mandal, 1903-1953, and Silver Jubilee Sir Ratan Tata Industrial Institute, 1928-1953, Volume* (Bombay, 1953), pp. 5-7 [Courtesy of Sir Ratan Tata Trust].
17. *Ibid.*
18. Chitalia, *Directory,* p. 17; Miss Engineer and Mrs. Choksi, "Seva Sadan and Other Social Work in Bombay," *Women in Modern India,* edited by E.C. Gedge and M. Choksi (Bombay, 1929), p. 47. Appendix 13, "A List of the Members of the Gandhi Seva Sena and a few details about the work of some of the individual Sevika," *AICC Files,* F-8/1929, Pts. 1 & 2. [NNML].
19. Interview with Ambabai, Udipi, Karnataka, May 24, 1976, translated by M. Ashotn and L. Bhat.
20. See Gail Minault, "Sisterhood or Separatism? The All-India Muslim Ladies Conference and the Nationalist Movement," in *The Extended Family,* edited by Gail Minault (Columbia, Missouri, 1981), pp. 83–108; Jahan Ara Shahnawaz, *Father and Daughter, A Political Autobiography* (Lahore, 1971), pp. 13–23, 42–50.
21. Mithan Tata Lam, "Biodata of Mrs. Herabai A. Tata," unpublished paper from author; interview with Mithan Lam, Bombay, February 22, 1980.
22. *Golden Jubilee Stri Zarthosthi Mandal,* pp. 25-26.
23. Ghulam Murshid, *Reluctant Debutante: Response of Bengali Women to Modernization, 1849-1905* (Rajshahi University, Rajshahi: Sahitya Samsad, 1983), pp. 95-96. Murshid has included a membership list of this organization, pp. 250-251.
24. "Swarnakumari Devi," *Dictionary of National Biography, India,* Vol. 1, p. 59; Saraladevi Chaudhurani, *Jibaner Jharapara* (Kalikata, 1958); Borthwick, *Changing Role,* p. 285.
25. Borthwick, *Changing Role,* p. 285.
26. Murshid, *Reluctant Debutante,* p. 96.
27. Neera Desai, *Social Change in Gujarat* (Bombay, 1978), p. 348.
28. Annette Akroyd, *Indian Notebooks,* December 27, 1872, Annette and Henry Beveridge Papers, c. 176/104, India Office Library.
29. Borthwick, *Changing Role,* p. 281.
30. "The Sorrow of a Widow," *The Indian Social Reformer* [hereafter I.S.R.] February 13, 1903, pp. 228-229.
31. Copy of a letter from Rena Carswell, April 3, 1916, Fawcett Papers, Fawcett Society Library, London, Box 90).
32. "The Women's Ranade Memorial Movement," I.S.R., August 11, 1901, p. 396.
33. *Ibid.*

34. *Ibid.*
35. J.C. Bagal, "Sarala Devi Chaudhurani," *Sahitya Sadhak Charitmala,* No. 99 (Calcutta, 1966), p. 24; Saraladevi, "Women's Movement," p. 347.
36. Saraladevi, "Women's Movement," p. 344.
37. "An Account of the Work among Women in Calcutta," *I.L.M.*, 8 May-June, 1935, p. 76; "The Bharat Stree Mahamandal," *The Modern Review,* September 1912, p. 312; Saraladevi, *Jibaner Jharapata,* pp. 196-197; Saraladevi, "Women's Movement," p. 348.
38. Shudha Mazumdar, *A Pattern of Life: The Memories of an Indian Woman,* edited by Geraldine Forbes (New Delhi, 1977).
39. *Ibid.* pp, 140–142.
40. *Ibid.*
41. Mrs. Kamalabai L. Rau, *Memoirs of a Brihan Maharashtrian,* translated by Mrs. Indira M. Rau, unpublished MS. from Dr. Krishnabai Nimbkar, pp. 9–11.
42. Mazumdar, *Pattern of Life,* p. 146.
43. *Ibid.*, pp. 143-144, 162–165.
44. Interview with Latika Ghosh Basu, Calcutta, February 29, 1976.
45. G.S. Dutt, *A Woman of India, Being the Life of Saroj Nalini* (London, 1941), pp. 91–98; interview with Mrs. Arati Dutt, August 15, 1972: "A Woman's Welfare Association," *Modern Review*, Vol. 45, (January-June 1929), p. 282; *Saroj Nalini Dutt Memorial Association for Women's Work in Bengal, Report for 1925,* pp. 2–17.
46. See Geraldine Forbes, "The Women's Movement in India: Traditional Symbols and New Roles," *Social Movements in India,* Vol. 2, edited by M.S.A. Rao (New Delhi, 1979), pp. 149–165.
47. Vina Mazumdar, "Comment on Suttee," *Signs,* 4:2 (Winter 1978), p. 269.
48. Murshid, *Reluctant Debutante,* pp. 184–197.
49. See article by Dagmar Engels, "The Age of Consent Act of 1891: Colonial Ideology in Bengal," *South Asia Research,* 3:2 (November 1983), pp. 107–132.

Punjab Politics and the Press, 1880–1910

N. GERALD BARRIER

The balance between cultural unity and diversity that has contributed to the vitality of Indian civilization involves the effective communication of ideas and symbols over time and space. In classical India, norms and cultural images were perpetuated by the great epics and religious classics as well as through folktales, drama, and song, often in local language, that linked the villager with centers of great learning. Such traditions also took the form of classical and vernacular literatures perpetuated by highly educated specialists as well as local literati. Beginning in the 19th century, the interaction between pan-Indian and regional traditions were important elements in new institutions and modes of communication. Tracts, books, and newspapers became major avenues for the transfer of ideas, and for the defense and strengthening of indigenous culture.[1]

Concern with Indian nationalism and the challenges confronting contemporary India have led many historians to emphasize the role of the press in creating a national public opinion that eventually paved the way for independence from England. Circulation figures, British prosecutions, official analysis of press trends, and secondary evidence are used to demonstrate journalism's support for secular nationalism and a concomitant sense of "being Indian."[2] Much of the current research on Indian politics, however, suggests alternative interpretations. In the nineteenth century, and probably much later, rather than bringing together the public and being at the vanguard of nationalism, newspapers more frequently reflected the opinion and concerns of organizations, groups, and individuals. As suggested in the work of Uma Datta, Suntharalingam, Bayly, and others, editorials and news coverage tended to play up local events and to reflect parochial interests rather than a commitment to nationalist goals.[3]

The formative stages of Punjab politics and Punjab journalism exemplify this pattern. Punjabi journalists generally were concerned with particular problems, issues, and associations, both subnational and parochial. This paper reviews the evolution of Punjab political patterns and the role of the press in that process. Particular attention is paid to developments within one community, the Sikhs, and also the inability of a newspaper that attempted to rise above sectarian viewpoint, the Lahore *Tribune,* to influence political affairs. A final section raises questions about parallel developments in other provinces and suggests difficulties in generalizing about the Indian press.

PUNJAB POLITICS IN THE NINETEENTH CENTURY

As often the case in other parts of India, Punjab politics mirrored commitments and patterns involving locality, community, and region.[4] In the Punjab, two elements stood out from the beginning — the prominence of rural politicians and a variety of religious communalism that strongly influenced first urban and subsequently rural political life.

The allocation of resources and political influence tended to be in the hands of specific rural elites. In the west, Jat and Rajput Muslim families owned considerable amounts of land. Although smaller than the holdings of large landowners in the United Provinces, these estates grew appreciably under the regime of Ranjit Singh and later under the British. Among Muslims, the *biraderi* or kinship groups influenced alliances and distribution of resources, as did attachment to local shrines and religious leaders. The central districts had a mixed pattern of landholding, with occasionally large estates and smaller domains controlled by Hindu, Sikh, and Muslim tribes (particularly Jats). *Biraderis* also were important there, and in the eastern districts, where Hindu Jats predominated.

In addition, each community had commercial or urban-oriented castes and classes. Muslim Kashmiris and Arains were notable examples. Although less influenced by rural social and religious networks, Arain professionals, such as those from the Mian family, managed to bridge town and countryside. Among Hindus and Sikhs, Khatri and Arora *biraderis* created commercial and social networks linking many Punjab towns. Within the context of traditional society, these groups played a vital economic role, but their political influence tended to be slight. Wealth and influence arose from landownership and agrarian linkages.[5]

Although British rule contributed to the religious conflicts later affecting Punjab life, the basis for division lay imbedded in the historical experience of Punjabis prior to the 1850s. In the past, even with the mixing of social and religious traditions in some locales, Muslims and Hindus (along with Sikhs) had maintained boundaries separating them from others and reinforcing sectarian identification. Each had their own religious elites and shrines, along with festivals, traditions of worship, educational institutions, and patterns of pilgrimage. Demarcation between Hindus and Sikhs tended to be less clear, with Sikhs being seen as in danger of losing their separate identity by the 1860s. Although social and religious cleavages existed within each community, differences along religious lines were understood and influenced local life. In addition, decades of struggle, local tension, and competition for converts had produced a legacy of distrust and insecurity, particularly within the minority Hindu community. Although more secure, partially because of their strengthened economic and political power under Ranjit Singh, Sikhs also had a sense of martyrdom and a tradition of sacrifice for religion. The ideology and institutional base for subsequent communal politics drew on these traditions. As Punjabis re-evaluated their history, and unsorted who they were and what they wanted in the new world associated with British rule, this heritage became accentuated and influenced decisions and ultimately political trends.[6]

The British presence reinforced existing patterns and added fresh elements that gave Punjab politics its distinct cast. On the one hand, the new rulers found or developed support groups within the traditional segments of Punjab society. In their quest for "natural leaders" and indigenous institutions to facilitate governance, the British cultivated the landed aristocracy through patronage and special educational institutions such as Aitchison College. Similarly, defending the interests of "peasant proprietors" in order to insure stability and loyalty became a keynote of Punjab administration, as did the defense of the village community and related political networks. Support of those supplying recruits for the military and police also was vital, leading to specific policies and a generally paternistic attitude toward the rural population.

At the same time, the government created changes that disrupted order and complicated decision making. The transfer of institutions and ideas about procedure and politics helped foster a new political environment. The British were seen as sources of patronage in areas ranging from the presentation of honors to jobs and pensions. In addition, accompanying British rule were new arenas of power and competition (such as the bureaucracy and municipal committees) that pointed toward and even encouraged fresh forms of political orientation. The government distrusted the emergence of Western-style politics surrounding the new institutions, and tried to minimize its spread by relying further on traditional support groups.[7] Competition and political organization nevertheless soon became a fact of life in Punjab.

As in other regions of India, most activities centered around a relatively small group of western-educated professionals residing in urban areas. Initially these tended to be Bengali, but by the end of the century, they were replaced by a distinctly Punjabi elite, most of whom were Vaishya castes that had a tradition of administration and a flair for innovation. Joining the Hindu Khatris and Aroras, and a few Sikhs, was a small but influential assortment of Muslims involved in law, bureaucracy, and journalism. These "new men" moved quickly to adopt Western modes of organization and tactics. They formed associations, conducted public meetings, and presented their views in a mild, constitutional manner. Resembling other Indians who had undergone similiar experience, Punjabis were concerned with local issues of social or economic consequence, and, more rarely, with provincial matters. They communicated among themselves, and with the British, through recognized mechanisms such as petitions, correspondence, and ultimately the print media.[8]

Besides these characteristics found elsewhere, from the outset Punjab political culture had a parochial style and imagery that tended to cut Punjabis off from organizations and groups in other provinces and frequently threatened local cooperation. Punjab aggressiveness and a pride in being brave and militant seems to have derived from a variety of sources, including folk literature, and the contemporary customs of Rajput and Jat tribes. Also important was the frontier orientation of the province with emphasis on physical strength and military tradition, coupled with a sense of falling behind the rest of India — an insecurity fostered by the relative lack of education and sophistication among educated Punjabis. Public statements and correspondence contained allusions to Punjabis as "rough and ready," crude, strong, and brave. Part of the imagery was positive — the sword arm, "the lions of the Punjab," the defender of India — and part negative — crudeness, lack of culture, a poor command of English, and general awkwardness. Also present was an emphasis upon practicality and common sense, possibly derived in part from the commercial traditions among the Vaishya castes.[9]

Factionalism and the belligerence common of Punjab public life influenced how local politicians operated. During the period 1870–1900, literally hundreds of organizations dotted the province. In many, whether secular or religious, factionalism, manipulation of rules, and internal struggle for control were common. A good fight was valued, not only within associations but in public arenas as well. Punjabis tended to go public in a very personal and aggressive fashion. Editorial columns and news reports in publications frequently referred to controversy, and contained personal attacks, slander, and innuendo. The history of public institutions in Punjab was littered with incidents of confrontation and fission — outside the province, Punjabis had a reputation for bullish, aggressive, and erratic behavior.[10]

Local politicians had a particular view of how their personal or institutional struggles related to British authority. Accepting the official view of government as *ma-bap,* the paternal sources of justice and ultimate patronage, Punjabis tended to emphasize their own loyalty and attachment to the *raj* while simultaneously tarring their opponents with the label of "sedition" or "trouble making." Friends of the British supposedly would be protected and supported, whereas opponents would be injured by governmental fiat. Whether in situations involving cow riots, or control of enterprises, or infighting within an organization, Punjabis were quick to charge opponents with "being political" (translated to mean "anti-British").[11] Such charges, ranking in popularity with other tactics such as legal ensnarement, led to rounds of charges and countercharges. Prior to 1900, the British generally were amused by the incidents and only infrequently investigated the charges. The accusations nevertheless became a pattern, giving the British information as well as reinforcing their central role as arbiter among various competing factions and communities.

Much of the competition involved religious revival and communal organizations. It should be emphasized, however, that viewing Punjabis as singlemindedly polarized into communal groups would be inaccurate. They never were, and they are not today. Urban politicians could and did cooperate, either over specific issues such as racism or a tax bill, or sporadically in a broad-based association such as the Lahore Indian Association.[12] And divisions within sect or community often were at least as heated, if not more so, than those between Hindus and Muslims. The dominant pattern nevertheless involved the spread of communal consciousness and related institution-building among urban Punjabis.[13]

Numerous scholars have explored the tendency for Western-educated Punjabis to identify with a religion or sect rather than with a professional class as a whole. Hindus frequently joined the Arya Samaj, a revivalist association stressing social reform, education, and a more modern view of Hinduism; Muslims formed societies or anjumans with similar concerns, and Sikhs belonged to Singh Sabhas that denounced apostasy, championed the Punjabi language, and re-evaluated tradition and contemporary practices. The patterns of participation reflected the degree of communal identity already prevalent, but participation in the associations reinforced that identification. Militantly anti-Muslim and committed to insuring the inclusion of Sikhs within Hinduism, the Arya Samaj propagated a vision of a Hindu nation; Muslim anjumans had a similar mobilizing role, as did the efforts of Sikhs to purify and spread their religion. Each organization adopted Western agitational techniques, sending out missionaries and attacking opponents with a flood of posters, literature, and street preachers.

An increase in rioting also tended to align Hindus and Sikhs and to widen the gap between them and Muslims. Over two dozen riots occurred between 1883 and 1893 over kine slaughter, processions, and related issues. Mass communication made things worse. Rapid transmission of news and rumor charged the atmosphere and set off sympathy demonstrations and occasionally other riots.[14] The intense rioting temporarily subsided after 1893, but unrest and bitterness remained.

Most communal activities involved the urban population directly affected by recent intellectual and economic challenges. Hindus, Muslims, and Sikhs contested elections to local councils and agitated for a larger share of power and resources arising from Western education and new employment opportunities. Urban politicians felt no urgent need to mobilize beyond their immediate locality and reference group. If and when the rules and structure of politics changed, the urban elites would face appreciable obstacles in developing a broader base. Hindu organizations, with a leadership drawn primarily from the commercial castes, were almost exclusively urban-based, as were most Muslim anjumans. Only the Sikhs, through the Singh Sabhas dotting the countryside, had the potential for rapid mobilization of the rural population.[15]

What, then, was the relationship between local politicians and the Congress in this formative phase of Punjab politics? Between 1885 and 1900, local support for the nationalist cause tended to come from a small assortment of leaders who had close personal and business ties with the Bengali community or with specific individuals such as Dyal Singh and his industrial and political heir apparent, Harkishen Lal. The Congress appeal for a program that involved secular values, moderate criticisms of the British *raj,* and cooperation across sectarian and regional lines tended to go unheeded for several reasons. First, Punjabis often judged the Congress irrelevant to what needed to be done. Building up education, new occupations, and industry, and cooperating closely with the British and official patronage seemed to be the most effective means of investing political capital. Other Punjabis actively distrusted the Congress, either because of bad experiences with its oligarchical leadership, or because of its secular priorities. Energetic politicians such as Lajpat Rai were involved in strengthening their own community or, at best, developing economic and political linkages at the local level. Finally, Congress participation and seemingly anti-British politics could conceivably endanger existing programs. In an atmosphere charged with fierce competition and tension, perhaps the most frequent charges against opponents, whether an opposing Sikh or Arya Samaj faction, or another religion, were the labels "seditious" and "anti-British." In the press and public meetings, use of the term "Congress wallah" joined the more traditional aspersions about parentage, morals, or the historical roots of an individual or association as favorite tactics to embarrass and undermine opponents.[16]

Interest in the Congress quickened in 1893 and 1900, when the organization held its annual conference in Lahore. In both instances, however, local concerns, controversies, and distrust prevented any long-term identification with nationalist goals. From approximately 1903 onward, the entry of a new generation of politicians into public life (often with Hindu and Arya Samaj interests) led to another renewal of interest in Congress. Their participation, occurring simultaneouly with British actions that culminated in the brief 1907 disturbances, led to the creation of a network of local Congress associations and interest in national politics.[17] Within a year after the disturbances, however, communal concerns and factionalism became the dominant pattern, as Punjabis speeded up the bolstering of their community or local group in preparation for new constitutional arrangements. The nationalist organization and the national cause remained virtually irrelevant to the dynamics of Punjab politics for at least another eleven years.

THE PRESS AND PUNJAB PUBLIC LIFE

The dynamism characterizing the intellectual, economic, and political life of urban Punjabis by the end of the nineteenth century involved a sorting out of priorities and identities. This often was reflected in the formation of Western-style associations that attempted to deal with current or projected issues in light of real or reconstructed past experience. Newspapers both contributed to that process and reflected the issues and priorities of concerned groups. The spread of literacy and the new means of communication, such as those afforded by the printing press and the postal and railway systems, helped set the stage for a steady increase in journalistic enterprise. By the end of the century, the number of newspapers and journals in the Punjab exceeded 100; by 1905, this had reached approximately 250, and by 1920, over 350 newspapers and frequently published journals (generally weekly or bi-weekly) dotted the province.[18] Most papers did not survive more than a few years, but those that did generally had financial support from a patron, an organization, or a particular interest group. Many had a message and a defined role, often disseminating the views of one association, facilitating communication among like-minded individuals, and attacking the ideas of opponents. Organizations often had their spokesmen, in the form of tract societies, journals, and newspapers. The Arya Samaj, for example, at one time or another prior to 1910 had at least twenty papers and magazines that discussed the goals and perspectives of the Samaj as a whole or represented one of its contesting factions. A similar pattern can be found for Muslims and Sikhs. Another key element in the politics and socio-economic development of Punjab, the associations, also had their literary network. Within this context, it is not surprising therefore that when journalists wrote about politics, the interpretations and, on many occasions, the facts mirrored the ideological stance of the papers' backers. Politicians and journalists alike were concerned with the local event, the parochial issue, the immediate controversy.

The Sikh experience illustrates the point. The current vitality and unrest among Sikhs has its roots in the revivalism that began in the nineteenth century. Sikhs faced a crisis of identity that led them to re-evaluate their history, basic assumptions about theology and social practice, and particularly their relationship with Hinduism. Asserting "ham Hindu nahin" (we are not Hindus), first a small band of activists and later a sizable proportion of the community emphasized the distinctiveness of Sikhism by delineating and defending boundaries that marked them from other religions. Caste was attacked, as was participation in Hindu festivals. Service for the *panth,* progress of the community, defense of Sikhism, building the Sikh nation — these slogans filled the literature of the period.[19]

Between 1873 and 1921, Sikh religious, social, and political activities tended to revolve around the Singh Sabhas and their coordinating body, the Chief Khalsa Diwan founded in 1902. Conversions to Christianity and anti-Sikh speeches of Hindu propagandists precipitated the creating of the first Sabha in Amritsar in 1873. The basis for the association is reflected in the following list of principles:

1. Arouse love of religion among Sikhs
2. Propagate true Sikhism everywhere
3. Print books on the greatness and truth of the Sikh religion
4. Propagate the words of the Gurus
5. Publish periodicals to further the Panjabi language
6. Exclude from membership those who oppose Sikhism, or who have associated with other religions, broken Sikh laws, or who have been excluded from Sikh holy spots.
7. Refusal to speak against other religions
8. Refusal to discuss matters relating to government[20]

The Lahore Singh Sabha (1879) adopted a similar program, as did a hundred other sabhas operating by 1900. Depending on local conditions, the sabhas held religious meetings, established schools and orphanages, and sent out preaching teams. Financial support came from individual subscriptions, donations, and sporadic grants from rajas or wealthy "gentry." The sabhas were distributed throughout the Punjab and neighboring provinces, with branches in both rural and urban areas.

Despite similarities of composition and purpose, each Sikh association had its own personality and peculiar interest. This coloring came from the local leadership and the particular conditions within which every sabha operated. Differences of opinion, factionalism, and conflict within the community were commonplace. The Lahore and Amritsar Singh Sabhas, for example, developed two constellations of associated sabhas and fought with each other over issues such as caste, Hindu influence, and more generally, over control of institutions and legitimacy. The Chief Khalsa Diwan attempted to minimize such conflict and to focus Sikhs instead on creating central institutions, reaching common theological and social agreements, and defending Sikhism against attackers. The Sikhs nevertheless enjoyed a good fight, and spent as much time confronting each other as they did responding to external challenges.

Although Sikhs had an effective informal communication network that tied together the sabhas and various groups, newspapers and journals came to play a major role within the community. From the outset, Sikhs appreciated the possibilities of using printed matter as a means to broadcast their message, circulate information, and as necessary, raise an alarm or answer opponents. Singh Sabha leaders rushed to establish presses and papers. Lack of experience and improper financing accounts for the rapid rise and fall of papers that characterized early Sikh journalism. Most ventures tended to be started for a particular purpose, and unless subsidized by a patron, ran on a slim budget. Accordingly, when interest in a cause waned, or when subscriptions dropped off, papers suspended operating, to reappear if circumstance permitted.[21] Newspapers generally were in Urdu or Panjabi and had small circulations (150–400). Most were weekly, bi-monthly, or monthly with occasional bulletins or supplements. The papers had similar formats — a page or two of scripture, editorials, perhaps special articles, local news, and a perennial letter column in which correspondents challenged the editor and others on a range of issues. In the 1880s, for example, Professor Gurmukh Singh and his Lahore associates established two journals, the *Vidya Pracharak* and the *Gurmukhi Akhbar,* to support education and Panjabi as a literary language. Although the former soon collapsed, the *Gurmukhi Akhbar* ran sporadically from 1880 until 1895. In 1883 Gurmukh Singh joined with Bhai Jhanda Singh and Bhai Ditt Singh to found the Khalsa Press and the *Khalsa Akhbar,* which remained the premier vehicle for the Lahore Singh Sabha until Ditt Singh's death in 1901. Other papers were short-lived, as, for example, Bhagat Lakshman Singh's English-language *Khalsa* (1899–1901) and the Panjabi *Shuddhi Pattar,* an organ of the Lahore Shuddhi Sabha (1896–1898).

The first decades of this century witnessed an upsurge of Sikh journalism. Approximately thirty newspapers and journals appeared prior to 1920, many focusing on specific issues (such as formal education, the military, caste) or speaking for one segment of the community (for example, Ramgarhia periodicals such as *Ramgarhia Patrika*). Despite failures, these papers tended to circulate more broadly and for longer periods of time — the Urdu *Lyall Gazette,* the Panjabi *Khalsa Samachar* begun by Wazir Singh and Vir Singh in Amritsar in 1899, and the *Khalsa Advocate,* an English weekly begun in 1893 and running until 1921, when it merged with the *Khalsa* to form the Panjabi *Khalsa Te Khalsa Advocate.*

The growth of the Sikh press was not matched by a broadening of interest and an effort to reach beyond the community. On the contrary, the general thrust of Sikh journalism did not change markedly from its inception until at least the 1920s. Religious ideology and controversy were prominent, as was concern with particular institutions (such as the Sikh Educational Conference, the Khalsa College, and the Chief Khalsa Diwan). As an illustration, during the period when the Congress and provincial politics attracted support from many Punjabis (1905–1907), Sikh editors and correspondents continued to address local issues, either arguing over ideology and practice or attacking a perennial foe, the Arya Samaj.[22] The Congress remained suspect, largely because Sikhs believed that ongoing success in securing educational patronage and providing recruits for the military, police, and bureaucracy required a loyalist posture. Editorials and letters critical of British policy toward Khalsa College in 1905, for example, still called on Sikhs to support the *raj.*[23] Also much in evidence was the Punjabi tendency to label opponents as seditious and by definition unworthy of British help. This emerged most clearly during the 1907 disturbances when the Sikh press charged the Arya Samaj with plotting revolution, and cheered the deportation of Lajpat Rai; however, a similar emphasis upon loyalty and disapproval of Congress activities can be found in coverage of incidents more directly affecting Sikhs, such as damage to the Sisganj Gurdwara, the details of the Morley-Minto reforms, and the Anand Marriage Act. Even as late as 1919, in an atmosphere charged with pro-Congress sentiment and Sikh impatience with British support for Hindu control of shrines, key papers such as the *Khalsa Advocate* and the *Khalsa Samachar* cautioned against an alliance with the nationalist cause.

Only one major newspaper, the Lahore *Tribune,* can be identified as a consistent supporter of Congress efforts. The English-language paper was associated with several campaigns to organize regionally, and in general, to forge a link between Punjabis and the nascent Congress. In fact, Dyal Singh founded the paper in 1881 for the explicit purpose of breaking down the parochialism of Western-educated Punjabis.[24] The venture succeeded in that the paper became financially secure and provided leadership in disseminating news about secular and provincial events. From another perspective, however, the *Tribune's* attempts to enhance local participation in and commitment to the Congress did not meet with success; the paper became embroiled in sectarian controversy, and the groups that supported the paper either died off or played an increasingly marginal role in provincial and nationalist politics.

Prior to 1900, the *Tribune* espoused the secular values and mildly critical approach toward the British associated with Dyal Singh, Jaishi Ram, and Harkishen Lal. The newspaper challenged Punjabis to put together delegations to the annual meetings, and in 1893, helped mobilize local support for the Lahore session. To the horror of pro-Congress Punjabis, however, instead of helping institutionalize Congress support, the Lahore meetings had the opposite effect. Local delegates played little role in the debates, and two Punjab proposals were rejected — support for industrial development and the establishment of a Congress constitution that would have given provincial politicians a voice in allocation of funds. Stung by the rejection of their suggestions, Punjabis would not turn over receipts from the conference and declined to attend future sessions.

The *Tribune* sporadically attempted to stir local interest in the Congress, but its lukewarm editorials proved ineffectual until 1899. At that point, concern over alleged anti-Hindu policies (dramatized by the Punjab Alienation of Land Bill) and a shaky coalition between various Hindu factions led to a successful bid for the Congress to come to Lahore in December 1900. Following the Congress *tamasha,* however, the persistent patterns of factional struggle, controversy over funding, and frustration with Congress leaders led to a rapid dissipation of Punjab involvement in the nationalist organization. The *Tribune* mirrored the dynamics of local politics, attacking the Arya Samaj critics of Harkishen Lal (who controlled the paper) and judging the Congress "a plaything of a clique."[25]

Historical accounts of the Indian press usually portray the *Tribune* as a powerful voice for nationalism in Punjab. Its early history suggests, to the contrary, that with primarily Bengali editors and associated with a small group of Hindu professionals, the *Tribune* served a limited constituency and had a minimal impact on political mobilization. While trying to remain above communal and factional struggle, the paper was pro-Hindu and distrusted by many Muslims as well as a significant network of Hindu politicians. The *Tribune's* limited base and appeal became even more evident in the turbulent events of Punjab politics after 1900.

Between 1904 and 1908, the Punjab witnessed a sustained effort at provincewide politicalization and eventually yet another resurgence of

Congress support. In typical Punjab fashion, the provincial Congress quickly evolved into two warring factions, each with its own nationalist newspaper. The heirs of Dyal Singh — Harkishen Lal and his Hindu, Sikh, and Brahmo colleagues — claimed to be the authentic Punjab representatives of the Congress. The *Tribune* endorsed them and took a moderate position in the ensuing battle between Tilak and Gokhale at the national level. The newer and more prominent generation of politicians consisted of Hindu lawyers and businessmen with some ties to the Arya Samaj, who championed self-help, industrialization, and attacks on the pro-rural stance of the Punjab government. Their paper, the *Panjabee,* blazed away with equal fervor at moderate rivals, the *Tribune,* and the *raj.* In its desire to arouse urban Punjabis, the paper published a series of distorted or inaccurate articles on British *zulum* (atrocities) that eventually led to the arrest and imprisonment of its staff. Despite the nationalist rhetoric, the two rival papers and their supporters spent more time attacking each other and putting forth inflated claims to leadership than creating a broad-based political organization.

The 1907 disturbances and their aftermath virtually destroyed the Lajpat Rai/*Panjabee* faction and drove it from tentative support of the Congress toward a more openly pro-Hindu stance; the *Tribune* and the Harkishen Lal faction fared little better, stuck with the label of being a pro-British, anti-Hindu group interested only in personal fortune and glory.[26] After 1908, the *Tribune* struggle with the Arya Samaj continued, as did its battle with Sikh reformers who were committed to strengthening their community at any cost.

Except for situations in which Punjabis discovered a common need to join hands against the British, such as that in the spring of 1919, the factions, the urban/rural split, and the communal tendencies already evidenced in Punjab politics continued to dominate local events. The *Tribune* briefly re-established itself as a leading nationalist paper in 1919, but once again, with the demise of a popular outbreak, the paper ceased to speak for anyone but a small portion of Punjab politicians.

THE PUNJAB EXPERIENCE IN PERSPECTIVE

How does the development of the Punjab press compare with the rest of India? The province did have specific patterns that distinguish its political history from that of neighbors. Most important were sub-regional economic and social networks, the shifting population balance of the major religious communities, and particular British policies affecting the constitutional context and milieu within which local politics flourished. Also increasingly important were two new factors — the creation of educational institutions associated with particular sects and interest groups, and the tendency of religious communities to identify with one language and literature (Muslims, Urdu; Hindus, Hindi; Sikhs, Panjabi). The essentially vernacular Punjab press both reflected and reinforced these trends.

Nevertheless, if one examines the recent literature on provincial politics across India, although the details and trends in the Punjab differ from other areas, the process of politicalization does not. The growth of elites, conflict among factions, reinforcement of regional languages and literary expression, and the British role in politics seem quite consistent.[27] Similarly, the resulting patterns of Punjab journalism may not be very different in kind or degree from those elsewhere. Although most Indian papers probably were parochial and only mildly nationalist, at best, in the nineteenth century, it is difficult to reach sound conclusions because with some notable exceptions, histories of the Indian press tend to be general and uninformative. Either they contain brief essays of uneven quality that narrate the history of a provincial press, or they are catalogues of individual press histories.[28] Another approach involves evaluating editorials and coverage of specific issues. Even one of the best, and most recent, studies on regional press development (K. Subramanyam, *The Press and the National Movement in South India, Andhra, 1905–1932*) suffers from the same tendencies. Although he presents an array of statistics and data, mixed with detailed narrative on editorial policy and British prosecutions, the author does not explain how the press actually functioned either as a profession or as an element within a regional political system.

If, as the Punjab case suggests, the Indian press should be seen within the evolving political and communication infrastructure of a region or province, then much needs to be done before a useful comparison or synthesis of case studies can be made. At least two pitfalls should be avoided in such research. First, scholars have to examine a frequently held assumption about the role of the press in political mobilization and the creation of public opinion. A broadening communication network does not necessarily lead to the growth of nationalism, and the existence of articulate champions of nationalism does not necessarily mold the political perspective of a population. On the contrary, what appears from the Punjab case is that the means of reaching a diverse population involves a complex of networks and linkages, in which the press may play only a small part. In fact, its role may be to reinforce existing cleavages and to exacerbate tensions rather than facilitate broad-based political action. Similarly, the effects of editorials and news coverage should be examined critically. That requires intimate knowledge of local politics and journalism as well as an ability to sort through both statistical data and personal accounts such as are found in memoirs and private papers.

Too often the scholar takes a short cut by relying on readily accessible British records. That suggests a second danger, namely, basing evaluation of press developments upon the documentation and perceptions of Imperial officialdom. In an effort to understand and at times to control the Indian press, the bureaucracy produced at least three types of record:

1. Weekly translations from the vernacular press (chosen for importance, organized by topic, and then circulated in printed form to district officials and intelligence specialists). These are found in state and national archives.
2. Annual reports on the Indian press, including background on editors and publishers, circulation, recent history, and comments on the "tone" and importance of each paper. Circulated confidentially, the reports became the basis for annual statistical compilations and political analysis, and have been preserved in police and political files.
3. Imperial, provincial, and district home/political/police files containing a voluminous assortment of documents on press prosecution, background on journals and journalists, and evaluation of trends.[29]

The difficulties inherent in using this material, probably the most coherent and comprehensive available to scholars interested in Third World journalism, should be obvious. The translations are random and usually out of context. Understanding their significance, especially when original files of the paper are not available, necessarily involves the tedious task of preparing background data on the paper as well as recreating the context within which it operated. The annual reports probably contain more or less accurate data on editors, proprietors, and the general history of papers (although that may vary sharply in quality and quantity), but the assessments suffer from the two inherent factors affecting the validity of political files in general — the degree to which British impressions and assumptions influenced the content and overall character of documents, and the persistent breakdown of an intelligence system that depended largely on informal networks and ultimately Indian informants.

We should know better, and yet virtually every study of the Indian press rests heavily on official sources. As in the case of any type of documentation, the British material has to be treated gingerly and evaluated against other material. With regard to journalism, this includes the back files of newspapers, biographies and manuscripts, and associational records. In many instances, these are available if the scholar leaves the archives and the comfortable library and follows a trail that may end in a dusty almirah or a long-forgotten record room. If that can be accomplished, and if the press can be placed accurately within the political and cultural milieu of the times, then we shall have a much better picture not only of how the Congress evolved, and of the role of journalism in that process, but also a better grasp of the problems and dynamics affecting the Indian press today.

NOTES

1. Surveyed in the following: Kenneth Jones, *Arya Dharm: Hindu Consciousness in the 19th Century Punjab* (Berkeley and Los Angeles, 1976); Ellen Gumperz, "The Modernization of Communication," *Asian Survey,* 2 (1968), 589–606; Ellen McDonald, "The Growth of Regional Consciousness in Maharashtra," *Indian Economic and Social History Review,* 5 (1968), 223–243; Yogendra Malik, ed., *South Asian Intellectuals and Social Change* (Columbia, Mo., 1972).
2. For example, discussion in S. Natarajan, *A History of the Press in India* (Bombay, 1962); Prem Narain, *Press and Politics in India, 1885-1905* (Delhi, 1970).
3. C. A. Bayly, *The Local Roots of Indian Politics* (London, 1975); Uma Dasgupta, "The Indian Press, 1870–1880," *Modern Asian Studies,* 11 (1977), 213–235, and *Rise of an Indian Public* (Calcutta, 1977); R. Suntharalingam, *Politics and Nationalist Awakening in South India, 1852–1891* (Tucson, 1974).
4. The historiography is reviewed in Barrier, "Regional Political History: New Trends in the Study of British India," in Paul Wallace, ed., *Region and Nation in India* (Columbia, Mo., 1985), 111–152; Howard Spodek, "Pluralist Politics in British India," *American Historical Review,* 84 (1979), 608–707. Especially noteworthy are recent books from Oxford and Cambridge, and articles in *Modern Asian Studies* (Cambridge University Press).
5. In addition to my publications on Punjab cited in this essay, two unpublished dissertations are particularly helpful on the indigenous roots of Punjab politics: Ian Talbot, "The Punjab and the Raj" and David Gilmartin, "Tribe, Land and Religion in the Punjab" (California, 1980). Also relevant are the sources and issues reviewed in Eric Gustafson and Kenneth Jones, *Sources on Punjab History* (Delhi, 1975).
6. See Barrier, *The Sikhs and Their Literature* (Delhi, 1970) and Jones, *Arya Dharm*.
7. Barrier, "The Punjab Government and Communal Politics," *Journal of Asian Studies,* 27 (1967-68), 523–39. Similar themes are discussed in the dissertations of Talbot and Gilmartin.
8. Barrier, "Punjab Politics and the Disturbances of 1907," (Ph.D. dissertation, Duke University, 1966), pp. 11–30.
9. Barrier, "The Arya Samaj and Congress Politics," *Journal of Asian Studies,* 26 (1967), 364–66. Also see V. C. Joshi ed., *Lajpat Rai Autobiographical Writings* (Delhi, 1965) and *Tribune* articles, December 1895, as well as the proceedings of the early Punjab political conferences (1895–1905).
10. Correspondence among Congress leaders (Naoroji Papers, Mehta Papers, National Archives of India) reflects disdain for Punjab tactics and leaders. On factions, see Jones, *Arya Dharm,* Gustafson and Jones, *Sources;* and Barrier, *The Punjab in 19th Century Tracts* (East Lansing, Mich., 1969).
11. For example, the numerous comments on opponents in the *Selections from the Punjab*

Vernacular Press, 1893 (National Archives of India), and the treatment in Kenneth Jones, "Communalism in the Punjab," *Journal of Asian Studies,* 28 (1968), 39–53, and Barrier, "Muslim Politics in the Punjab," *Punjab Past and Present,* 5 (1971), 84–127.

12. Patterns of earlier politics are discussed in Barrier, *The Punjab Alienation of Land Bill of 1900* (Durham, N.C., 1966).
13. On communalism, Barrier, *The Sikhs;* Jones, *Arya Dharm;* Gustafson and Jones, *Sources;* Barrier, *Punjab in Tracts.*
14. Barrier, "Punjab Government and Communal Politics," and Jones, "Communalism in the Punjab."
15. Awkward attempts of urban politicians to affect or represent rural interests are discussed in Barrier, "Punjab Politics," 45-110. On the Singh Sabhas, Barrier, *The Sikhs,* xxiii-xxxiv.
16. For example, consider the controversy over Muslim participation in the Congress, 1887-88 (Barrier, "Muslim Politics"), and the rancor surrounding the 1893 and 1900 Lahore Congress sessions (particularly letters to the editor and memorials in the *Tribune,* the *Arya Patrika,* the *Khalsa Akhbar,* and the *Civil and Military Gazette*).
17. On the Congress and the disturbances, see Barrier, "The Arya Samaj," and "The Punjab Disturbances of 1907," *Modern Asian Studies,* 1 (1967), 353–384.
18. Background on the Punjab press in Emmett Davis, *Press and Politics in British Western Punjab, 1836–1947* (Delhi, 1983) and Barrier and Paul Wallace, *The Punjab Press, 1880–1908* (East Lansing, Mich., 1970).
19. Extensive discussion of sources and issues may be found in Barrier, *The Sikhs.*
20. Jagjit Singh and Harbans Singh, "Singh Sabha Lahir," in Ganda Singh, ed. *Panjab 1849–1960* (Ludhiana, 1962), 123–140.
21. Information on Sikh journalism appears in Barrier, *The Sikhs,* pp. 75–88. My two articles on the evolution of Sikh journalism will be published shortly in the *Encyclopedia of Sikhism.*
22. For example, references in the June and July 1907, issues of the *Khalsa Advocate* and the *Khalsa Samachar.* Along with other Punjabis, Sikhs persisted in submitting "loyalty" petitions or holding meetings that cheered the British.
23. Letters to the editor and meeting reports in the *Khalsa Samachar,* June-December 1905.
24. Background on the *Tribune* in Barrier, "Punjab Politics," pp. 27–58.
25. *Tribune,* April 23, 1903. Congress leaders seemed happy to wash their hands of the Punjab. Wacha to Naoroji, December 19, 1903 (Naoroji Papers). Events and controversy summarized in Barrier, "Punjab Politics," pp. 101–110.
26. Barrier, "The Arya Samaj," p. 376.
27. For example, see four excellent studies on U.P. politics: Bayly, *Local Roots;* Francis Robinson, *Separatism among Indian Muslims* (Cambridge, 1974); Paul Brass, *Language, Religion and Politics in North India* (Berkeley and Los Angeles, 1974); Gyanendra Pandey, *The Ascendancy of the Congress in Uttar Pradesh, 1926–34* (London, 1978).
28. For example, S.P. Sen, ed., *The Indian Press* (Calcutta, 1967).
29. For problems inherent in utilizing papers as primary sources, see Edwin Hirschmann, "Using South Asian Newspapers for Historical Research," *Journal of Asian Studies* 31 (1971), 143–150. Background on the British documents and Imperial surveillance of the press is in Barrier, *Punjab Press,* pp. 2–4; and *Banned: Political Control and Controversial Literature in British India, 1907–1947* (Columbia, Mo., 1974).

The Diplomacy of Dependency: Content and Style in Nineteenth-Century Foreign Relations in India

AINSLIE T. EMBREE

In Rose Macaulay's novel, *The Towers of Trebizond*, Father Chantry-Pigg, the High Anglican clergyman, had trouble with the notice board outside his church when he used such words as Mass and Confessions. Young Roman Catholic vandals would write on it, "You have no Mass," or "He has no power to obsolve," while Protestants altered the reference to confession to read, "The Minister will be in church to give counsel."[1] One expects an analogous fate in announcing the topic: Indian foreign policy in the nineteenth century. It invites the obvious comment that India had no foreign policy in the nineteenth century, since it was the dependency of a great imperial power or, that, if it is admitted that there was a foreign policy, then it was British, not Indian. What this essay suggests is that the foreign relations of the Government of India, despite ulitmate control by Great Britain, expressed needs and interests rooted in the subcontinent, and that the content and style of this diplomacy was a formative legacy for modern India.

THE NINETEENTH-CENTURY STYLE

The argument for this particular interpretation of the foreign relations of the Government of India depends upon certain assertions that can be justified through copious archival material, but here the references must be both selective and somewhat capricious. The first of these assertions is that the Government of India pursued policies in foreign affairs in the nineteenth century that reflected the political, economic, and geographic realities of the Indian situation, with the impulse for these policies coming from within the structures of the bureaucracy of the Government of India, not of Great Britain. The second assertion is that these policies were the product of territorial control by a well-organized authority, and, given the fact of power, the alien origin of the ruling group is not the decisive factor. Certainly the fact that they were British made important differences in the attitudes of that ruling group to their perception of their responsibilities and the mode of their execution of policies, but one suspects that any strong power would have behaved much the same in relation to neighboring states. This argument depends to a considerable extent on a third assertion, that has to do with the way foreign policy was made and executed in India in the nineteenth century. When foreign policy became visible, that is, when the stage was reached for public pronouncement of policy aims and for the defence of their execution, London often seemed to be the place of origin. But in almost all major issues this is misleading. The conclusion that forces itself upon the close reader of the voluminous documentation of the external policies of the Government of India is that, to a quite extraordinary degree, decisions were made in Calcutta, but that these in turn reflected pressures from district officers, agents on the frontiers, and officials at the provincial capitals. The role of London was to demonstrate how actions that had been taken in India, often on the frontier itself, were the products of national policy, when in fact either the Home Government had been ignorant of the course of events or actively disapproved of them, but felt compelled to accept them. Curzon's activities in Tibet are, on one level, an exception to this generalization, but that they could proceed so far, and that the governor-general could have have expected approval, suggests, on another level, how the impulses for activities with repercussions not just for India but also for Great Britain, came from India.

But having said this, it is necessary to guard against pushing the argument too far in the opposite direction and to suggest that a concern for India was a major determinant of British foreign policy as a whole in the second half of the nineteenth century. This is an infinitely complex question, and it is arguable that British policies having to do, for example, with the Eastern Question, were no more determined by Indian considerations than was American involvement in Southeast Asia a product of concern for the integrity of South Vietnam. Linkages and relationships in foreign policies may be more apparent than real, masking issues quite other than those that seem to be determining events. There was an obvious need, based on the dependency relationship, for the foreign policy of the Government of India to seem to be congruent at every point with that of Great Britain; it is almost the reverse situation from that a modern client state that may wish, for internal political reasons, to assert its independence of the major power on which it is dependent. By the end of the nineteenth century, India had become a modern state in terms of bureaucratic structure, political stability, and, above all, through economic relations with the world community. Use of the rubric of imperialism has always tended to conceal the extent and signficance of India's entry into the modern system; for our purposes, it indicates India's links with the European state system as a whole, rather than just with imperial Britain.

A fourth assertion is that out of this background of an active and, in many ways, autonomous foreign policy, although masked by India's political situation, came what I have called a diplomacy of dependency. It is this that has provided the inheritance for India's foreign policy since 1947. Out of the nineteenth century came a style of diplomacy, a way of conducting foreign relation, that has shaped India's foreign contacts. This assertion, while tantalizingly relevant, is only touched upon in passing in this paper.

In attempting to characterize the foreign policy of India in the nineteenth century it is perhaps unnecessary to point out that "policy" is an obvious misnomer; that, like other countries, at best India followed "policies," which changed according to the dictates of external and internal pressures. But having made this admission, I believe it is possible to argue that two general statements can be made concerning the foreign relations of the Government of India at most periods from about 1830, that is, from the time when its authority was secure within penninsular India, up to the end of the First World War, when the energy of the government was increasingly absorbed in internal affairs.

The first of these statements is that the Government of India was unwilling to permit any genuinely independent country to exist on its borders. There was probably no explicit statement of this policy, but it is an interpretation that fits the realities of the Indian historical experience. The usual formulation of policy was that the government did not desire to control its neighbors; it did, however, insist on governments that were not hostile. The translation of this insistence on friendly neighbors into policy often led to outright conquest, as in the case of Burma, or, as in the case of Afghanistan, a combination of military intervention and diplomatic pressures.

The second characteristic of Indian foreign policy in the nineteenth century is expansionism. This is obviously related to the argument that the government was unwilling to have independent countries on its borders, but expansionism in the nineteenth century has another dimension. It has often been seen as a reflection of British imperialism, of the aggressive outward thrust of European power, and it would be perversely tendentious to deny validity to this conventional wisdom. But what can be argued from the inner history of that expansionism is that, to a remarkable degree, it grew out of pressures generated in India, not in Great Britain, and served what can only be described as Indian interests. The classic statement of the two points of view — the one that sees expansionism as an expression of foreign imperialism and the other that understands it is a definition of India's national needs — came in the interchange of documents in 1959 before the Sino-Indian border conflict. For the Chinese, the border dispute was, in Chou En-lai's words, "a complicated question left over by history," the result of acts committed when Britain had used India as its base for aggression.[2] For the Indians, however, these particular actions of the Government of India in the nineteenth century had been wholly consonant with national needs, since the borders defined territory that had been Indian for three thousand years, and enclosed peoples who had always regarded themselves as Indians.[3]

This insistence by the political heirs of the Indian National Congress on the inviolability of nineteenth-century frontiers has a note of peculiar irony since Indian nationalists from the 1880s up to the time of independence had expressed frequent hostility to the government's border policies.[4] The war with Afghanistan in 1878-1879 evoked more criticism from Indians than any previous action of the government; it was denounced as an extravagance that India could not afford, especially at a time when the government was unable to relieve the victims of the famine that had recently desolated large areas of India.[5] The annexation of Burma was condemned at the very first session of the Indian National Congress as "unwise, unjust, and immoral," and it was argued that since the annexations of Sind and Punjab were the outcome of the Afghanistan war, "the aggression of Russia might be said to be traceable to these early aggressions of our own British government."[6] The same sentiments were expressed twenty years later, when the Younghusband expedition to Tibet was denounced as "foreign aggression."[7] But this attitude should not be taken as wholly representative of Indian opinion, for there are frequent expressions of an almost strident militarism to be found in some Indian language newspapers in the 1860s and seventies. A Bengali newpaper chastised the government in 1864 for not having dealt severely enough with the Bhutanese who intruded into India, on the grounds that they were barbarous people understanding only force. In 1878 another paper called for a war to teach Russia not to interfere on the northern frontiers; if it did, Maratha horsemen would soon ride about the streets of Moscow.[8]

As was stressed in the beginning, the active foreign policy of the nineteenth century was the product of dynamism generated by a powerful Indian government that had mobilized the resources of the subcontinent, even though there was always the necessity fo making it appear to be congruent with British national interests and the product of initiatives from London, not Calcutta. The result was a peculiar pattern of diplomatic activity, a diplomacy of dependency. The nature of this style deserves full study in all its aspects, but here it will be illustrated by special reference to the search for frontiers for India in the middle years of the nineteenth century. The selection is not wholly arbitrary, since border problems occupied an enormous amount of the attention of the Government of India. This search for a defined frontier has usually been understood in terms of security, but other forces were at work in the process that reflected concerns other than security.

In the confrontation with China after 1969, India was undertaking what has been called the most difficut task a successor state can be required to perform: "the assumption of responsibility for a former imperial frontier."[9] During the years of the nationalist struggle, energies had been concentrated on relations with the administrative structures of the imperial power and, especially in the crucial years immediately before the transfer of power, on the tensions involved the competing nationalisms represented by the Indian National Congress on the one hand and the Muslim League on the other. Furthermore, the most urgent foreign policy issues in the last thirty years of imperial rule — the period of the coming to political age of most of the nationalist leaders — were almost wholly centered far beyond the Indian periphery. The militarism of Japan in the 1930s, the Spanish Civil War, and the rise of Hitler, were of passionate intellectual concern to men like Nehru, but they did not impinge in any immediate geographical sense on India. Concern with external frontiers was, on the whole, a new and disquieting problem for Indian nationalism.

The identification of national interests within India with the boundaries created by the former imperial power to define the limits of its expansion is an indication of their importance for the process of nation-building. In the perspective of historical development, territorial expansion, the most imperialistic of activities, and one almost wholly ignored by analysts of nationalism, was a crucial element in the making of India. In India, as in Europe, the nation-state is a modern phenomenon, and the delimitation of fixed and widely accepted boundaries is one of the most important characteristics of such states. Neither the ancient world nor feudal Europe, nor even the great powers represented at the Congress of Vienna in 1815, thought of nationality as coterminous with political frontiers. The boundary as a fixed line, marked on the ground, accurately represented on a map, and described in a treaty by two contiguous sovereignties recognizing each other's territory, is a feature intimately associated with the rise of the modern nation-state. Its introduction into the subcontinent profoundly altered interstate relationships. Territorial sovereignty in the subcontinent before the nineteenth century had meant, in pragmatic terms, the ability to collect revenue and to command the loyalty of local chieftains. The outer limits of such control could expand or contract, leaving untouched the central territories of a ruler. The modern concept of a border as a fixed line between two sovereignties was a political novelty that did not make good sense to traditional ideas of state power. This was the point the Burmese envoys were making when asked by the British in 1823 to show them where the boundary was, replied, "Our king knows the extent of his own dominion, and no one can set limits to it but himself."[10]

THE QUEST FOR STABILITY: 1765-1833

Students in India used to be asked as an examination question to trace Indian constitutional development from the Regulating Act of 1773 to the India Act of 1935, thus emphasizing the continuity of the legal framework of the Government of India. The same kind of question might be phrased for diplomatic history, because by 1773 the East India Company had begun to engage in diplomatic activity that suggested an autonomous power, if not a sovereign one. Even before the grant of the Diwani, the Company officials had signed a treaty with Manipur in 1762, with both parties treating each other as if they were sovereign states.[11] One of the claimants in a succession dispute had sought the Company's help, and the officials agreed, hoping, with an optimism based on a faulty knowledge of geography, that the new arrangement might lead to trade with China through the hills. It was also seen as a defensive alliance against the Burmese, who were then expanding their power into the hill areas. In this, as in subsequent exercises in diplomacy, stability, not just security, was the goal. The two are obviously related, but the distinction is useful in emphasizing a concern to create political conditions that would require a minimum use of resources on defence. "All revolutions must henceforward be at an end," Clive told the Directors in reporting the events of 1765, and, with the complicated exception of 1857, this proved true. I have suggested that the two characteristic features of the foreign policy of the Government of India in the nineteenth century were expansionism and the refusal to permit independent states to exist on its borders. In a somewhat paradoxical fashion, the aggression implicit in these attitudes was an expression of a quest for frontier stability. In the thirty years after Buxar, as the Bengal Government sought to define its Mughal inheritance, it made frequent wars on its neighbors, despite the prohibitions and denunciations from London. The style of diplomatic activity was not to vary much during the next century.

The first conflict between the Bengal Government and the Burmese was in 1749, when a Burmese army crossed the Naf River into Chittagong district in pursuit of refugees who had fled from Arakan.

In the crisis caused by the Burmese intrusion, the role of the district officers was, as in almost all such cases, decisive; their actions, not decisions by the Bengal government, set the pattern for later development. The civilian official in charge of the Chittagong district was Edward Colebrooke, and the commanding officer of the little army brigade was Lt. Col. James Erskine, whose field reports are detailed and perceptive. Although Colebrooke and Erskine differed sharply over details, they agreed that the Burmese intrusion should not become the occasion for a war with Burma. Not only had the Burmese commander not known that the British regarded the Naf as their frontier, but he saw no reason why they should object to his crossing it to recover his own subjects. His action, Colebrooke wrote to the Council in Calcutta, "tho' inexcusable under the admitted rules of conduct between polished nations may be explained without attaching any idea of premeditated invasion to the authority which deputed him."[12] The British were concerned with concepts of territorial integrity that meant little to the Burmese, who thought of sovereignty largely in terms of rights over subjects, which could not be abrogated by a boundary line. Colebrooke's insistence on taking into account the Burmese conceptions of sovereignty could not, however, be translated into actual negotiations. The Burmese government was unwilling to negotiate frontier problems; for them, this seemed an admission of the British frontier claims and of the rights of their subjects who fled from their territories.

The result was that no real contacts were made with the central Burmese government at Ava during these years, even though two missions were sent from Bengal, one under Captain Michael Symes in 1795 and the other under Captain Hiram Cox in 1796. Symes found the Burmese open and friendly, ready to make arrangements for trade and commerce; Cox a year or so later reported a hostile reception at the royal court, which he characterized as "an assembly of clowns," marked by cruelty, bad faith, and dishonesty.[13] Part of the explanation for the very different interpretations of the Burmese situation is to be found simply in the temperaments and styles of the two envoys. Having established contacts with the Burmese, Symes was content with being treated as a private visitor, whereas Cox was insistent on his role as a diplomatic emissary. The Burmese apparently had no objection to personal relations with foreigners, but formalized diplomatic and commercial relations with Bengal could not be fitted into their state system.

Perhaps more than any other single factor, the concern with borders and frontiers gave the East India Company in Bengal what Warren Hastings had called a polity "worthy of a rising state."[14] When the officials in London were still fretfully reminding their servants in Calcutta that "you should never appear as principals yourselves in any matter relative to the administration of the government,"[15] the Company had assumed the functions of actual political power. By 1800, the continuous pressures for definition of borders and the opening up of trade with China through the countries to the north had also given the officials in Calcutta experience in diplomatic negotiations. Almost without exception, the impetus for the actual negotiations had come from Bengal, not from London, with the Company's agents in such frontier districts as Purnea, Rangpur, and Chittagong making the decisive decisions.

From the arrival of Wellesley in 1798 to the end of the First Burmese War in 1826, the diplomacy of dependency was to a large extent submerged by the wars that transformed the Government of Bengal into the Government of India. But the wars themselves, as the famous polemics of the Wellesley era so spectacularly show, were the product of policies that had their origins in the autonomy of the Bengal Government and in the activities of its servants. Passing over the Wellesley era as well as the war with Nepal, the outbreak of war with Burma in 1823 provides another example of the nature of diplomacy in nineteenth-century India.

By the early 1820s political conditions made for an unstable frontier in the northeast. On the one side was British power in Bengal, engaged in a quest for internal stability, and emphatic in its need to prevent any intrusion into its territory. On the other side was Burma, with a dynasty no less desirous of asserting its internal authority and jealous of any restriction on its sovereignty. In such a situation, it was not the lack of natural frontiers but the existence of intervening territories with weak governments — Assam and the conglomeration of hill states of indeterminate political status — that led to conflict. The refusal of Burma to have normal trading relations, which was perhaps the major cause of the Second Burmese War 1852, was not a significant factor in the 1820s. Economic considerations find virtually no mention in the contemporary records. The emphasis is on borders, and the problem generated by what the British, from their point of view, regarded as the aggressive expansion of the Burmese, and the Burmese, from theirs, saw as a refusal by the British to acknowledge this legitimate sphere of influence.

The Burmese had intervened in the complex internal power struggles in Assam in 1817 when they supported a claimant to the throne by sending in an armed force. The significant British response to the Burmese annexation of Assam came from David Scott, who as magistrate at Rangpur was the chief British official in the border area, for it was his report that provided the Calcutta Government — and beyond it, London — with the interpretation of the Burmese presence on the Bengal frontier which largely determined the policy followed in subsequent years. Sensitive to changes taking place in his area, and possibly magnifying their importance, he urged upon the Calcutta officials the necessity of measures that they at first regarded as unwise but eventually accepted as inevitable. By 1822 it was clear to him that the Burmese were in control of Assam and had made it a province of their empire. This, Scott insisted, had radically altered the whole political situation in the area, with Bengal now having as neighbor, instead of the feeble Assamese administration, a powerful and warlike country.[16] What was needed was a forward movement into the whole area from Assam itself through the eastern hill states. This policy might lead to war with Burma, but Scott felt that the possibility of driving out the Burmese, and restoring a weak and presumably grateful government on a vulnerable frontier was worth the chance.

The logic of Scott's position became more attractive when the Burmese moved against the hill states of Manipur, Cachar, and Jaintia. The Bengal government was thus faced with the likelihood of having Burma as an immediate neighbor on an undefined and vague frontier in the eastern hills as well as in Assam. By this time David Scott was the agent of the governor-general for the whole eastern frontier region, and in continuation of the policy he had advocated for Assam, he urged that the Bengal government should work for the establishment of regimes in Cachar and Jaintia that would be independent of both the Burmese and the British, thus providing a neutral buffer zone between the two states. Coupled with this was his conviction that the people of Cachar, as of Assam, would rise in suport of any attempt to overthrow the Burmese.[17]

This belief in the possibility of establishing states that would be committed to friendship with India, but accepted by other powers as genuinely independent, is one of the most persistent of political ideas in nineteenth-century India, appearing again and again in the context of frontier policy. It would be difficult to imagine a situation in Indian frontier history where its application would have been practical, and certainly as Lord Amherst, the new governor-general, recognized, there was nothing in the events of recent years that suggested that the Burmese have been willing to agree to the neutralization of a frontier zone. His own solution for the problem of the hill states was to declare Cachar and Jaintia to be a "protected state" wholly within Bengal's "general system of defensive arrangements for the frontier."[18] The frontier of eastern Bengal was now thrust deeply into the hills.

How largely the acquisition of new frontiers on the eastern border was the product of forces within the Bengal government itself is shown by the reaction of the London administration of the East India Company to the reports of events during 1823 and early 1824. The Burmese, they pointed out, could hardly have been expected not to object to the vital annexation of the hill states by Bengal. The argument that Cachar had to be taken because it commanded the passes through which Burma might invade Bengal seemed to them particularly weak. "This may be said," they pointed out, "of any petty state lying between our frontier and the territory of any considerable power." The best way of avoiding disputes in this situation was not to get involved in the politics of the intermediate country.[19] But the London administration could do little more than protest the acquisition of territory and the declaration of war. The reversal of forward movements on frontiers was seldom a political possibility.

Here, as elsewhere, the problem of defending and defining frontiers had moved the East India Company toward the assumption of the role of an Indian power. The pressures came from within the context of Indian political life, and were not an extension of the interest of the British government. The whole sequence of events leading to the war with Burma demonstrated how far the Bengal government had moved in the direction of becoming an autonomous entity, motivated by the same political impulses that characterize any independent state. The concern with frontiers at one level can be seen as a problem in defence of the interests the East India Company had built up in Bengal, but there is more to it than this. The reactions of the officials and the arguments they used were those of the defenders of a nation-state, with such abstractions as "national honor" becoming applied to their conduct. It would be difficult to demonstrate any significant difference between the attitude of the foreign rulers of Bengal in the 1820s and those of the Indian Government in the 1960s in relation to borders and frontiers.

DIPLOMACY IN THE NORTHWEST

That statement is equally true of the shift of diplomatic interest to the northwest after 1833. During the next thirty-five years, the frontiers reached their approximate limits but were not very precisely demarcated, nor was there even general agreement as to what the limits of actual territorial control should be. During the next period, roughly from 1870 to 1914, the first actual demarcation of boundaries in the mountains, as distinct from the demarcation along the mountain edge that had taken place after the war with Nepal, was carried out. Even then much remained vague, but as far as British power in India was concerned, this marked the end of over a century of debate and negotiation.

The explanation that has seemed most satisfactory to historians, as it was for contemporaries, of the shift in interest that took place in the 1830s toward the northwest is that it was the product of fear of Russian expansion through Central Asia toward India. Russia was the only great power that had to be taken into serious consideration in India throughout most of the nineteenth century. The way in which this fear of Russia, or perhaps more exactly, the desire to prevent Russian expansion into areas where the Government of India was considered to have special interests, preoccupied the thinking of officials in India is easy enough to document. The printed literature is vast and the unpublished records provide almost inexhaustible sources for an explication of "the Great Game in Asia."

But despite the seemingly overwhelming evidence for giving fear of a Russian invasion the dominant place in any explanation of the foreign policy of the Government of India, this was not only — perhaps not even the major — determinant in the fascination the northwest exercised over so many minds. Some importance must be given to the old expectation for trade through the mountains to Central Asia. That later knowledge proved these hopes illusory does not detract from their reality. When Lord William Bentinck spoke as late as 1831 of the need for information about the countries between the Indus and Caspian "in aid of war or commerce,"[20] his equal emphasis on the two factors of trade and defense against Russia was probably justified. For men like Bentinck, to explain imperial expansion in terms of trade was not to give away a guilty secret but to provide it with moral justification.

An important aspect of the Government of India's diplomacy was fear of the effect Russian expansion might have on Indian opinion. References to "public opinion" are few in state papers meant for public circulation, as the Government of India neither then nor later wished to give any indication that it was responsive to public criticism, but there was widespread anxiety concerning the "moral effect" Russian expansion might have on the people and princes of India.[21] Continual talk of the Russian danger, it was feared, might tempt Indians to a reassessment of British power and the possibilities of seeking assistance from Russia.

Another factor in northwest frontier policy that must be taken seriously, even though it is more intangible and less amenable to definition and documentation, "the challenge of the frontier," the attitude of which Turner in the United States was the historian and eulogist.[22] "The challenge of the frontier" is a vague explanation, but it suggests something of the compelling appeal incited by unexplored regions, particularly mountains, on the periphery of known territory. Two quite separate facets of the meaning of this challenge are recognizable in the Indian situation, one personal — related to the individuals involved — the other political — part of the historical experience of the Government of India as an Indian power. The personal element included the appeal that the unknown and dangerous has always held for some men. Scarcely separable from this was the impulse toward geographical exploration that remained an abiding British passion. Intermingled with both was the shrewd assessment that reports from areas like Afghanistan and Central Asia might prove useful in advancing one's career.[23]

The element rooted in the Indian historical experience is more complex and tenuous: it depends upon the argument that strong powers in India move toward completion of territorial control of the whole subcontinent. Boundaries of Indian kingdoms were always essentially unstable, with the possession of power carrying with it almost a compulsion to expansion. But there was always a sense of incompleteness of empire, of a need to find frontiers where power could rest with the assurance that it had reached its logical limits. The mountain wall seemed a far more certain line of demarcation than did the rivers of the Punjab plains. Even before they were reached, it was argued that the frontier must be found beyond the mountains, or in the great plateaus beyond.

The long search for a "buffer state" in the northwest was the result. Metcalfe had argued that the Sutlej was the true northern frontier of India, with the Sikh kingdom of Ranjit Singh, and to a lesser extent the territories of the Amirs of Sind, providing all that was needed by way of a buffer.[24] But by the 1830s the durability of the Sikh Kingdom was being questioned, and the political structures of Sind were regarded as confused anachronisms. The obvious answer was to look beyond them to the Afghan country, to find in the mountains and plateaus a barrier to the Indian plains through the formation of connections that would, in Sir Alfred Lyall's phrase, create a buffer state, which would be placed under "political taboo as far as concerns rival powers whose hostility may be serious," and which by reciprocal understanding would be guaranteed against foreign aggression.[25] There were two possible general lines of action that might be taken in the creation of a client state: through subsidies and guarantees to make the acceptance of client status worthwhile to an incumbent ruler; or to overthrow a ruler and replace him with someone with claims to legitimate succession. Both policies were pursued in Afghanistan and the Punjab, providing the fullest scope for the diplomacy of dependency.

The archives of the Government of India and the abundant private papers of the period provide detailed evidence of the processes by which information was collected and decisions made. The agents on the frontiers were far more than collectors of data. They expressed their opinions vigorously, and the information they sent to their superiors was weighted to back up their views. In many cases, the reports that reached provincial headquarters or Calcutta were also intended to reach officials known to be sympathetic to the agents' views. "I presume to state my opinion," an agent wrote about the territory between Herat and Kabul, "that the occupation of these countries is an absolute necessity if there be any danger of an attack on the British possessions from the west or northwest."[26] The agent at Herat used the magic phrase: "Herat was the key to India."[27] Alexander Burnes, who had been appointed commercial agent at Kabul, filled his reports with accounts of Herat as a trade entrepot for Persia, Russia, India, and Central Asia. If it fell into Russian hands, he argued, India would lose all hope of participation.[28] That the fear of Russia was fed by agents, both British and Indian, is clear from the hundreds of intelligence reports emphasizing the Russian influence in the border lands.[29]

A curious by-product of this interest in Central Asia was what must be the first historical work to show that the Government of India had a special concern for its Muslim subjects. It was written by Arthur Conolly, the agent to the Khanates of Central Asia in the 1840s, to counteract the impression among the khans that the British were anti-Muslim since they had overthrown the Muslim rulers of India.[30]

The idea that the existence of a powerful state in India had transformed relations with the neighboring states so that expansion was a necessity found a vigorous, if eccentric, exponent in Sir Charles Napier. Beyond the existing political frontiers of the Government of India were, he argued, natural boundaries: on the northwest, the Indus; on the north, the Himalayas, on the east the Brahmaputra.[31] The space between was filled by "weak, uncivilized nations," that opposed commerce and left idle great tracts of land which could have yielded crops and a great river which could have been a highway for trade. This argument, that a nation by refusing to trade was acting in defiance of the law of nations, was often heard later in the nineteenth century, and found notable expression in Commodore Perry's mission to Japan. In India it was combined with the idea of natural frontiers. A powerful state did not even necessarily have to advance to its natural frontiers, for, in Napier's metaphor, a natural law was demonstrated in that "the larger body attracts the smaller."[32] In another physical science he found a further justification for extending the frontiers: "There is also as it were a chemical affinity to the larger one, for the people of Scinde, one and all, are our own in their hopes and aspirations."[33]

This has curiously modern ring, for in the early years of expansion in India, the argument, so familiar in later boundary discussions, that ethnic and cultural similarities of peoples should be considered in boundry making, was not often heard. By one of those curious ambiguities with which British rule in India is marked, it was Ellenborough, the model imperialist, who seems first to have seen that the choice of frontiers had implications for the development of India as a national unit. The new boundaries that were the legacy of the annexation of Sind would, he insisted, embrace all the peoples of India, giving them a new unity through freedom of internal trade and a uniform currency.[34] A careful regard for the interest of the people, "not the pecuniary advantages of the nation of strangers," could, he said, give India a future of limitless prosperity.[35] The contradictions between such sentiments and the aggression that ended in the annexation of Sind were resolved by the larger union of the Indian peoples that would follow from the introduction of the mundane instruments of internal free trade and a uniform currency, "I ought to look only to India," he wrote Wellington, "I must . . . act in the spirit of a native, not a foreign, governor.[36] This thought let to another: Delhi could soon became the capital of the Government of India. "To have in our hands the ancient seat of empire, and to administer the government from it, has ever seemed to me to be very great object."[37] Expansion toward the limits of the Mughal empire brought with it dreams of Mughal grandeur. This meant he must "act like Akbar."[38] "I must write and act for India, not for England," he said on another occasion, indicating how British governors-general became Indian rulers.[39]

This enthusiasm for conquest fits the conventional stereotype of the imperialist, but it is also a by-product of expansionist nationalism, with its search for national identity and its fulfilment of manifest destiny. Since Ellenborough and his lieutenants were British, their expansionist policy is not seen as nationalism, but any ruler of a strong Indian state might have acted in a very similar fashion. The British had reactivated that dream of an empire encompassing the whole of the subcontinent which has haunted the political consciousness of Indian rulers. Ellenborough's evocation of Akbar was more than bombast; it was a claim for territorial sovereignty that would define a nation.

The annexation of the Punjab provides another illustration of what can, with little violence to facts, be called Indian expansionism. According to Lord Dalhousie, only "old women and young ladies," among whom were included Henry Lawrence and members of the British Cabinet, opposed the annexation; the logic of events made it inevitable.[40] The government's agents in the area, notably Herbert Edwardes and James Abbot, supplied the evidence that could be used to justify annexation, while at the same time initiating actions that forced the Sikhs into offensive positions. In the diplomacy of dependency, such actions had to find a rationale in self-defence and morality, but Dalhousie's correspondence expresses what can only be called a nationalist ardor for rounding out the natural frontiers of India.[41]

THREE FRONTIERS

Throughout the last half of the nineteenth century, and on into the twentieth, the concern for frontiers remained central in the diplomacy of the Government of India, even though the main decisions had been made by 1860. By then, a peculiar characteristic of Indian frontiers that was of fundamental importance for all diplomatic activity was becoming increasingly explicit. This was that the Government of India in practice recognized three kinds of frontiers, necessitating quite special forms of diplomatic activity. These three kinds had long been foreshadowed in the government's practices, but in the last quarter of the century they received both practical manifestation and theoretical justification. There were, first of all, the frontiers of administration, with linear boundaries demarcated on the ground and defined on maps.[42] Up to these frontiers of administration, the government asserted its control with uniformity in laws and bureaucratic procedures with the rest of the country, with distinctions between citizen and noncitizen, and a clear notice to neighboring sovereignties that there could be no unauthorized intrusions. All of these are the commonplace features of a modern state. But beyond this frontier of administration in the northwest, north, and northeast was a kind of territory perhaps unique in the twentieth century to India: the unadministered frontier area. Such areas were not subject to regular administration, but when circumstances required, claims could be asserted, even when no outer boundary had been demarcated, to advance to a new defence position or for advantages in diplomatic negotiations. As the inheritor of unadministered frontiers after 1947, the Government of India found it expedient to insist that these areas had been an integral part of its inheritance.

To a nation-state, however, conscious of the need to assert national unity through the integration of all races, religions, and cultures into a common Indian nationality, the unadministered territories in the northeast, known as the Northeast Frontier Area, were a troublesome anachronism. The decision to incorporate the region in an administrative structure that corresponded to the rest of India met with fierce resistance from tribal leaders, who insisted that the new government was seeking to impose alien customs and language.

The third kind of frontier area was the one most lacking in geographic definition, and the source of most diplomatic concern. These were the frontiers of influence, beyond the frontiers of administration and the unadministered areas. These were the areas from which the Government of India sought to exclude any other great power, particularly Russia, and where, in effect, no genuinely independent power could exist without constant pressures and interference. Charles Trevelyan had argued earlier in the century, for example, for the complete subjugation of Nepal to prevent its becoming a base for intrigue against India.[43] For Trevelyan and others, the same argument held for making sure that Afghanistan was at least indirectly under the control of the Government of India. That more pressure was not applied against Nepal was probably due to its acceptance as belonging partly to the category of frontiers of influence, and partly, like Bhutan and Sikkim, to being recognized as an unadministered frontier area. The states in this third area were, in effect, to be protectorates of India.

After India became independent, Bhutan actually enhanced its status, gaining forms of sovereignty that it had not enjoyed in the nineteenth century, such as membership in the world diplomatic community, but the exigencies of border politics required Sikkim's formal absorption by India. The fate of both territories was, however, consonant with the stress lines of the nineteenth-century legacy.

The definition of the borders between Afghanistan and Russia in 1884 and the Durand Line in 1893 were the high-water marks of the frontier diplomacy of a dependent nation. The MacMahon Line, politically and geographically more dubious, was the final stage of the search for the frontiers of India under the last power to control the whole land mass of the Indian subcontinent. The whole process was marked by a discussion, partly practical, by a group of talented and knowledgeable men on the significance of the frontiers for India's future that was perhaps not equaled in relation to any of the numerous boundary decisions made elsewhere in the world during this period.[44]

Owen Lattimore, in his studies of China's frontier history, has insisted that to see the frontiers of the great empires only in terms of defence against intruders is to miss much of their significance. The frontier, whether a zone or a linear boundary, looks inward as well as outward: it is intended to set the limits for expansion from within. Efficient administration, taking into account economic resources and military requirements, has to decide how large a territory can be controlled and "to reach out too far beyond the periphery of this manageable whole is wasteful."[45] This is a quite precise way of rephrasing one of the great central arguments of modern Indian history. At the beginning of the modern period, one of the charges made against Warren Hastings was that he wasted the resources of Bengal on wars of expansion, and Wellesley had been recalled, after bringing vast new territories under British control, for the same reason. Then in the 1860s and 1870s came the great debate between the advocates of "Masterful Inactivity" and those of a "Forward Policy." One side, for which Sir John Lawrence was the spokesman, argued that India's resources did not justify expansion beyond the Indus; the other side, of which Sir Henry Rawlinson was a representative, insisted that the correct boundary of India's resources required such a "precautionary move."[46] Sir Alfred Lyall cautioned against making claims for territory without realizing that, whatever line was drawn, some expression of political authority had to be made. For this reason, he argued, "the political and financial condition of India renders it imperatively necessary to circumscribe as closely as may be possible, the extension of our dominion over the Afghan highlands, and this can only be done by settling authoritatively a consistent policy, based upon a plain recognition of definite objects, and careful, proportionate comparison of their value with the cost of obtaining them."[47] This is *realpoltik* of a kind to be commended to any expansionist.

In international politics, the new frontiers gave India a position in the world she had never enjoyed before. "On the west," Lord Curzon proclaimed, "India must exercise a predominant influence over the destinies of Persia and Afghanistan; on the north, it can veto any rival in Tibet; on the north-east and east it can exert great pressure upon China, and it is one of the guardians of the autonomous existence of Siam."[48] Modern Indian statesmen may share Curzon's sense of manifest destiny for India, but they would of necessity be more circumspect in expressing it.

From the very beginning of the British intrusion as a political force in Bengal in the middle of the eighteenth century, problems relating to the frontiers had absorbed the interests and the energies of the new administrators. Many of these problems were inherent in the geography of the regions they controlled; some were the product of the fact that the East India Company was, in a formal sense, the legatee of Mughal authority in Bengal; others derived from the position of Great Britain as a world power. Other problems, perhaps most, grew out of the understanding of sovereignty, especially in relation to neighboring powers, that was integral to the western state system but was a new factor in the political life of the whole Indian region. The search for solutions to frontier problems thus made diplomacy a central activity of the Government of India, even though it was often masked as an expression of British interests.

From this concentration on a narrow, if important, aspect of nineteenth-century diplomacy, are there any generalizations one can make about the diplomatic inheritance of independent India? The following are offered, with some trepidation. One is that the concern for the inviolability of frontiers that has been of such importance to contemporary India is one aspect of the nineteenth-century inheritance. As in the nineteenth century, more has been involved than security; the reality of boundaries is a reflection of the reality of the nation. Second, did not something of the nineteenth-century dislike of the pretensions of genuine independence by contiguous states linger on in the thinking of post-1947 India? And, with great hesitancy, is it possible that something of nineteenth-century expansionism, based, as I have argued, on a perception of Indian interests, has at times been present? Even if the response to these questions is an indignant denial, one can continue to argue that the style of foreign relations in India in the nineteenth century, at least in respect to frontiers, reflects concerns and interests that were essentially Indian, not British, in origin.

NOTES

1. Rose Macaulay, *The Towers of Trebizond* (London, 1956), p. 23.
2. *Notes, Memoranda and Letters Exchanged between the Governments of India and China, September-November 1959,* White Paper No. II (New Delhi, 1959), Letter from Chou En Lai to Nehru, 8 September, 1959.
3. *Ibid.*, Appendix F.
4. The government's border policies in many instances are cited in Bimla Prasad, *The Origins of Indian Foreign Policy* (Calcutta, 1960).
5. *Rast Goftar,* 29 December, 1878, in *Report on Native Newspapers: Bombay,* 1879.
6. *Proceedings of the First Indian National Congress* (Bombay, n.d., but apparently 1886).
7. *The Indian National Congress* (Madras, n.d., c. 1909), Part 3, p. 148.
8. *Som Prakash,* 28 December 1864, in *Report on Native Newspapers: Bengal,* 1863-64, and *Sabachar,* 1 April 1876, *ibid.*, 1878.
9. W. Kirk, "The Inner Asian Frontiers of India," in *Transactions and Papers of the Institute of British Geographers,* No. 31, 1962, p. 131.
10. Quoted in T.C. Robertson, *Political Incidents of the First Burmese War* (London, 1853), p. 18.
11. *National Archives, (hereafter N.A.); Home Public, Orig. Cons.*, 4 October 1762, No. 5.
12. N.A., For Pol. Proc., 27 March 1794.
13. *Quoted in* A.C. Banerjee, *The Eastern Frontier of British India* (Calcutta, 1964), pp. 138-139.
14. N.A., Home Dept., Orig. Cons., No. 1, 19 April 1779.
15. N.A., Home, Public, India Office Copies, 1766-67, 20 November 1767.
16. N.A., For. Pol. Cons., 26 July 1822, No. 50.
17. C.R.O., H.M.S. 660, Lord Amherst to Secret Committee, 23 February 1824, pp. 85–143.
18. *Ibid.*
19. C.R.O., H.M.S. 680, Secret Commitee to Gov. Gen., 4 August 1824, pp. 1–9.
20. N.A., For, Misc. Records, No. 261, Minute of Bentinck, 23 August 1831.
21. *Ibid.*, Memorandum, May 1831.
22. Frederick William Jackson, *The Frontier in American History* (New York, 1921)
23. R.H. Phillimore, *Historical Records of the Survey of India,* 4 vol. (Dehra Dun, 1948-1954) has many references of this kind.
24. J.W. Kaye, ed., *Selections from the Papers of Lord Metcalfe* (London, 1855), pp. 211-217.
25. Sir Alfred Lyall, "Frontiers and Protectorates," in *The Nineteenth Century,* 30 (1981), 315.
26. N.A., For. Dept., "Kabul Papers," Vol. 1, No. 1, Memoir by Lt. Pottinger, 3 December 1839.
27. *Ibid.*, No. 4, Memorandum by E.H. Todd, 2 October 1839.
28. N.A., For Dept., Pol. Cons., 31 January 1838, No. 38.
29. For a representative sampling of reports from agents stressing the Russian menace, see N.A., For. Dept., Pol. Proc., 11 Feb. 1935, Nos. 40–47, and 10 August 1835, Nos.

29–31. The accounts of the best-known Indian agent, Mohan Lal of Delhi, are found in Pol. Cons., 31 Dec. 1834, Nos. 104–105; 5 Dec. 1836, No. 7, as well as in the expurgated extracts published as *Travels in the Panjab, Afghanistan, and Turkistan* (London, 1846).
30. N.A., For Dept., "Kabul Papers," Vol. 3, No. 47, Conolly to MacNaughten, 26 December 1840.
31. Sir William Napier, *The Life and Opinions of Sir Charles James Napier* (London, 1857), II, 346.
32. *Ibid.*, p. 218.
33. *Ibid.*
34. Quoted in Robert Huttenback, *British Relations with Sind* (Berkeley and Los Angeles, 1962), p. 80.
35. Lord Colchester, ed., *History of the Indian Administration of Lord Ellenborough* (London, 1874), p. 65.
36. *Ibid.*, pp. 358–359.
37. *Ibid.*, p. 309.
38. Sir Algernon Law, *India under Lord Ellenborough* (London, 1926), p. 64.
39. British Museum, Add. Mss. 40471, Peel Mss., Ellenborough to Peel, 23 March 1843.
40. British Museum, Add. Mss. 36, 476, Broughton Papers, Dalhousie to Hobhouse, 15 August 1848, pp. 183–220.
41. *Ibid.*
42. Sir A. Henry McMahon, "International Boundaries," in *Journal of the Royal Arts*, 84, 1935, 4.
43. N.A., For. Dept. Sec. Cons., 25 October 1838, Trevelyan to John Hobhouse.
44. Ainslie T. Embree, "The British Concept of South Asian Borders," South Asia Seminar, University of Pennsylvania, 1982–1983, is a discussion of these ideas.
45. Owen Lattimore, *Studies in Frontier History* (London, 1962), p. 117.
46. Sir Henry Rawlinson, "The Results of the Afghan War," in *The Nineteenth Century*, 6, 1878, pp. 377–400.
47. Indian Office Library, Lyall Collection, Mss. Eur. F. 132137. Note by Sir Alfred Lyall, "On Afghan Affairs," 9 January 1879, and Minute, 8 Oct. 1897.
48. Lord Curzon, *The Place of India in the Empire* (London, 1909), p. 12.

A Conversation of Cultures: The United States and Southern Asia

MILTON SINGER

Mutual security depends on mutual understanding, and for understanding you have to have a conversation.

At home and abroad to talk and then to listen, to listen with the help of reason and reasonably to talk, is to strengthen us just where we can be so much stronger than the Soviets. It is to build the community of free minds, "the civilization of the dialogue."

Robert Redfield

It occurred to me as World War II was ending that in order to create a constituency for the concept of a United Nation we needed a program of this kind, in which people from all over the world could come to know one another and to understand and respect the traditions and cultures and values of other people.

Senator J. William Fulbright

Since the history, research activities, academic programs and degrees in Southern Asian Studies at the University of Chicago have been described in previous publications,* the present article will restrict itself to a brief account of the international climate of opinion in which the ideal of "a conversation of cultures" emerged, of how that ideal influenced foreign policy and educational programs in the United States, and in particular, the development of several experimental intercultural programs at the University of Chicago.

Emergence of the Ideal of a Conversation of Cultures after the Second World War

The idea of guiding the relations among nations by "a conversation of cultures" and "a civilization of dialogue" emerged as a worldwide ideal after the Second World War. The idea was articulated in the conference and round table discussions organized by UNESCO as well in the meetings of other international and national associations and societies, a few of which changed their names to bury their pasts as societies for colonial affairs.

At that time, in the 1940s, the idea of "a conversation of cultures" expressed the hope that international relations would be reconstructed on a basis different from that which led to the Second World War — imperialism and colonialism, master-race myths, psychological warfare, balance of power politics, chauvinistic nationalism. As an alternative means of conducting international relations, "the conversation of cultures" projected the old ideal of peace through mutual and equitable exchange of people, words, goods and services—an exchange that was both a precondition and a consequence of mutual knowledge among the nations of the world. Growing numbers of thoughtful people are now convinced that "to make conversation, not war" remains about the only survival path left open for mankind to follow in this nuclear age.

In the United States, post-World War II foreign policies included some attempts to contribute to "a conversation of cultures" with other nations. In addition to the Marshall Plan for Europe and Point Four programs, largely humanitarian programs for postwar reconstruction, there were also programs specifically designed to increase mutual exchange of people and knowledge. Among such programs were the United States Information Service libraries abroad, the State Department's cultural exchange program, the Peace Corps, the Fulbright and Hays fellowships, the Public Law 480 arrangement that bought publications from countries with counterpart funds accumulated from food loans and "gifts." Foreign and international programs funded by the Rockefeller, Ford, and Carnegie foundations and other nongovernmental organizations added significantly to these government fellowship, research, and aid programs.

In spite of the many difficulties and imperfections of these programs, deriving from maladministration, naiveté, and insensitivity, or from the operation of other policies which thwarted their aims, the programs have been widely regarded as sincere expressions of goodwill and a desire to help. But the critics of these programs have persistently asked whether goodwill and friendly gestures were enough, whether understanding of other cultures based on firsthand experience and scholarly knowledge was not also an indispensable ingredient for "a conversation of cultures." These critical questions were dramatized in literary portraits of an ugly American or European full of good intentions, carrying "the white man's burden" to help the "natives" but failing in the end because of his lack of knowledge and understanding of their history, their languages, their social customs and mores, their values and mentality, as well as their special conditions of living. Sometimes these portraits were set to cheerful music, as in "South Pacific" and "The King and I." Kipling's sad refrain, "East is East and West is West" somehow kept breaking through the musical comedy optimism, echoing the melancholy overtones of the white man in the East sounded by Conrad, Maugham, Forster, and by Puccini's "Madama Butterfly," and to some extent by Kipling himself, to mention only artists who were "white" themselves.

NATIONAL STEPS TOWARD INTERCULTURAL EDUCATION

Awareness of the problems of "the ugly American" and of the need to educate him in the cultures of other peoples broke into public consciousness and public policy with the passage by Congress of the first Fulbright Act in 1946. After that there followed about a decade's quick growth in cross-national programs for exchange of persons, for language and area training and research, for publications, performing arts, conferences, lectures, and seminars; libraries, professional associations, and journals. Some of these programs were authorized and funded by nationnal legislation, some by nongovernmental groups such as the Rockefeller, Ford, and Carnegie foundations; the learned societies, universities, and business corporations. Lines were not always easy to draw, since there were many joint and cooperative undertakings.

For Southern Asian Studies in the Unites States, this formative period was marked by a number of important milestones. These included the following:

1951 — Report of the Joint Committee on Southern Asia of the Social Science Research Council and the American Council of Learned Societies. The report surveyed present resources and needs, and made recommendations, most of which were in fact realized over the following decade. Professor W. Norman Brown, who had organized the first American university interdisciplinary program on South Asia at the University of Pennsylvania in 1946-1947, was the moving spirit behind the Joint Committee's report.

1956-1957 — The conversion of the Far Eastern Association into the Association for Asian Studies and the associated change in titles of the Association's journal from *The Far Eastern Quarterly* to *The Journal of Asian Studies.* These changes were made to accommodate the growing number of professional scholars working in Southern Asia, and were negotiated by an Ad Hoc Committee on Southern Asia under the leadership of Richard Park.

1956-1957 — National-level meetings of South Asianists to discuss mutual problems of teaching and research, such as the seminar on "Leadership and Political Institutions in India," Berkeley, organized by Richard Park; the conference on "Introducing India in Liberal Education" in Chicago, organized by myself and the staff of Chicago's Indian Civilization course; the conference on Library Resources for South Asia organized by Horace Poleman, Director of the Orientalia Division of the Library of Congress.

1958-1959 — The passage of the National Defense Education Act, which authorized, under Title VI, the designation and partial funding of Language and Area Centers at universities and colleges. Seven such centers were designated in 1959, including a South Asia Language and Area Center at Chicago, and more were designated later. Funds for predoctoral fellowships and for research were also made available under this act.

1962 — The passage of Public Law 480 (The Library of Congress Book Procurement Program), which brought to participating university libraries thousands of books and periodicals from South Asia (and other countries with counterpart funds). The titles were selected and, more recently, catalogued by a special staff of the Library of Congress (final decisions on which titles to retain were made by the university libraries). This has been the most important single program making contemporary publications from South Asia quickly available for American students and faculty.

1961-1962 — Establishment of the American Institute of Indian Studies (AIIS) by a group of American universities to support the teaching of Indian studies in the United States and research in India. The Institute offers fellowships for study in India to students and faculty with support chiefly provided from counterpart funds. In the 1960s the Institute added special programs of language instructions in India, a Center for Art and Archaeology in Banaras, seminars, and publications.

The proposal for establishing an American Institute of Indian Studies was first made in Norman Brown's 1951 Report to the Joint Committee on Southern Asia. The realization of this long-cherished dream of Professor Brown's owed much to the great esteem which both Indians and Americans felt for him as a gentleman, a scholar, and a leader.

A measure of what had been accomplished during the decade of formative growth of South Asian Studies in the United States from the joint SSRC-ACLS Committee Report of 1951 to the establishment of the American Institute of Indian Studies in 1961 will be found in *Resources for South Asian Language Studies in the United States* by W. Norman Brown (1960), and Richard Lambert's *Resources for South Asian Area Studies in the United States* (1962). Lambert also updated his report in 1973.

THE FORMATIVE PERIOD AT CHICAGO

The University of Chicago was an active participant in and contributor to the national-level programs and organizations on South and Southeast Asia that emerged after the Second World War. Chicago faculty people were active as members and officers in the national committees, associations, and societies such as the joint SSRC-ACLS Committee on Southern Asia, the Ad Hoc Committee on South Asia, the Committee on South Asian Languages, the Association for Asian Studies, the Asia Society, and the American Institute of Indian Studies, of which the University became a charter member.

In fact, the formative period for these developments of South and Southeast Asian Studies at the University more or less coincided with the formative period on the national scene, from the late 1940s through the 1950s. There had been some teaching and research on India, Burma, the Philippines, and Indonesia before the Second World War in several departments of the University. But this attention, while serious, had been intermittent, scattered, small-scale and unsupported by associated studies of the areas except for Sanskrit studies. With the organization of the University's Committee on Southern Asian Studies in 1954 to coordinate and support further development in this field, the University assembled over the next decade the faculty, library, and language resources that enabled it to offer undergraduate and graduate programs in Southern Asian studies. Most of the programs were distributed over twelve or thirteen departments in the Divisions of the Social Sciences and the Humanities.

Beyond making such programs available, these expanded and coordinated resources at the University improved the level of American conversations with the people of South and Southeast Asia in accuracy, depth, and mutual understanding.

Before attempting to describe the kind and level of intercultural conversation started at Chicago, it is important to take note of the special supporting conditions that facilitated Chicago's development of South Asian Studies (as well as its other area and international studies). Three conditions were basic, I believe: the availability of outside funds, the administrative structure and leadership of the University, and the initiatives and persistence of a small group of faculty.

No university in the United States is well enough endowed to afford from its regular budget the kind of expansion of faculty, library, language laboratory, and predoctoral and postdoctoral fellowships for training, travel and research, or to build on its own a first-rate language and area program. Without the institutional grant and fellowship programs of the major foundations — especially Rockefeller, Ford and Carnegie — and of the Fulbright-Hays Act, the National Defense Education Act, Title VI, or PL 480, neither the University of Chicago nor any other such institution would have progressed very far toward establishing a center for South Asian studies.

A second facilitating condition was the flexible and open administrative structure of the University of Chicago, which permitted the formation of interdisciplinary, interdepartmental, and interdivisional committees, centers, and institutes. Some of the University's administrative officers recognized that the organization of scholarly resources for the study of regions such as South and Southeast Asia could not be accommodated in separate departments and would require inter- and supra-departmental administrative structures. They also encouraged the innovative programs with the promise that those which proved educationally successful would be incorporated into regular University budgets.

One significant measure of such incorporation may be indicated by the fact that ten out of the fifteen members of the Department of South Asian Languages and Civilizations are now on tenured appointment, and two of these have recently been named Distinguished Service Professors (Edward C. Dimock and A.K. Ramanujan).

In addition to the availability of external funds and a flexible administrative structure, a third condition that facilitated the development of the University's program in Southern Asian studies was a small group of faculty willing to take the necessary initiative and to cooperate in coordinating programs of studies. Most of these were not specialists who had been trained in South Asia language and area programs. In many cases, their knowledge of the area, and its people and cultures, was derived from wartime and immediate postwar experience. They traveled and lived in the area in the armed services, or as civilians on special government assignments. Their experience as teachers or students in the army language schools, the Army Specialized Training programs, and the Civil Affairs Training programs showed them ways to improve educational methods. In the immediate postwar period, they took advantage of opportunities for travel, study, work, research under the Fulbright and other fellowships, the United Nations relief agencies, UNESCO, and other societies.

When these faculty members returned to their regular duties at the University they drew on their wartime experience and immediate postwar travels in their teaching and research. They joined with colleagues and educational leaders in discussion and cooperative planning of new forms of international education. At Chicago one of the early results of these cooperative efforts was the formation of the Committee on Southern Asian Studies in 1954. But this was only one of several such groups that were formed at the University in the 1950s. Fred Eggan established a

Philippine Studies Program; Bert Hoseltiz and several colleagues founded a journal and a Center for Economic Development and Cultural Change in the same year; Sylvia Thrupp founded her journal, *Comparative Studies in Society and History*. Comparative and international programs were also launched at this time for the Comparative Study of New Nations (Shils, Fallers, and Geertz), International Relations (Morgantheau and Kaplan), Economics (Schultz, Johnson), Law (Rheinstein), Linguistics (McQuown, Hamp), Literature (Stankiewicz, Dimock), and History of Religions (Kitagawa, Eliade). These new groupings were mutually reenforcing and sometimes overlapped, and were to some extent competing for the same sources of outside funding. Eventually they were administratively unified in a Center for International Studies with Chauncy D. Harris as director. This Center also included other language and area centers, and committees that had meanwhile been organized in Far Eastern, Middle Eastern, Slavic and Balkan, African, and Latin American studies.

A NEW KIND OF AREA STUDIES: THE REDFIELD MODEL

The problem of finding a basis for intellectual unification for these proliferating area, international, and comparative studies within a framework of concepts that would make scholarly and educational sense was a more difficult one, at Chicago and elsewhere. Robert Redfield, anthropologist and Dean of the Division of the Social Sciences from 1934 to 1946, was one of the first to question the adequacy of the wartime organization of "area studies" as a model for postwar programs in universities. At a 1944 conference on the organization of postwar area studies sponsored by the Social Sciences Research Council, Redfield proposed an alternative model: a long, integrated, and intensive study of the languages, history, economics, government, society, anthropology, and arts of Russia, China, India, and Latin America. In Redfield's model the different disciplines would be brought into considered relation to one another with reference to each of these regions, but the unifying conception of such studies would be anthropological and cultural.

"For the conception that would give unity to the effort would be not so much the spatial fact that China or Russia or Latin America is one part of the earth's surface, as the fact of culture. These students would all be concerned with a traditional way of life that had maintained a distinguishing character over a long time, to great consequence for mankind. A literate people expresses its traditional way of life in what is written; and every people expresses it in institutions and customs and everyday behavior. . . . The regional program in research may take the form of long study of the great world cultures.

"We shall . . . have one or more excellent sets of different colored glasses through which to see and correct our preconceived notions. What the study of primitive societies now contributes to education will then be attainable through study of important world civilizations with the aid of specialized disciplines" (quoted in Singer 1976).

The idea of studying traditional ways of life or cultures holistically and comparatively was, of course, already a familiar approach to anthropologists in the 1940s. But such an approach had been chiefly applied to nonliterate, primitive, and tribal cultures. Redfield's suggestion that the approach could be extended to the organization of area studies through interdisciplinary studies of a few selected living civilizations and their great literate traditions was a novel and challenging one, even for anthropologists.

In this own studies of peasant and urban communities in Mexico and Guatemala in the 1930s, Redfield had already taken the first step towards "a social anthropology of civilizations," as he later called the approach, by a simultaneous comparison of four Yucatan communities along a continuum or "gradient" of folk to urban culture. But since the "great tradition" of Mayan civilization had been pretty well decapitated by the Spanish conquest, Redfield did not feel a need to incorporate historical, literary, and textual studies into his approach. His conception of civilizations as historic structures and organizations of great and little communities, of great and little traditions, persisting, interacting, and changing, emerged when he turned after the Second World War to China, India, the Middle East, Europe, and "the great traditions" of their civilizations.[2]

Redfield's proposal for organizing "area" studies around groups of scholars from different disciplines prepared to devote themselves to long and intensive study of the cultures of selected living civilizations was not quickly taken up. The methodological and financial problems seemed forbidding. Redfield himself was given an opportunity to encourage the formation of such interdiciplinary groups when in 1951 the Ford Foundation made the first of several grants to the University of Chicago for intercultural studies under Redfield's direction. This grant of funds was not at the outset intended to support the intensive study of any particular civilization. It was rather intended to support the exploration and development of methods for characterizing and comparing civilizations. Redfield saw the problem as one of developing widespread knowledge of the differences and similarities among different civilizations and of the common humanity underlying them through a cooperative effort among scholars all over the world.

As these explorations of methods for characterizing and comparing civilizations proceeded, based chiefly in a continuing "Comparison of

Cultures" seminar at the University of Chicago, several groups of scholars were found who were already engaged on specialized intensive cultural studies of specific civilizations and who expressed a willingness to consider some of the questions being raised by the project. Such were The Committee on Chinese Thought, under the leadership of Arthur Wright and John Fairbank, a group of Islamicists organized by Gustave von Grunebaum, and several groups of social anthropologists and Indianists working in India who were assembled by McKim Marriott and myself. Besides these groups of specialized scholars of particular civilizations, the Redfield project also supported promising research by individual scholars on the world views of peasants in Middle America, (Charles Leslie, Calixta Guiteras-Holmes, E. Michel Mendelson), and on historical and philosophical methods of understanding other cultures (F.G. Friedman, Eliseo Vivas, Arnold Toynbee). A conference organized by Harry Hoijer of linguists, anthropologists, psychologists, and philosophers assessed the Sapir-Whorf theory of the relations of language to thought and behavior and provided the landmark volume *Language in Culture*, in 1953.

Redfield's participation in the Ford project was not confined to administrative and financial matters. He articulated the animating vision of "a conversation of cultures" and himself charted some of the unexplored territory to be traveled in his three books, *The Primitive World and Its Transformations*, 1953; *The Little Community*, 1955; and *Peasant Society and Culture*, 1956. In three lectures, delivered of the Behavioral Sciences Center just before his death in 1958, and intended as drafts for a little book on civilizations, he began to develop his ideas on how to think about a civilization.[3]

AN UNDERGRADUATE INTRODUCTION TO SOUTH ASIAN CIVILIZATIONS

Redfield's eassy on "Thinking about a Civilization" introduced the readings and lectures in the College's introductory course on Indian Civilization launched in the autumn quarter of 1956, and was also given as a paper at the University of Chicago conference on "Introducing India in Liberal Education," in 1957. The latter had been convened to consider alternative ways of organizing such courses. Indeed, the influence of Redfield's approach to understanding living civilizations as wholes went beyond the circumstance of being presented in an opening lecture. The spirit of that approach infused the entire early organization of the Indian Civilization course and, to a lesser degree, the cognate Islamic and Chinese civilization courses, which constituted the first phase of the College's non-Western Civilization program. In the first three years,

1956-1959, of the Indian Civilization course, for example, the organization of the syllabus, readings, lectures, and discussions roughly followed the model sketched in Redfield's "Thinking about a Civilization": a holistic and comparative conceptual framework for the civilization guided by a direct acquaintance with the culture and its expressive utterances and representations, and by collections of factual information about it.

The first quarter of the Indian Civilization course dealt with the changing dimensions of society and culture on the subcontinent (language, religions, culture; land and people; social structure; village and town; civilizational change; worldview and ethos). This first unit was taught by three anthropologists: Bernard Cohn, McKim Marriott, and myself. The second quarter dealt with the classical heritage ("The Great Tradition") of ancient and medieval India and was taught by two Sanskritists, George Bobrinskoy and J.A.B. van Buitenen; and the third quarter dealt with the emergence of the independent national states of India and Pakistan, taught by a modern historian, Stephen Hay, and a political scientist, Myron Weiner.

The threefold division of the course was not rigidly drawn, for much of the planning of the course was joint; we often listened to each other's lectures, followed a discussion section through the year, and tried to read all the course readings. Films, musical and dance performances, demonstrations of rituals and other expressive aspects of the culture were an integral part of the students, and the faculty's shared experience in the course. This undergraduate course quickly became a forum where the specialists' conversations about the cultures of South Asia established a community of scholars who in more specialized courses and study trips taught the languages, literatures, and the arts; the religions, philosophies, and sciences; the customs, laws, politics, economics, and history needed to carry on a dialogue about the cultures and civilizations of South Asia.

A measure of the vitality and viability of Redfield's civilizational approach is provided by the fact that about thirty years after his lecture on "Thinking about a Civilization," the Indian Civilization Course, now broadened into a South Asian Civilizations course, has kept the spirit of that approach alive and, in fact, returns to the three-part organization of 1956-1959. The Redfield approach also stimulated the organization of B.A., M.A., and Ph.D. programs in Southern Asian studies, and civilizational studies in other areas. These recent developments have increased the number of civilizations being studied intensively at the University and have also deepened the levels of analysis and understanding attained by the approach.

FROM ETHNOCENTRIC IMAGES TO SCHOLARLY KNOWLEDGE

For the civilizations of South and Southeast Asia, evidence of these developments is provided by the publications of COSAS members. Even when written for nonspecialists, their work shows a deep and intimate knowledge of the languages, culture, social institutions, and history of the people they deal with. It is not simply the direct acquaintance with a particular festival, person, literary or architectural expression which accounts for the achievement of understanding. One needs also to know how such particulars fit into a context of customs, institutions, language, and arts. Presupposed also in this process of getting to know another civilization is a command of some scholarly discipline — anthropology, art, history, linguistics, philosophy, theology, or politics. We have tended to assume that most of these disciplines as developed in the West have a universal validity and apply to all societies and cultures. Anthropology, geography, and history have occasionally questioned these assumptions, and have tried to counteract the ethnocentic bias of Western scholars. The formula proposed by anthropology for avoiding ethnocentrism was to try to understand other cultures in their own terms, "to grasp the native's view of *his* relation to *his* world," as Malinowski put it in his *Argonauts of the Western Pacific*.

The overcoming of ethnocentric bias and the acquisition of the kinds of direct acquaintance, information, and knowledge of the cultures of Southern Asia leading to an understanding of them in their own terms has been a difficult and long undertaking depending on the work of many different kinds of people. The missionary, the soldier and diplomat, the colonial administrator, the scholar have all contributed to the knowledge and opinion, the images and "scratches on our minds" through which the West has seen Southern Asia.

> A story which seems to have impressed both the Greeks and Romans concerns two Indian ascetics, called in Greek accounts "philosophers" and named Kalanos and Mandanis. The story is derived from Oneskritos, one of Alexander's officers who was sent to find the sages. Alexander had heard that they went about naked, were inured to hardships, and held in highest honor, but would not go to others when invited. Oneskritos found some outside of the city (Taksasila) sitting or lying naked in the hot sun and talked with two of them. Kalanos, the younger, told Oneskritos that if he wished to hear him he should strip off his clothes and lie down naked on the stones to listen. Mandanis, the oldest and wisest, rebuked Kalanos for his insolence and said he would talk with Oneskritos. He praised Alexander for

> desiring wisdom and for being the only philosopher in arms he had ever seen.
>
> "I am entitled," he added, "to indulgence, if while conversing by means of three interpreters who, except for language, understand nothing we say any more than the vulgar, I am unable to demonstrate the utility of philosophy. One might as well expect water to flow through mud."

Given the large number of languages in South Asia as well as the sophistication and variety of arts and sciences, Mandanis' complaint about the difficulties of communicating with Westerners is still current in South Asia. The complaint is somewhat mitigated by the fact that many in South Asia know European languages, especially English, and that some Westerners have acquired fluency in the languages and literatures of the region. Both kinds of mitigation are well illustrated by members of Chicago's Department of South Asian Languages and Civilizations, three of whom are tenured native speakers (A.K. Ramanujan, K. Bahl, C.M. Naim). In their cooperative contributions, members of the Department provide overall historical surveys of South Asian languages and literatures, as well as more specialized grammars, readers, and translations in Sanskrit, Hindi, Urdu, Bengali, Tamil, and Rajasthani. Less regular instruction has also been provided on demand in Gujarati, Maharathi, Kannada, and Oriya. The level of language proficiency required of Ph.D. students in the Department is set at the equivalent of four years continuous study of a language. In addition, a stream of original translations, commentaries, criticisms, and interpretations in prose and poetry, flows from the faculty of language and literary specialists, cultural and art historians, linguists and philosophers. A Southern Asian Reference Center was organized by Maureen Patterson in 1959, with a Reference Collection, Catalogues and Bibliographic Services. The long, integrated study of the languages and history of a great world culture, envisaged by Robert Redfield, began at Chicago in 1960.

From Outside to Inside Views

Redfield particularly emphasized the importance of grasping the "inside view" in trying to understand another culture. He did not, however, think that it was possible to dispense with the "outside view." The characteristic outlook of a people on their world, their "world view," should be grasped as far as possible from the "inside" as it appears to members of the culture; their conceptions of the good life, their value systems, should be formulated in indigenous terms. There are features of every society and culture, however, that are more appropriately described from an objective point of view: its demography, ecology, subsistence economics, kinship and social structure, even some of the psychology of personality. The anthropologist's conceptual and operational tools for describing and analyzing cultures and civilizations must therefore include both the subjective and the objective, the inside and the outside points of view.

The outside point of view is clearly represented by the objective kinds of information collected, analyzed, and interpreted, respectively, by demographers, economists, geographers, and economic anthropologists. It is equally clear, however, that these "hard science" kind of specialists become "softened" when their analyses and predictions are sensitive to considerations of political, social, cultural, and even psychological factors. Food, population, land and urban settlements seem irresistible enough forces, but they are forces that move in response to social and personal values, cultural beliefs and values, political organization, and technological innovation. There is a theology and ontology of cows and rice as well as an economics and agriculture.

Until about 1950, anthropologists, including Redfield, regarded the analysis of kinship and social structure as one of the more exact, universal, and scientific branches of anthropology. Kroeber's suggestion in 1909 that kinship systems were "psychological," "semantic" systems that varied with the culture was not taken very seriously until it was revived and elaborated in 1956 by Lounsbury and Goodenough. Levi-Strauss led the field in the same direction when he suggested in the 1940s that behind kinship terminology and kinship behavior, as well as other cultural phenomena, lurked the hidden "deep structures" of the unconscious categories of the human mind. Extending these views to American and other systems of kinship, David Schneider and his students dissolved the last vestiges of an objective, universal biological basis for kinship systems. What kinship is all about, according to Schneider, is a system of "diffuse, enduring solidarity" defined by and symbolically expressed in the terms of a given culture (Schneider, *American Kinship: A Cultural Account* [1984]; *A Critique of the Study of Kinship* [Ann Arbor, 1968, 1980]).

Ron Inden and Ralph Nicholas as students at Chicago were stimulated by Schneider's conception of kinship and by his study of American kinship in particular, and eventually tried to study Bengali kinship in terms of Bengali culture as Schneider studied American kinship in terms of American culture. The fact that their study of Bengali kinship turned up significant differences from American kinship is not as surprising as that a conception and method of kinship analysis developed for the study of one culture should turn out to be fruitful in the study of another culture — precisely because the results highlighted the differences between Bengali views of kinship and American views. The study of kinship was converted from an objective study of biological facts of genealogical descent to a cultural analysis of "native categories," conscious and unconscious.

The feasibility of such a shift from an "outside" to an "inside" point of view depends on the intimacy of direct acquaintance with a culture and its symbolic representations. Where the anthropologist is a "native" of the society he studies, as is the case with Schneider's study of American kinship, or M.N. Srinivas' study of Indian social structure, he usually already has a level of familiarity with the culture that is quickly deepened with specialized study. Where the anthropologist is not a "native," he has to begin with almost a child's level of knowledge of the culture and slowly learn his way around — unless he has previously studied the language, history, and society. Inden and Nicholas did not begin their studies of Bengali kinship at a child's level. As students in Chicago's South Asia program, they both studied Bengali language and literature, North Indian social and cultural history, Hindi and Sanskrit. Inden, as an historian, specialized in ancient and medieval Sanskrit and Bengali texts, but also did fieldwork among rural and urban groups. As an anthropologist, Nicholas made several field studies of ecology and ritual in West Bengal, but complemented his observations and interviews with the use of medieval Bengali texts.

TOWARD A SOCIAL ANTHROPOLOGY OF CIVILIZATIONS

This unusual combination of fieldwork with textual studies, of anthropology and history, prefigured in Redfield's conception of a social anthropology of civilizations, is becoming a distinctive mark of the teaching and research in Chicago's program of Southern Asian studies. While the textualists illuminate their translations of linguistic and literary texts with a knowledge of social and cultural contexts, the social scientists are extending their studies of social, political, and economic institutions to include knowledge of relevant historical and classical texts.

McKim Marriott, who has applied this approach to a new interpretation of South Asian caste systems (see Marriott and Inden, "Caste Systems," *Encyclopedia Brittanica,* 15th edition, 1974) organized a seminar at Chicago during the spring quarter of 1977 on "Person and Interpersonal Relations in South Asia: An Exploration of Indigenous Conceptual System," in which Sanskritists, linguists, anthropologists, sociologists and psychologists participated. Some of these were "native" South Asianists. The seminar was sponsored as one of a series by the ACLS-SSRC Joint Committee on South Asia. The planning group of the Joint Committee recommended seminars and workshops to explore and test the value and limits of various South Asian conceptual systems, that is, the tools or frame of thought, or the structures of ideas, that define order, and create meaning in individual and social perceptions in South Asia (Szanton, "South and Southeast Asia: New Concerns of the Council," SSRC, *Items*, 1976).

This growing interest in indigenous conceptual systems among social scientists reflects "a widespread recognition of the limitations of Western concepts — too often presumed to be universal — in the study of non-Western societies, and an attempt to develop alternative means of analysis." The planning group is also convinced that special attention to this difficult area "could lead to major breakthroughs in (a) interpreting the meaning of a great deal of social and cultural phenomena" in South and Southeast Asia, and (b) "developing new analytical frameworks applicable beyond the region" (Szanton, *ibid.*).

Whether these high expectations will be realized remains to be seen. The preliminary results of this approach in terms of a deeper understanding of Bengali kinship and South Asian caste systems certainly justify its continued exploration and application to other domains of South Asian civilizations and to other civilizations as well.[5]

SYMBOLS, MYTHS, AND CULTURAL PERFORMANCES

The social scientist's interest in reading and using indigenous texts to deepen his understanding of a given civilization's systems of thought is being extended to the interpretation of political, economic, cultural, and psychological systems. A recurring theme in this mode of interpretation is that the human artifacts and events of the earthly world are microcosmic icons of a wider heavenly cosmos peopled by gods and other superhuman beings, and that the meaning and norms of human affairs in the earthly world are to be discovered for the peoples concerned in the cosmic patterns and divine acts that govern the heavenly cosmos. When human affairs go awry, they can be set aright by the intercession of the gods descending to earth in human form or by the powers of those saintly human beings — Bodhisattvas, jivan muktis, Mahaviras — who linger on earth to help ordinary mortals.

Underlying such interpretations of South and Southeast Asian cultures is a method of analysis which takes as its units of observation "cultural performances," those multimedia enactments in which the members of a society exhibit to themselves and to outsiders aspects of their history, values, cosmology, and social structure encapsulated in symbolic representations.[6]

The Redfield approach to the study of civilizations as historic structures of small and large communities, of little and great cultural traditions, has proved most fruitful in Southern Asia. The applications of the approach included in such volumes as *Village India* (1955) edited by Marriott, *Traditional India* (1959) and *Krishna: Myths, Rites and Attitudes* (1966) edited by myself, and *Structure and Change in Indian Society* (1968), edited by Singer and Cohn, testify to the potential value of the method for integrating the objective and subjective views, and contextual with textual analysis.

CONCLUSION: TOWARD A CIVILIZATION OF THE DIALOGUE

The general movement toward an understanding of the civilizations of Southern Asia represented by publications and research in recent years goes, then, from the European and American "outsiders' " unconscious images and conscious concepts whose construction is guided by direct experience and information, to the "insiders' " ultimate theological and cosmological beliefs and world views. Between these two poles are the translations and interpretations of selected texts of the great and the little traditions and the objective social science analysis of food and population, of rural and urban problems.

Jawaharlal Nehru, in the closing speech at a UNESCO conference in New Delhi in 1951, *The Concept of Man and the Philosophy of Education in East and West,* said that he had always resisted the idea of dividing the world into the Orient and the Occident, and that he was convinced that the world faced two great common problems: whether we can avert the disaster that threatens to result from progress, and whether the democratic process can be saved from deterioration consequent on its unthinking use by the mass of mankind. During the sessions of the Indian Philosophical Congress in 1954 a plan was formed to study the problems "Human Relations and International Responsibility." Richard P. McKeon, Professor of Philosophy and Greek in the University of Chicago, was asked to conduct preliminary symposia in eighteen colleges and universities in India: Mysore, Bangalore, Madras, Calcutta, Visva-Bharata, Andhra, Nagpur, Bombay, Poona, and Hyderabad, and he presented a report of the results to the meeting of the Indian Philosophical Congress in Pardeniya, Ceylon, in December, 1954.[7]

Seven specific issues were discussed in these conferences: equality, neighborliness, violence, international communication, the universality of art and religion, cultural loyalties, and the humanities and the classics. The dialogues of these meetings exhibited a tendency to get behind the opposition of philosophical disputation and partisan propaganda to the discussion of common problems. It is in meetings and discussions such as these that the conversation of cultures can become a civilization of the dialogue.

POSTSCRIPT

In spite of a quarter century's creative growth and development of Southern Asian Studies at the University of Chicago, and in spite of the substantial institutional incorporation of these studies into undergraduate and graduate programs, the field is now facing two imminent shocks — the possible dismantling of the PL 480 library acquisitions program administered by the Library of Congress, and the exhaustion of funds for the American Institute of Indian Studies. Both of these eventualities may occur because of the exhaustion of the PL 480 excess currency fund of rupees. As Richard Lambert's 1984 report *Beyond Growth: The Next Stage in Language and Area Studies* concludes, if the AIIS were to disappear, "the most important collective activities in South Asian Studies would disappear with it" (p. 418). When the Library of Congress PL 480 acquisition program expires, equally, "a major new acquisition and cataloging program for the field, supported in the main from the centers' own funds, will have to be developed" (Lambert 1984: 419).

Not only Chicago's South Asian Languages and Area Center but all American South Asian centers would be placed in equal jeopardy by the loss of the American Institute of Indian Studies and the Library of Congress Acquisitions Program. It is quite unlikely that most of these centers would have the capacity to replace these services with their own funds and staffs. The negative impact of these events would also compel the existing domestic centers to retrench their teaching and research activities when they should be increasing their enrollment and supporting the formation of new centers.

The exhaustion of PL 480 counterpart funds will also inhibit the development of domestic and overseas language and area centers in other regions than South Asia at a time when such centers have become financially and politically vulnerable.[8]

The language and area centers that were established in some American universities after World War II, and their associated overseas centers for training and research, together with the library acquisitions program administered by the Library of Congress, have proved themselves to be a most effective and economical means to carry on a conversation of cultures with the people of other countries. These centers have given Americans the hearing aid which Robert Redfield said in 1958 they needed for the conversation and mutual understanding that is the condition of mutual security.[9]

The organization in 1985 of The Festival of India by the Indo-U.S. Subcommission on Education and Culture, supported by Prime Minister Gandhi and President Reagan, encourages the hope that the conversation and mutual understanding will continue.

NOTES

*An earlier version of this paper was drafted in 1977 as the introduction to a volume of selections, mostly previously published, by members of the Committee on Southern Asian Studies (COSAS) at the University of Chicago. The volume was intended as a companion to the Committee's *Programs and Dissertations in Southern Asian Studies at the University of Chicago* (1977). It was not possible to publish the volume at that time, though an updated and revised version of the volume may still be published.

I am particularly pleased to have this paper included in a collection of essays honoring my colleague, Edward C. Dimock. As scholar, teacher, and administrator he has played a vital and creative role in America's conversations of culture with South Asia. At Chicago, beginning as a Carnegie Intern in the Indian Civilization course in 1958, he quickly assumed a primary responsibility for teaching, organization, and publication in the field of Bengali language and literature. His many administrative appointments at the University of Chicago are too numerous to list, but as Director of the South Asian Language and Area Center, and as Chairman of the Committee on South Asian Studies and of the Department of South Asian Languages and Civilizations, he provided the imaginative and stabilizing leadership the South Asian program needed in its formative years. He has played an equally vital role at the national and international levels as President of the American Institute of Indian Studies since 1972 and as a member of the Indo-U.S. Subcommission on Education and Culture and of other national committees. His recent award by the Tarak Nath Das Foundation, making him only the fourth American scholar to be so honored (A.K. Ramanujan was the third) is an indication that Professor Dimock's contributions are amply appreciated by the Indian community also. Professor Dimock's publications have been distinguished for their sensitivity and fluent translations, a deep understanding of the Bengali and general Indian literary and theological heritage, and his broad knowledge of Indian cultural history.

He represents a living embodiment of the ideal language and area specialist and he continues to be an inspiration to both students and colleagues.

I am indebted to Chauncy Harris who as Director of the Center for International Studies in the 1970s asked me to assemble and edit the volume on "The Conversation of Cultures" and made many helpful suggestions.

1. Some earlier discussions of these programs will be found in the following publications which I helped to edit or draft.

   1955 "Seminar on Interdisciplinary Indian Studies" (Summary Report). Poona.

   1957 *Introducing India in Liberal Education*. Chicago.

   1959 "The Asian Civilizations Program at the University of Chicago." In E.P. Boardman, ed., *Asian Studies in Liberal Education*. Washington, D.C.

   1964 "The Social Sciences in Non-Western Studies." In Bicglow and Legters, eds. *The Non-Western World in Higher Education. Annals* 356: 30-44.

   1967 "On Understanding Other Cultures and One's Won." *The Journal of General Education 19: 1-23.*

   1976 "Robert Redfield's Development of a Social Anthropology of Civilization.' Murra, ed. *American Anthropology: The Early Years*. St. Paul.

   1977 *Programs and Dissertations in Southern Asian Studies at the University of Chicago. Committee on Southern Asian Studies.*

   Richard H. Davis has recently traced the origins of COSAS in his *South Asia at Chicago: A History* (Committee on Southern Asian Studies, 1985)

2. This later phase of Redfield's thought is traced in my paper, "Robert Redfield's De-

velopment of a Social Anthropology of Civilizations" in Murra, ed., *American Anthropology, the Early Years*.

3. These lectures were published in the collection of Redfield's papers assembled and edited by his wife, Margaret Park Redfield, under the title *Human Nature and the Study of Society* (Chicago, 1962).
4. The story is told in J.W.N. Crindle, *Ancient India as Described in Classical Literature*, p. 74. See my "Passage to More Than India" for an account of this and other images of India in Singer, *When a Great Tradition Modernizes, (Chicago,* [1972], 1980).
5. For a recent application of the approach, see E.V. Daniel and J.F. Pugh, eds., "South Asian Systems of Healing" in *Contributions to Asian Studies,* 18 (1984). Other reports of recent research on indigenous South Asian concepts include *Karma and Rebirth in Classical Indian Traditions,* edited by Wendy O'Flaherty, 1980; *Karma and Anthropological Inquiry,* edited by C.F. Keys and E.V. Daniel, 1983; and *Moral Conduct and Authority: The Place of Adab in South Asian Islam,* edited by Barbara Metcalf, 1981, all published by the University of California Press.
6. See my *When a Great Tradition Modernizes* ([1972], 1980) and *Man's Glassy Essence: Explorations in Semiotic Anthropology* (Indiana, 1984) for further applications of the method to the interpretation of Indian and American cultural identities.
7. *Human Relations and International Obligations. A Report of the UNESCO-Indian Philosophical Congress Symposium held at Ceylon December 1954.* Edited by N.A. Nikam, 1956, pp. 257-303.
8. See *Corners of a Foreign Field: Discussions About American Overseas Advanced Research Centers in the Humanities and Social Sciences.* Edited by R. McC. Adams and C. S. Schelling, New York, 1979.
9. Robert Redfield, "Does America Need a Hearing Aid?" Reprinted in Redfield, *The Social Uses of Social Science.* Chicago, 1963.

Envoi

WENDY O'FLAHERTY

Ed Dimock saved my life once. It was in Calcutta, at a time (1963-1964) when the latest episode in the war betwen India and Pakistan had touched off riots which cost many Calcutta Muslims their lives. I had wandered across town on some foolish errand, and suddenly found myself in imminent danger of being trampled (presumably to death) by an enormous hysterical crowd. As I prepared to meet my maker (and wondered if he would be Śiva), the Marines landed, in the form of a jeep and a driver and Ed, who scooped me up and swept me back to relative safety in Swinhoe Street.

My experience, though real enough to me, might serve as a metaphor for what Ed Dimock has done for just about every American scholar who has carried out research in India during the past two decades. By keeping the American Institute of Indian Studies alive for us he has made it possible for us to live our lives in India; and to do this he has often had to scoop the entire program out of the jaws of disaster, at the hands of one government agency or another (on either side of the planet earth). More important, if less dramatic, than these cosmic battles were their microcosmic parallels, the painstaking, tedious, discouraging, infuriating little daily problems that he alone could solve — the law's delay, the insolence of office, and all that a foreign country demands as initiation fee for anyone who would study with her. Think what it means to add together all that each individual has had to do in order to adjust to Indian concepts of time and place, and multiply that to some nth degree, and that is what Ed Dimock has done for all of us. It is a debt that truly boggles the mind; and we owe it to him in India, in units of value that we can never repay back here in America.

But he has personally helped so many of us, as pupils and colleagues, that I suspect that my anecdote could be matched, and topped, by many others on a level far more specific than the metaphor of the AIIS as a whole. And there have also been many lighter moments. I recall one Durgapuja when we had all drunk rather more *shiddhi* than we realized, and we were driving past the Maidan in that same jeep; the round, dark space of the park set against the lights of the city was mistaken, by Ed, for Lake Michigan (and Calcutta, apparently, for Chicago); he wanted to jump out of the jeep and swim in the Maidan (just as Caitanya jumped into the sea at Puri, mistaking it for the Yamunā). (Another Chicago colleague, McKim Marriott, recorded a similar sort of fieldwork during the Holi celebrations.) Hundreds of us have had such *darshan* of Ed Dimock in India, have been taken in by him and Loraine, into their home, when we were sick or out of luck; have been fed, and encouraged, and introduced to just the people that we needed to meet, and shown wonderful things. How can a great scholar find so much time to nurse all those lost souls in that vast subcontinent? How can the man who wrote *The Place of the Hidden Moon* and *The Thief of Love* and *In Praise of Krishna* (and a still unpublished, definitive translation of the entire *Caitanyacaritāmṛta)* also seem to take by the hand every scholar on an AIIS grant, as Krishna took each gopī? How can a man on whose shoulders so much rests also manage to have so many bizarre and exquisite experiences in India, and to distribute to us his own sense of the joy that one can have there, as Krishna distributed the butter to the monkeys?

The joy is there, too, in his books — in the poetry, and the erotica, and the folktales, and the religious esctasy, even in the terrifying glory of Manasha. In generations to come, people will be very glad indeed to have those books, and to glimpse the author through them. But we are fortunate enough to have a closer glimpse of the man himself — of his brilliance, of his courage, of his sadness, of his vitality, and above all, of his love for India.